S0-FKB-206

Library of
Davidson College

THE KINGS AND THE COVENANT

THE KINGS AND THE COVENANT

by

HAMISH SWANSTON

LONDON · BURNS & OATES

BURNS & OATES LIMITED

25 Ashley Place, London S.W.1

First published 1968

Nihil obstat: LIONEL SWAIN, S.T.L., L.S.S., Censor
Imprimatur: ✠ PATRICK CASEY, Vicar General
Westminster, 1 June 1968

The Nihil obstat *and* Imprimatur *are a declaration that a book or pamphlet is considered to be free from doctrinal or moral error. It is not implied that those who have granted the* Nihil obstat *and* Imprimatur *agree with the contents, opinions or statements expressed.*

221.95
8972 b

69-914

© Hamish Swanston 1968

SBN: 223 29755 0

Made and printed in Great Britain by
William Clowes and Sons, Limited, London and Beccles

ACKNOWLEDGEMENT

Since, after reading the first version of the text, he encouraged me to think that such a book would not be despised by intelligent members of senior school classes, and since he made the first versions of the maps, I think it only right, and certainly pleasurable, to dedicate this account of the Hebrew Monarchy to
ROGER BODEN, of Keble College

CONTENTS

INTRODUCTION

Israel's Historians and Israel's History

THE PEOPLE OF ISRAEL came into Canaan not all at one time nor all together, but in scattered groups. This makes it all the more notable that the original Canaanite population was unable to assimilate the intruders. The Israelites remained as alien minorities, refusing to be taken into the society around them. Against all likelihood, the Canaanite society was swallowed up by the Israelites—though it must be allowed that some elements of Canaanite tradition and practice were rather indigestible.

The Israelites were able to achieve this taking over of Canaanite territory precisely because they were not dependent upon territory for a realization of their identity as a people. The Canaanites were Canaanites because they lived in Canaan. They were the men of the land and they worshipped the gods of the land in lively fertility rites. Every acre of land lost to some other people diminished their claim to be men of the land and diminished their national confidence. The land was the evidence they needed to show they were a people.

The Israelites had no need of land to be a people. They simply needed land on which the people could practise their way of life. They did not worship the gods of fields and byres, they worshipped the God of the people. Although at the beginning of their history the separate tribes worshipped before various shrines and called on various names in their liturgy, all those who later came to be called Israelites had this faith in common: God is not tied down to any place, he is with his people.

The little separate groups of invaders were unknown to each other before they came their separate ways into Canaan. There were two main groups of tribes, the *Leah* group (Reuben, Simeon, Levi, Judah, Issachar and Zebulon), and the *Rachel* group (Ephraim,

Manasseh and Benjamin). The Leah tribes were the first to arrive in the land and accepted the Rachel narratives of God's presence at Sinai, the oasis of Kadesh and the Reed Sea as their stories, just as they accepted the men of the Rachel group as their people. These tribes, with others who joined them, came to be called *Israel*. Their recognition, their sharing of the same understanding of God, enabled them to come together as a people. Their way of worship made them acceptable to each other. They recognized as one the God whom they worshipped at the distinct local shrines of the tribes as the God of Abraham, the God of Nahor, the God of Isaac and the God of Jacob; they recognized that he who was worshipped as the Kinsman of Isaac in one place was worshipped as the Mighty One of Jacob at another. The title 'Kinsman' is indicative of their sense of personal relationship with God. They recognized, too, that the gods of the land, the gods tied down to places, were quite different from the one God who was present to his people. They joined together. They refused to have anything to do with the Canaanites.

We can see this process of combining and separating at work in the story of the Exodus. Moses' group, under Joshua's leadership, easily joins with the already settled groups to form Israel because the traditions of the earlier invaders and those coming from Egypt are so alike, the God of Sinai who marches with his people is the God who led Abraham from Haran, and is not the same as those fertility godlings whose shrines were set up 'under every green tree'.

Much later in Israel's history, in the seventh century B.C., the Assyrians besieged Jerusalem and their leader mocked the men of Israel for supposing that God would help them; 'Where', he sneered, 'are the gods of Hamath and Arpad? Where are the gods of Sepharvaim and Hena and Ivvah? Where are the gods of the land of Samaria? . . . Tell me which, of all the gods of any country, have saved their countries from my hands, for Yahweh to be able to save Jerusalem?' The men in Jerusalem know that Yahweh, their God, will not save Jerusalem, a city of bricks and stones, but they go into his presence and ask him to save *his people*, and the prophet Isaiah gives them Yahweh's answer. He tells them that their whole history has been a holy war in which Egyptian troops have been thrown into the sea and Canaanite towns have collapsed before the army of

Israel, 'like fields of corn before the strong East wind', but that God is with them as a people in all they do and he will save his people. The Assyrians do not capture the men of this city. This narrative brings out clearly the continuing belief of the Israelites that pagans may worship feeble gods of fields and towns, but that thay have no such local deity.

Of course there were Israelites who mistakenly supposed that Jerusalem was a holy city which must of necessity be protected by Yahweh for his own honour. But Micah cannot have been the only Israelite who fully expected the fall of Jerusalem precisely because men had begun to trust in its holy walls instead of in Yahweh who dwelt among them. The message of this prophet was simply that unless the people became aware of Israel's moral obligations to the personal love of Yahweh, the city must collapse. Those who thought in terms of battlements were false to Israel's understanding of history, and were in for a nasty surprise in 586 B.C.

In the Exile which followed the sack of the city in that year, some Israelites certainly came to think of their worship of Yahweh as integrally connected with the stones of Jerusalem and its Temple (for example, those who in Psalm 137 refuse to sing the songs of the liturgy because they are not in the holy city but are in exile 'by the waters of Babylon'). These Israelites thought only of return to Jerusalem and the restoration of its walls. But others, more faithful to their true tradition, realized that though away from the holy place they could still celebrate the worship of Yahweh in little groups assembled round the scribes who read Yahweh's loving word on the Sabbath.

This is not to suggest that the land had no importance. But it had secondary importance as an expression of Yahweh's primary relation with his people. It was the 'holy land' only because it was a sign in the world of Yahweh's giving of himself to Israel. This is brought out in the story of Naboth's vineyard in 1 Kings 21; King Ahab wants to extend his property and asks his neighbour to exchange or sell his land. It could well be argued on Ahab's side that he offers a very fair price, that small plot economy is not really viable, and that only by the strengthening of the royal central control, and supporting the designs of Ahab, was there any chance of the country maintaining its independence of the great empires of Mesopotamia. But Naboth refuses to sell on the ground that his small holding is a gift from Yahweh and to give it up for money would be to opt out of the presence of Yahweh. Just as the land of Canaan is a sign of Yahweh's self-giving to the whole people, so each man's share of the land is a share in the giving of Yahweh himself. He says to the king, 'God forbid that I should let you have the vineyard of my fathers'. It is significant that Ahab, the Israelite king, understands and accepts this attitude while his pagan Tyrian wife, Jezebel, cannot comprehend what is going on.

The Israelites expressed their sense of near relationship between Yahweh and Israel in the covenant. The covenant is the acknowledgement, sometimes actually written out, sometimes not, that Yahweh's presence has been met by man's trusting response. The Israelites centred their whole political structure (and it is with this structure and its workings that this short description of Israelite society is concerned) on the belief that Yahweh had promised to be present with them in their history, and that Abraham acted for all Israel when he committed himself in the light of this promise to loving obedience to Yahweh. Israel exists because of the covenant. Israel is the visible effect of the Promise.

These ideas affected the very notion of history in Israel. Other Near-Eastern societies produced lists of kings, annals of large (and therefore significant) events, and ceremonial inscriptions declaring that this battle was won this year at this place or this palace was built by this prince. These are not indications of historical thinking. Almost the reverse. These are endeavours to keep things static. They answer questions like 'What happened last year?', and 'How did we do it last time?' History is a process.

A society which is concerned with a personal relationship at the centre is a society which can create historical writing. The Israelites are the first historians of our antiquity. They are concerned with origins in order to explain the present. The Fall Story, for example, was not so much set down to tell us what happened once at the beginning but rather to tell us why events are now as they are.

The society which is concerned with the personal relationship of God and man is the society which will provide historical explanations in terms of God. The Israelites are the first men of our antiquity to produce a consistent view of God's will and providence and love. It is precisely because of their faith in Yahweh of the covenant that the Israelites were able to understand that there was such a significant process as history.

Their historical writing was a declaration of faith in Yahweh's presence in their historical events. The same structure is employed in their statements of belief as in their descriptions of events. The primitive creed, for example, recited by Joshua and his people, and set out in Joshua 24 and, with some variations, in Deuteronomy 26, is based on the three major events (the call of Abraham, the deliverance at the Exodus, and the gift of Canaan) which shape the structure of the Hexateuch, the first six history books of our Old Testament. The historical writing of the Israelites is the setting down of the evidence for that divine love which the Israelite worshipper knew to be present in his life. The writing of history was begun, therefore, as a process of simplification and unification of the old oral traditions of the tribes to one continuous story of Yahweh's saving presence in every moment of his people.

The relationship between Israelite historical writing and worship was not all one way. As the historians set down their witness to Yahweh, those responsible for the arrangement of the liturgy reorganized the services to make room for the recitation of the historical narrative for songs of thankfulness for Yahweh's activity among his people, or, less often, reproaches at the way he has treated his people, as in *Lamentations*. In turn the liturgical celebration of the historian's witness might affect the way in which the historian set down the 'second edition' of his history, or when another revised his work. A good example of such intermingling of cultic and historical influences on a narrative is the story of Gideon, which is at the same time a saga of a hero, a celebration of Yahweh's intervention at a critical moment in Israel's history, and an explanation of how a liturgical vestment called the ephod came to be at Ophrah. The hero history and the hymn to Yahweh are woven inextricably into our present text. The liturgical expression of the story told by the first historian has been assimilated by the later historian.

Sometimes the historian's own participation in the celebration of an event in the liturgy enabled him to be much more accurate in his account of the past. For example, when the editor of the royal chronicle of Solomon was putting his work together horses were the common mounts of kings. But the coronation ritual of Judah still included the ceremonial entry of the king riding on an ass. The historian therefore knew that when Solomon was anointed as king he rode into Jerusalem, not on a horse, as the historian would have expected, but on the traditional beast still used in the liturgy.

Sometimes the historian employs his material to bring his own contemporaries to a better appreciation of their liturgical service. Thus the later versions of parts of the Exodus story which are in our present text, for example, the story of the manna in Deuteronomy 8, show the writers thought a plain unvarnished historical narrative would be mere historicism of the worst conservative kind, the earlier narrative of the manna (in which it was simply taken to be food for the journey) must be made relevant by the comment that man does not live by bread alone but by listening to the present word of Yahweh. Life in the wilderness may be very remote from the settled Israelites in their farmsteads, and it may appear alien to those who carry on in life without miracles, so it is part of the duty of the historian to recall the reader of his narrative to an awareness of Yahweh's presence in contemporary farming prosperity.

The writing of history and the celebrating of the liturgy are never considered as autonomous in Israelite thinking. The liturgy had to be a celebration of the history or it was not liturgy. We can see this line of thought at work in the story of Jeroboam in 1 Kings 12 where, in a successful effort to bring the northern tribes to accept the religious services performed at Bethel and dissuade them from going to Jerusalem, the new king introduces references to the Exodus events into the patriarchal story which was already recited at the shrine. The Israelites recognized the proper worship of Yahweh in the celebration of his work as Lord of History.

The conviction that the historian's duty was to speak in a relevant way to his contemporaries led the Israelite historians to be rather more free with their arranging and adapting of their sources than is regarded as proper in our post-Acton days. The Israelite historians felt free to manipulate their materials if, *and only if*, by doing so they made the meaning of events clearer to their readers. They wanted other men to share their understanding of Yahweh's work. Perhaps the best-known example of this kind of re-interpretation of earlier historians' work is the southern scribes' adoption of the northern chronicles after the collapse of Samaria in 721 B.C. The archives of the record-office of the northern kingdom, the literary complexes of the Elijah and Elisha stories, the text of Hosea's prophesyings, were accepted by the southern historians from the northern scribes who fled south from Sichem with their texts, and then re-shaped to fit into the southern view of history. The final version was produced by the priestly scribes of Jerusalem in the first decades after the return from the Exile and used in the new liturgy of the second Temple. With patience we can disentangle the various components of our present texts, but to do so would certainly be to go against the historian's duty as both north and south conceived it. It would be to seek a static condition for the Promise.

Into the pattern of the Promise the historians shaped all the old traditions and histories—the great story of Joseph, for example, was told so that it should lead, after so many strange incidents and adventures by which Joseph became the chief minister of Egypt, to the affirmation: 'Yahweh sent me here to preserve some few Israelites alive, a remnant that shall grow into a great people. Not you but Yahweh brought me here.'

So, very much later, the historians who set down the events that followed the death of Elijah saw in the rise of the fierce enemy king, Hazael of Syria, the *coup d'état* of Jehu, and the prophetic message of Elisha, the realization of Elijah's understanding that Yahweh would punish Israel for apostasy and leave only a remnant to build afresh the society of Yahweh's people.

The historians were at pains to demonstrate the providential character of history. Yahweh was ever ready to rescue those who trusted in him, but so often it happened that few men could be found to trust him. This is the intention behind the different historians' use of the concept of 'the remnant'. Originally the term was used to describe those left alive after the sack of a city. The Assyrian kings were always boasting that after their army had laid siege 'not even a remnant was left in the town'. Sometimes the remnant became the nucleus through which a community was reconstituted, like 'the remnant of the coastland of Caphtor' among the Philistines, and it is as such new beginnings that Noah and his sons, Lot and his daughters, or Jacob and his sons, are described in Genesis. Yahweh works his purpose out with whatever men are ready to trust him and renew the life of the covenant. Yahweh waits on men.

2—K.C.

The Israelite historians were totally committed to the importance of human participation in events. They did not often posit interference by Yahweh. Yahweh had no need to rush to the rescue of his design for the world; it would work itself out in the end. Ordinary historical events were the way in which Yahweh's design came into completion. For example, the way in which Yahweh's will for the Davidic line as kings of his people came to be known by the people was not by a sudden clap of thunder and a mighty voice from the clouds, but by the men who had grown prosperous in the security of David's empire realizing that if any other man than David's son was elected King of Judah *and* King of Israel, the empire would cease to exist for the fief of Ziglag and the city of Jerusalem would be inherited by David's son and lost to a non-Davidic ruler, and the Philistine towns and Transjordanian territories might very well regain their independence unless they were kept under by the united forces of Judah and Israel. Solomon succeeded because of the economic sense of the Israelites. The Israelites came to understand that the empire Yahweh had willed them to possess could only be maintained by a son of David inheriting the whole of it. They thus came to speak of Yahweh having willed the line of David to be rulers in his kingdom. The historians moved from economic and political events to divine causation.

This history, from the election of Saul to the captivity of Jehoiachin, is the result of extremely intelligent men attempting to understand events, and their coming to do so in terms of the covenant within which they themselves lived. Their historicist principle is perhaps best expressed in the words of Solomon: 'You spoke with your mouth. And you have with your hand today fulfilled your word.'

H.F.G.S.

Eliot College, Canterbury

BEFORE THE MONARCHY

THE ISRAELITES' BELIEF that Yahweh was working their good in his covenant derived generally from their story of what had happened in the distant past, and, more immediately, from their view of the events of the Exodus and the manifestation of Yahweh at Sinai. They were a people before they were a race, a people before they were a nation, because for them blood and soil came after faith in the Yahweh of the covenant.

It must not be imagined that the Law of the covenant alliance was simply a set of regulations and demands for obedience. The men of the covenant understood that what Yahweh wanted from Israel was love. The wonderful events of the Exodus and the delights of the Promised Land were presented to the Israelites as showing how Yahweh loved them. The expected response was that they should love Yahweh. The history of the tribal confederation ought to be viewed as a history of Israel's response to the demands of the covenant of love made with Yahweh. Nothing is less like the original intention of those who took part in the covenant than the legalistic and narrow manner in which the Law was interpreted, for example, by the leaders of the Jews in the time of Christ. In the beginning of the history of Israel the covenant is thought of as demanding a free adult response from each Israelite as a member of the great community. The covenant makes the community. The regular assembly of the tribal community is the time for the renewal of the covenant, for the declaration by the people that they are still loyal to Yahweh. This is what we find described in several places in the early narratives. One of the most famous of these renewals is recorded at the end of *Joshua*. The army general takes the lead in the declaration by the assembled people that they will keep the covenant:

Your fathers lived in Mesopotamia and Yahweh led Abraham to Canaan and gave him many descendants, Isaac and Jacob, Joseph in Egypt, and Moses to bring you out of Egypt. Yahweh rescued you at the reed sea and was with you in the wilderness. Yahweh has given you victory here and brought you home at last. You have a land though you have not ploughed, cities though you have not built, vines and olive trees though you have not planted. Now, therefore, serve Yahweh in sincerity and love.

And the people shouted in answer their promise to be loyal: 'We will serve Yahweh, for he has brought us out of slavery and cared for us in all our wanderings.'

Yahweh has been with his people in Egypt and in the desert. He is with them now. It is noticeable that both Joshua's introductory speech and the people's acclamation suggest that the work of Yahweh is to be discovered in the events of their history. They acknowledge that Yahweh has made them a people by guiding them from one event to another.

After the first acclamation Joshua moves through the liturgical formulation of the oath. They all went through a ceremony something like this:

'Do you accept that Yahweh will punish any man who is disloyal to this covenant?'

'We accept all this.'

'Do you accept that this oath cannot be broken without sin?'

'We accept all this.'

'Do you accept that you owe love and loyalty to Yahweh and to him alone?'

'We accept all this. We shall serve him and no one else.'

So the covenant is renewed in the formal phrases that grew up through the years at the often repeated ceremony. By taking part in this ritual the Israelites at the assembly proclaimed their tribal confederation to the kindom of Yahweh. It was, therefore, difficult later for the conservative leaders of the confederation, Samuel for instance, or Nathan perhaps, to welcome the establishment of the kingdom of Saul or of the Davidic house. These kings seemed to threaten the kingdom of Yahweh. This early tension and its results will be outlined later in this history as the Israelites themselves described it.

During the period of the confederation the worship of Yahweh was built round signs of his kingly power: the ark was a throne, the rod of Moses was a sceptre, and in the liturgy Yahweh was acclaimed as King. In the old song celebrating the miracle at the Exodus the final verse sung by all the people spoke of the whole land as his holy place and kingdom: 'The land, Yahweh, where you have your home is a sanctuary where you will reign for ever.' And the song of Balaam, equally old, speaks of the Israelite encampment during a campaign against the princes of Moab, in similar terms. They are the royal army of Yahweh: 'Yahweh their God is with them, their king urges them on.'

Similar things are to be found throughout early Hebrew literature. They express the firm conviction of the people that their nation belongs to Yahweh, and not to any man. This is the central thought of the covenant ritual in its first form and, despite the development of the monarchy and its claims, this was never entirely lost sight of.

The covenant was not, of course, simply an effect of past activity by Yahweh, it was also a promise for the future. The early makers of songs, the men who played on primitive harps round the camp fires and at village festivals, encouraged the people to look forward to a long summer in the land under the blessing of Yahweh.

These songs emphasize that Yahweh had chosen to live among his people, to share their settlement. They thought of him as present over the Ark, his throne. This was the central shrine of the league of tribes. When peace was achieved the shrine of the Ark was set up at the central town of Shiloh; here was its customary home, though it certainly was moved to other places for short sojourns during the period of the Judges. Here the prayers were offered for the whole confederation. At lesser shrines throughout the countryside the priests offered prayer for the local tribesmen. It was at these smaller religious sites that many of the individual traditions of the conquest of Canaan and the settlement were preserved until incorporated in the great historical work we now have. Israel began in Canaan with a great store of pre-entry traditions reaching back at least five hundred years, deriving from the time when men of their race first set out from Mesopotamia. These had been kept going by tribal communities and preserved apart from the native Canaanite traditions by the first settlers. When the men of Moses' group came into Canaan they could easily find acceptance among the earlier immigrants to form a unifying Israel because their traditions were similar and because these other pre-Israelites had refused to be assimilated in the Canaanite culture.

It is not possible to understand properly the way in which the

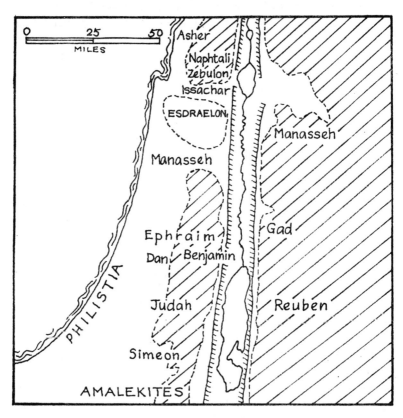

sagas originated that are now included in the great sweep of biblical history, without taking into account the economic, political and, most important, the geographical conditions of the tribes where the traditions were shaped. The fragmentary character of the narratives of Israel before Saul is a reflection of the fragmentary character of the early settlement in Canaan.

The settlers in Galilee were separated from the rest by a group of

Canaanite villages in Jezreel or Esdraelon. The eastern tribes were largely cut off from the western tribes by the Jordan rift. In the central mountainous districts communication was always difficult. These conditions led naturally to the formation of small self-contained groups round local shrines. This in turn had the effect of making it a rare thing for the tribes to combine for any purpose once they had settled down in the conquered land. It thus affected, too, the nature of the traditions of Israel that were handed down. Since these were mainly about local events and were preserved by the priestly guardians of the local shrines the stories are extremely difficult to fit together. The writer who put the history of the Judges period into its final literary form is to be much admired for his considerable success in an enterprise of such difficulty. When he set about making his account of the beginnings of Israel he was confronted with all kinds of stories, some in verse, some in prose, some collections of anecdotes, others quite long narratives, some developed in the north of Palestine, some in the south, some belonging to a tribe before it arrived in the land. Each one unlike the other and independent of the other.

The editor has reduced the historical traditions of the various localities to a unified scheme which treats of Israel from Moses to the end of the monarchy. His artifice, although it has not totally disguised the character of his sources, has produced an impressive arrangement of many disparate traditions.

The separation of the religious shrines of the various tribes from each other and from the central shrine had a great influence on the development of the people's religious attitudes. The separated local shrines must have been subject to local pressures in a way that a network of closely linked shrines of a national religious establishment would not have been. The local inhabitants must have included many who were recent converts to the conquering Yahwism and these must have treasured memories of the old rituals and superstitions. They would have introduced their old stories to the local liturgy, and not felt these pagan elements to be incongruous. The history of religion in Israel at this time confirms such a suspicion. The particular menace which attracted most attention in this matter was the reappearance of the Canaanite fertility rites once the semi-nomadic Israelites had acquired farms of their own and were personally concerned in the crop cycle of an agricultural community. Many of them accepted the general pagan notion that the gods of the harvest must be propitiated so that the crop would be a good one. While not abandoning Yahweh and his worship they attempted to combine with this the former cults of the Canaanite religion. These country rites gained so firm a hold on the local shrines that in the time of the monarchy it was generally accepted in Jerusalem that if Yahwism was to be upheld the only way to achieve this was the destruction of the local hill shrines which were nominally for the worship of Yahweh but practically pagan.

The liturgy of the central shrine was made up chiefly of various ceremonies that developed round the renewal of the covenant between Yahweh and the people. This too had its effect on our histories. Many of the narratives of the pre-settlement period have their present shape because they have been adapted for repetition at the covenant renewal feasts. The whole of the Exodus tradition has been written in this manner—indeed it has been suggested that the whole account of the Exodus has been composed by placing various separate stories in an order suggested by the later pilgrimage to the covenant renewal, culminating in the repetition of the Sinai Law as the basis of the covenant society. Whether this be the case or not, it is certainly true that the renewal of the covenant in the liturgy inevitably brought the Law into prominence in the life of Israel. The generalized commandments were expounded in ever greater detail so that specific cases were covered by an enormous legal system dispensed by the village elders. From the beginning the confederation accepted the necessity of law if man were to live as the society of Yahweh.

The Philistines

Just as the Israelites had settled themselves in the land a new wave of invaders came down the eastern coast passing through on their way to Egypt. These were the Philistines. Ramses III, the Pharaoh at this time, beat them back from Egypt but was not strong enough to push them further north so he compromised and accepted their occupation of the sea coast of Palestine while in return the Philistines agreed to accept him as their nominal overlord. This uneasy situation did not last long. In 1144 B.C. the Pharaoh was assassinated and his successors gave up their claim to Palestine. The Philistines settled down and looked about them. Various pockets of the original Canaanite inhabitants survived the two large invasions of Israelites and Philistines. The Phoenician cities in the north-east made a quick recovery but for the moment the Philistines were secure on the coast. The Israelites occupied the mountain areas, though here too some Canaanite towns held out, for example, Jerusalem.

The Philistines set up five great towns, Gaza, Ashkelon, Ashdod, Ekron and Gath, linked by a military alliance. They established themselves in a monopoly of sea trade and iron manufacture. This gave them a position of some strength in Palestine.

It must be appreciated, therefore, that while the Philistines were geographically and economically well-knit and able to exert a united political and military pressure on their neighbours, the Israelites had no such advantages. Settled in their widely separated villages, brought up in isolated tribal societies which had few ties with those of the other tribes, the Israelite had only one reason for combining with his fellows, only one demand for his community loyalty, and this was the confederation as expressed in the covenant. In this way it became clear to each man that it was only through the covenant with Yahweh that Israel was a nation.

Any form of government that was to make an appeal to the men of the tribes must have three characteristics: (1) It must acknowledge that the nation belonged to Yahweh and could only survive by his protection; (2) it must acknowledge the supremacy of Law in Israelite society—no man could put aside the will of Yahweh expressed in the terms of the covenant; (3) it must be adapted to conditions of continual war since all the neighbours of the Israelites were worshippers of foreign gods and jealous of their lands and resources.

To these requirements two answers were found, the Judges and the Kings. The first was only supplanted by the second because of the necessity of waging a highly organized war in defence of the covenant and the Law.

The Judges

In such a situation of disparate and unassociated tribal interests it was obviously impossible for national heroes to appear. Those described in the chronicle of Judges as having by their personal response to Yahweh produced a flourishing Israelite attack on the pagan neighbours are evidently local heroes. The stories of these men were adopted by the whole confederation in rather the same way as the stories of Abraham, Isaac and Jacob were felt by later generations to be concerned with ancestors of all the tribes even though historically this was certainly false. Three of these popular local tales are presented here as examples of the kind of material available to the chroniclers.

1. Ehud

Early in the twelfth century the men of Moab defeated the tribe of Reuben and began to encroach on the territory of Benjamin across the Jordan.

After Eglon, chieftain of the Moabites, had occupied Benjamite lands, the men of this tribe were forced to send him tribute. This demand was continued for nearly twenty years. In the eighteenth year the tribute was to be brought to Eglon by Ehud, an Israelite with the characteristic of being left-handed, a thing evidently rare among the Israelites. Ehud had a short sword made which he hid on his right thigh under his clothes and thus secretly armed he went with the other Benjamite bearers to Eglon's court.

After the ceremonial handing over of the tribute to the fat king on his throne, Ehud sent all the other Benjamites away and presenting himself to the unsuspecting king as an informer asked for a private audience. Eglon dismissed all his attendants and took Ehud up to his pent-house on the roof of the palace. Ehud came near him announcing that he had a message from Yahweh and reaching beneath his clothes for his short sword he thrust it into the king's belly. Eglon was so fat that the hilt disappeared among the laps of flesh and his guts burst out. Ehud left the room, locked the door behind him and walked out of the palace.

After Ehud had left, the courtiers of Moab waited for Eglon to summon them. Ehud had a good start on them once they did brave the king's anger and burst open the door.

The confusion in Moab at the assassination of the king was so great that the Benjamites were able to revolt against the occupying power and drive them out of Benjamite territory across the river and make sure that no Moabite would return by setting guards at every ford.

It appears that the tribe of Reuben was unable to take advantage of this situation for Moab remained in control of the eastern bank of the Jordan. Later the tribe of Gad took over the Moabite lands on this side of the river. It is at any rate significant as a pointer to the independence of each tribe that it did not occur to the Benjamites to cross the river and free the men of Reuben from foreign occupation.

2. Deborah and Barak

The villain and victim of this story is the general Sisera, an aristocratic member of the Philistine government. He was chieftain at Harosheth at the north-western end of the plain of Jezreel. Twenty-five years before he had commanded the chariots of Jabin against Joshua. When that city was defeated Sisera had got together a small state of his own. He seems to have been able to command an army composed of both Philistines and Canaanites from the plains of Esdraelon and Acco. Probably the Canaanites were press-ganged into military service for the Philistines.

It seems likely that the Galilean tribes found themselves in subjection to the cities of the plains and appealed for help to the independent tribe of Naphtali. At any rate a Naphtali soldier, Barak, inspired by a fiery woman named Deborah, came with men from Naphtali and Zebulun to attack Sisera.

This tale is noteworthy because it introduces two important elements in the Israelite view of the world. Barak is a man who had no official status; he is not a general of a regular army, he is simply the man of the moment. His power to persuade men to follow him is given for a particular purpose and is seen to come direct from Yahweh. He has a vocation to be the leader, and the tribesmen understand that this vocation comes from Yahweh. Therefore they follow him. Secondly, the war that such a leader embarks upon is, by definition, Yahweh's war. The Israelites thus introduced the notion of a 'Holy War' when Yahweh himself was believed to march with his troops and gain the victory for them. The plan of campaign, therefore, was to consult the oracles of Yahweh, follow the divine instructions, and then offer the booty to Yahweh after the defeat of the enemy.

On this occasion Sisera heard that the infantry of Naphtali and Zebulun were coming from Kedesh, having consecrated themselves on the holy mountain of Tabor. He immediately drew up his great force of chariots on the plain of Jezreel. The Naphtali footsoldiers had never been able to defeat this chariot force before. So the enemy had always held the plain of Esdraelon, dividing the confederation almost in two. On this occasion Yahweh himself won the victory. Torrential rain came down and the chariots became unusable in the mud of the plain. The men of Naphtali were able to leap down upon the charioteers and their drivers and so inflict a crippling defeat on the Philistines.

Seeing the hopelessness of his case, Sisera got down from his chariot and ran from the battle. While Deborah remained to urge on the killing in the field: 'At 'em! For today Yahweh goes before you and Sisera is done for!' Barak chased those who escaped and slew them before they reached Harosheth. Sisera himself ran to the tent of a Kenite pitched near the field of war. This Kenite was a friend to Israel, that is, he worshipped Yahweh. His wife Jael was in the tent when Sisera came running.

'Come in here, come in here. You will be safe with me.'

'Many thanks. Give me a drink. I am very dry.'

'Here, my lord, drink this.'

'Thanks and thanks again. Can I sleep here a little while?'

'Do. Wrap yourself in those skins. I will watch by the door.'

'Do not let anyone know I am here.'

Sisera slept, tired out by his fighting and his running. Jael took a tent peg and a mallet and crept up to the sleeping general. Quickly she held the tent peg to his forehead and smashed down the mallet. The tent peg went right through Sisera's head and stuck into the ground beneath.

It would seem that after this battle the dependence of the Galilean tribes on the cities of the plains was over. The Israelites had established their claim to a place in Canaan.

The significance of the victory for the men of Naphtali and Zebulun was the demonstration that they really could defeat the Canaanite chariot forces. Yahweh was with them and they could do anything. The gain in confidence that resulted gave the Israelites a psychological advantage over their enemies and so empowered them to overthrow the rule of the original inhabitants in many areas of Palestine. They had still, of course, to reckon with the Philistine menace.

3. Gideon

The confederation of the cities of the plain of Esdraelon collapsed under the raids of the Midianites: camel-riding nomads from the desert. The Israelites were terrified of the new animal and were defeated time and again by the Midianites. After a few years of this, whenever the camels were sighted the Israelites hid in caves till they had passed. It appears that the nomads always attacked at harvest time and either carried off the grain or destroyed the crops, so that the Israelites, who depended on the crop for their year's food and barter, were being ruined. The story of the hero Gideon tells how Yahweh rescued his people from their pitiful condition. This is the great 'Holy War' saga of *Judges*. The story is told so that no one will ascribe the relief to any human effort. The victory is wholly won by Yahweh's direct intervention. At the decisive moment in the campaign it is Yahweh and not the hero who inflicts the defeat.

The story of Gideon from beginning to end is written to point Yahweh's constant care of his people in war.

When the people cried to Yahweh because of the Midianite raiders, he sent a prophet to them: 'Thus says Yahweh of Israel: I have brought you from Egypt, I have given you this land. If only you would serve me I would see to it that you should be free from all oppression.'

Gideon, a young farmer, was threshing corn in secret for fear of the raiders, as he heard the prophet's cry. An angel of Yahweh appeared to him.

'Hail, Yahweh is with you.'

'If, sir, Yahweh is with us why are we so unhappy and our livelihood ruined? All we hear now is talk of what Yahweh once did, why does he do nothing now?'

'Yahweh will help you now. You must make war against the Midianites.'

'How can this be? I am a member of an insignificant family in a small clan. How can I deliver Israel?'

'I am with you. My power will be with you in the fight.'

Then the angel left him. Gideon offered sacrifice to Yahweh.

He summoned the men of his tribe and their neighbours, picked a few men to follow him in Yahweh's war, and crossed the Jordan to set up camp on the plain of Esdraelon. Then with the group of warriors—the small number of men with Gideon is stressed in the narrative to emphasize that it was through Yahweh and not armed forces that the enemy was scattered— he walked into the Midianite camp one night as they slept beside the well of Harod, at the western footlands of Mount Gilboa. He divided his little force into three parts and gave each man not a sword—for Yahweh had no need of swords— but a trumpet and a light in a jar. On a signal the Israelites blew their trumpets at every point in the camp and lit their lights. The sudden awakening brought panic on the enemy so that each man seized his sword and struck out in the dark at anyone who moved near him. Yahweh set every nomad's sword against his own comrade, so that many were killed and the rest so frightened that they got on their camels and fled as far as the Jordan and crossed to the further bank.

That was the last time the Israelites heard of the Midianites. This story is told so that the climax comes with Yahweh's intervention. Yahweh brings panic on the enemy and the victory is won. The men of Yahweh are merely required to take up symbolic positions round the scene. They are like priests of the liturgy, with trumpets blaring and lights lit for the ceremonial victory of Yahweh.

The decisive act in the battle does not belong to any man. Therefore Gideon retires into private life after this episode and the notion of making him king is explicitly rejected as an affront to the honour of Yahweh. As long as victory could be achieved in this manner so long the monarchy was delayed.

By the end of this period in Israel's history not much more territory had been gained than Israel had occupied at the time of the settlement. Nowhere had the Canaanites been totally defeated and driven from their enclaves, and the Philistines were equally secure, a young, aggressive power on the coastal strip, ready for war. It is remarkable, therefore, that the sporadic efforts of various independent leaders were enough to keep the individual tribes going, and particularly remarkable that the confederation should have survived. The one force which preserved the tribe, the great man working for his fellows, would have been an additional factor working against the continuance of the alliance with other tribes.

The confederation did not, indeed, work very well at this time. The local shrines continued to encourage the old pagan rites and this lessened the hold of the covenant with Yahweh on the tribesmen. The tribes refused to join together for any war effort and directed their energies towards preserving their own territories and possessions. Worse, there were occasions when the tribes actually went to war with one another. Therefore the two hundred years between the settlement and the monarchy are astounding because of the power to survive that is seen in the covenant society.

However, the coming of one threat to all the tribes altered the situation and brought about a new phase in the history of the covenant. The Philistine crisis changed the tribal pattern and produced a situation for which new solutions had to be found within the covenant framework.

The Philistine Crisis

Highly organized by the aristocratic Aegean military men who had settled in Palestine just after the arrival of the Israelites, the Canaanite population had been shaped into a powerful army to destroy the Israelite confederation. The menace of the five Philistine warlords was made the greater by the superiority of their weapons. They had attached to themselves the old Hittite monopoly of iron, and the Canaanite chariot force. The ill-disciplined Israelites, in mutually-jealous tribal connections, were unable to deal with such an enemy.

At first the battle between Philistine and Israelite was confined to local skirmishes on the borders of their territories. The stories of Samson contain remembrances of such encounters. The real engagement took place at Aphek about 1040 B.C. The Israelite account of this campaign is given in the history of the Ark at the time of Eli. It was a total disaster for the Israelites. The Ark was lost, Shiloh destroyed and the army scattered. The Philistines occupied vast areas which had formerly been thought secure for Israel. In order to prevent the resurgence of an Israelite power all the smithies were closed and all weapons confiscated. This was the end of the old confederation. The central covenant shrine had been occupied and the sacred area laid in ruins. Even when the Ark was returned to Israelite hands there was no attempt to restore the confederation of Yahweh. Israel had lost confidence in the old order.

The sole representative of the past who continued to receive Israel's respect as he worked for a restoration was Samuel, the surviving member of the clergy at Shiloh. Even Samuel could not, however, turn back the clock. Despite his protests (which later anti-monarchists elaborated with some relish) the people adopted a new constitution and elected a king for themselves. At this point the history of the monarchy begins.

THE FIRST KING

Saul becomes King

NAHASH, THE LEADER of an Ammonite raiding party, camped his men around the small Israelite town of Jabesh, intending to sack it. The townsmen were very alarmed when they saw the foreign ruffians and sent a message to Nahash asking why they could not all live at peace together and be friends. 'We shall be friends', replied Nahash, 'when you have let me gouge out your right eyes so that everyone may understand what an Ammonite can do to an Israelite.' The town councillors saw that there was no treating with such a man. They asked for a week's armistice from the Ammonite. If they could get no help in that time then they would surrender.

The armistice was agreed and the men of Jabesh sent out messengers to all the Israelite towns asking for help.

One of the messengers came to Gibeah, another small town, and told the people the terrible things going on at Jabesh. Soon everybody was talking about it. In the evening the men came in from the fields and were told the news. One of the farmers, Saul, coming in with the oxen that pulled his plough, was suddenly filled with a determination to rout the enemies of Israel. He seized a great knife and killed his oxen. Hacking the carcasses in pieces, he sent each of his men off with a piece, telling them to shout out this message in the neighbouring towns: 'Join me or I'll do the same to your oxen.' The Israelites were filled with enthusiasm and hurried to meet Saul as he marched with his men through the countryside.

He stopped at Bezek and the Israelites came in crowds from all the tribes of the North and the South. Saul said to the messenger who had brought the news from Jabesh: 'Tell the

3—K.C.

townsmen that by noon tomorrow you shall be rescued.' He was as good as his word. The Ammonites were cut to bits by the peasant army Saul had raised.

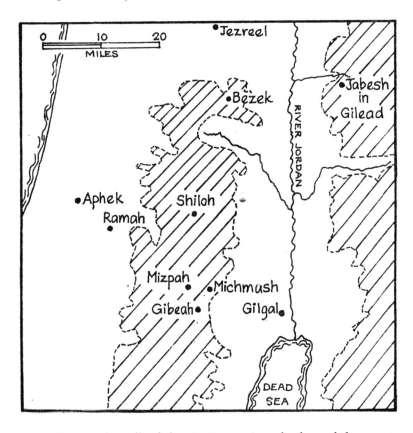

The people realized that Saul was a born leader and they went to the old Judge Samuel at Mizpah and said, 'We will have this man for our king.' So Samuel led the people to the shrine at Gilgal and there Saul was consecrated as king of the people. They sacrificed to Yahweh and had an enormous party.

During the celebrations the old Judge Samuel called for silence and announced his retirement from political life. He looked back over his long career and judged himself as he had judged others. He wanted to be sure that no one would make an opportunity to harass him once he had handed over power.

Samuel stood up and said: 'You have a king now and I am old. Let me settle all scores and retire. Come forward any man whose ox or ass I have taken from him, or any man with whom I have dealt unfairly or who has had to bribe me to get justice done; who accuses me of this?'

The people replied, 'No one accuses you. You have been just.' The last of the Judges retired and the people of the covenant had a king.

The Covenant

Just as the period of the free confederation of tribes was introduced by an affirmation of loyalty to the covenant of Sinai, so the chronicler has set at the beginning of the monarchy a ceremony of dedication and renewal.

The narrator's intention is that the reader should realize that though the political institutions of Israel are being altered in a radical manner, the covenant continues to be the central principle of Israelite society. After the abdication of Samuel the old man reminds the Israelites that whatever happens they must not turn their backs upon their history. It is still the event of the covenant which makes them a community. Samuel begins the ceremony of enthronement by reciting the acts of Yahweh, just as Joshua had inaugurated the new year of the tribal confederation with a liturgy in which the litany of past events led up to a renewal of the covenant oath by the assembly. For Samuel history is longer than for Joshua but the main idea is the same

Stand and hear what Yahweh has done for us in the past. When the Egyptians oppressed us and made us their slaves Yahweh sent Moses to bring your fathers out of Egypt and gave them this land to settle in. But they forgot their oath to serve Yahweh only and he punished them, letting kings come and defeat them so that they cried to Yahweh for rescue. He sent the Judges to save them. Now you, in this generation, are oppressed by enemies and you ask for a king from Yahweh. Here, then, is the king that Yahweh has given to you.

It is evident that the chronicler did not approve of the demand of the people for a king when they already belonged to Yahweh, but Samuel makes the best of the situation that confronts him.

The new development is placed at the end of the historical line. The monarchy is linked by the chronicler to the Sinai covenant: 'If you serve Yahweh and keep his commandments, you and your king, all will go well for you, but if you rebel against Yahweh, you and your king, then Yahweh will be against you and your king.'

The writer has now made it evident that the king is to be a man of the covenant, to keep his loyalty firm to Yahweh and that the people are to see in their loyalty to the king the eternal expression of their loyalty to Yahweh. The king is enthroned as the personal representative of Yahweh, but at the same time the opportunity is taken to declare to the people that if the king does not serve Yahweh loyally then chaos will come again. The pattern of the liturgy of Joshua is thus repeated here. Once the covenant is accepted the conditions of service must be obeyed or punishment follows. As the people accept all the conditions announced by Joshua so the king and people must accept the conditions announced by Samuel. The chronicler has set the king firmly in the pattern of covenant obedience, before Yahweh his responsibilities are great, he must answer for his government. The king is not to be an autocratic ruler whose only law is a whim of iron but the chief servant of Yahweh.

Saul sent the people home, but kept back two companies of strong men for his army. The larger company he took with him to Michmash in the hill country of Bethel and the rest he sent to garrison Gibeah, the capital of his new kingdom. These he placed under the command of his son Jonathan.

Jonathan was a successful young commander who took his men out of Gibeah on a sortie and defeated the Philistines who had set up a fort on a nearby hill. Saul was very pleased with his son's success and trumpeted through the land so that everyone should know how the royal family had won another battle. Of course, the more successful the Israelites were in these small frays the more the Philistines thought it necessary to put a stop to their activities. The Philistines prepared for war. The Israelites were summoned to join Saul at the shrine of Gilgal.

The army of the Philistines seemed as numberless as the sands upon the seashore. They were encamped all over the countryside of Michmash. The Israelites in the villages looked

at them, and crept into caves and in holes in the rock faces and
into deserted tomb-chambers or fled across the tributary streams
of the Jordan by the fords which led to Gilgal where Saul was
encamped. Even in Saul's camp they were afraid.

Saul offends Samuel

Samuel had said he would arrive in the camp at Gilgal by
the end of the week, to perform the sacrifice to Yahweh before
the fight with the Philistines began. He was late. The people
were beginning to desert Saul and scurry home to their farms.
Saul saw that his army was fast disappearing, so the king himself burnt the offering as a sacrifice to Yahweh. As he finished the
ceremony Samuel came up.

He was very angry that the king had not waited for him to offer
the sacrifice. The king had usurped the prophet's office. He had
taken more than kingly powers upon himself in making the offering.
To Samuel it showed that Saul was not ready enough to trust
Yahweh. He feared that Yahweh would not entrust Saul's family
with the hereditary government of his people.

Samuel went sadly from the camp at Gilgal. By this time
Saul's army mustered only six hundred men so the Philistines
were free to ravage the countryside.

The Philistines had a great advantage over the rebel force.
While they had control of events in the Israelite settlements,
they had forbidden the blacksmiths to make any weapons. Only
Saul and Jonathan had proper swords. But the desperate
Israelites turned their ploughshares into swords, and took up
their sickles, and tree-axes to make a fight of it.

They looked such a savage crew that the Philistines withdrew
from Michmash.

Saul and the Amalekite King

Hearing this, Samuel sent a message to Saul suggesting that
there was now an opportunity for him to use his men against
their old enemy the pagan Amalekites.

The Amalekites had harassed the Hebrews during the Exodus
and when they had settled in Canaan and were making farms for

themselves. Whenever the Hebrews sowed seed, the Amalekites would come from the hills to attack them in the fields. There was no love between them. It was not surprising that Samuel should think of them as the first enemies of God's people:

'Go and attack the Amalekites, and destroy them, spare no one, kill men and women, children and babies and all their animals. Yahweh will be with you.'

Saul defeated the Amalekites and chased them from Havilah to Shur in the Sinai peninsula, slicing them up as they fell before him. The foot soldiers and camp followers were killed in great numbers, but Agag their chieftain was captured and a great many fine sheep and oxen.

Saul was very pleased with himself and erected a monument at Carmel to commemorate his victory, then returned with his prisoner and booty to Gilgal. Samuel came to his camp. 'Now,' said Saul, 'you can see that Yahweh is with us and has given us the victory.' 'If Yahweh has given you the victory,' replied Samuel, 'why haven't you given him the spoil?'

Saul began to realize that Samuel's message from Yahweh was meant to be obeyed in every detail. He was to kill every one of the pagan enemy. So Saul tried to put the guilt of his disobedience on the soldiers.

Saul answered: 'The people brought back the animals from the battle. They meant to sacrifice the best sheep and oxen to Yahweh. Everything else has been destroyed.'

Samuel had been praying all night for Yahweh to forgive Saul and take him back into favour but now he gave his message from Yahweh unhesitatingly:

'You are the king of Israel, the leader of the people, anointed as the man of Yahweh. Yahweh sent you on a mission to destroy the Amalekites utterly and you have kept back the spoil.'

Saul defended himself:

'I have done the will of Yahweh. I have captured the king and destroyed the whole army of the Amalekites. The people have kept the sheep and oxen back to sacrifice here at Gilgal before Yahweh.'

Samuel would have none of this argument: 'Yahweh does not need sacrifices, he requires obedience. As you have rejected him so he has rejected you.'

Saul was horrified. He flung himself on the ground: 'I admit I have sinned, I tried to please the people rather than Yahweh. Do not leave me now. Come and sacrifice to Yahweh for me.'

'No,' said Samuel, 'there is no turning back. You have rejected Yahweh and Yahweh will not leave you to rule over his people.'

He turned abruptly away and Saul caught hold of the bottom of his robe so that it tore. Samuel turned to him and said: 'As you have torn my robe from me so has Yahweh torn the kingdom from you and has chosen another man to rule.'

Saul saw that pleading was useless. He could only hope that the people would not learn of his punishment. He had to keep up appearances:

'I have sinned. I am punished. But yet come with me to the sacrifice before Yahweh so that the people may not know this.'

So Samuel, who liked the unhappy king, went with Saul to the sacrifice.

As they walked from the altar, Samuel saw Agag the Amalekite chief in his path. Agag by now was sure that everything would be well. He thought that the Israelites would not keep him prisoner so long only to kill him. He grinned at Samuel. Samuel took an axe from a soldier standing by and hacked Agag into little pieces.

Then Samuel went to his house at Ramah and Saul went back to Gibeah. Samuel did not see Saul again. He kept to his house sorrowing that Yahweh had turned from the king.

Probably the manner of this narrative reflects the later opposition of prophets and kings; the matter is primitive enough, however, since it shows us a time when it was still possible for the old Holy War ideal to clash with the new secular conduct of the king's war.

David meets Saul

The Philistines mustered a new army and encamped in Judah, a great number of them stretching from Socoh to Azekah.

Saul brought up his men to face them and drew up his line of battle along one ridge of the valley of Elah. The Philistines then stood along the other ridge of the valley. So the armies faced one another and neither wanted to go down into the valley and climb up against the other.

Then from the Philistine ranks a man stepped out. He was well over seven foot tall and broad with it, and he was armed in bronze from helmet to the greaves on his legs. His spear was a beam of wood with a great bronze spear head upon it. It took a strong man to lift his shield. He was named Goliath of Gath.

Goliath came to the front of the Philistine spearsmen and shouted across to the Israelites on the other ridge: 'Why bother with battle-lines? Find a champion for yourselves and let him try his strength in single combat with me. If he kill me we shall serve you but if I kill him then you shall serve us. I challenge Israel to find a man who will fight with me on these terms.'

When Saul and his men heard this loud boasting they were afraid. They knew there was no one in the camp who could stand up to Goliath.

Day after day the armies faced one another across the valley. Each morning and each evening Goliath came out to mock Israel with his challenge. And no one dared accept it.

Among the Israelite soldiers there were three brothers, sons of a Benjamite farmer named Jesse. One day while the armies waited at Elah, Jesse sent his youngest son with provisions for the three brothers in the army and a cheese for their company commander. David found his brothers in the Israelite battle line and while he was talking with them Goliath came out on the other side of the valley and shouted his challenge across to Israel. The soldiers knew how real a threat this was. David asked them if there were a reward for killing Goliath. The soldiers were sure that the king would give wealth and his daughter to any man who could kill Goliath. They said so to the young David. He became eager to try his skill. David's elder brother Eliab was furious at the idea of this youngster setting himself up before all the experienced armed men of Israel. 'You're a romantic fool,' he said, 'come to see the fun of a battle.'

David shrugged his shoulders, 'I was only talking,' he said. Saul was told of his talk. The king sent for David.

David was full of confidence. 'I'll fight this Philistine,' he declared.

'You're only a boy,' said Saul, 'and Goliath is an experienced warrior.'

'I keep my father's sheep on the hill,' said David, 'and I've killed many a lion or bear that has come to steal one of the lambs. I'll leave this Goliath like a dead lion, sir. Yahweh has given me strength to deal with lions and bears, he will give me strength to deal with this uncircumcised Philistine who defies the army of Yahweh.'

Saul decided to let him try it: 'Go, and Yahweh be with you.'

The king loaded David with his own armour; he put on him his bronze helmet and his coat of mail and gave him his own sword to wield. When David tried to go out of Saul's tent he found he could not move, the armour was so heavy. So he said to the king: 'I can't take these. I'm not used to armour.' So David uncased himself and taking his own staff in his hand and putting five smooth stones from the brook in his shepherd's wallet and his sling over his shoulder, he went out to meet the Philistine.

Goliath came on with his shield-bearer and looked at David and mocked him. He looked so small and useless in a fight.

But David answered: 'You come to fight with sword and spear and javelin but I am armed with the name of Yahweh, the God of Battles, whom you mock here. This day Yahweh will deliver you into my hand and I will cut off your head and feed your body to the birds of the air so that everyone shall know that Yahweh is with Israel, Yahweh, who has no need of sword and spear.'

Then as Goliath came at him, David took a stone from his wallet, slung it across the valley and hit the Philistine in the forehead. The stone smashed into his skull and Goliath fell on his face in the mud.

David ran forward, snatched Goliath's own sword from the Philistine's belt, and sliced off his head with it. At this the line of Philistines turned and ran and the men of Israel leapt up and chased the Philistines as far as Gath and the gates of Ekron and the road was littered with the dying and the dead of Philistia all along the way.

Then the Israelites returned from the chase and plundered the Philistine camp. David took the head of Goliath and came with it to the king's tent. Saul's counsellor Abner brought him into Saul and the king said to David: 'Whose son are you, young

man?' 'I am the son of your servant Jesse of Bethlehem,' said
David. Saul made David a member of his royal household. His
policy was to attach professional soldiers to himself, granting
them baronial fiefs. Thus he began to erect a feudal system to
assure himself of some personal independence of the national
militia.

Jonathan, standing by Saul's side, thought David a fine fellow
and determined to be his friend. In the days that followed the
two young men went everywhere together and did everything
together. The king's son gave David his own robes and armour
to wear.

David went out to the wars again and had many successful
skirmishes with the king's enemies, and Saul gave him his
daughter Michal to be his wife. As David walked in the streets
of Jerusalem the Israelite women sang songs about him. One
of them had as a chorus the lines, 'Saul has slain his thousands,
but David has slain his ten thousands.'

Saul did not care for this song at all. He grew jealous of the
young soldier who was everybody's favourite. 'Next,' he
thought, 'they will offer him my kingdom.'

Saul planned to have David assassinated. Jonathan warned
David not to come to the court and went himself to persuade
the king to put aside his plan: 'David has done nothing against
you, he has always served you and won battles for you. You have
been pleased with him before, why turn against him now?'

Saul listened to Jonathan, and his words brought David
back into Saul's favour. The king put him again in charge of
the war with the Philistines.

The Camp Story of Samson

As the Israelite men sat in the camp at night they told one another
old stories of how their ancestors had beaten the Philistines in
earlier wars. Some of these stories, which encouraged them for their
present campaign, have come down to us. A set of these stories is
concerned with Samson and his great strength. Here is one of
them.

Once there was a man of Zorah, of the tribe of Dan, whose
name was Manoah. His wife was barren. Then an angel of
Yahweh came to her. He told her: 'Behold you shall conceive

and bear a son. He shall never shave his head and he shall be
the man to deliver Israel from the Philistines.'

Manoah and his wife did not guess that it was an angel who
had come to them. They asked the angel to take a meal with them
but he would not eat and told them to prepare a sacrifice for
Yahweh. As the sacrifice was burning the angel went up in the
flame of the altar and Manoah and his wife knew that they had
entertained an angel.

Their son was born. They named him Samson and he grew
up a brave youth. Now, strangely, Samson fell for a girl of
foreign Philistia, who lived in the village of Timnah, and he
went courting. As he walked one day to Timnah he passed
through the vineyard outside the village and met a lion roaring
in his path. He picked up the brute and tore it apart as another
man might tear a young goat. Then he went on his way and
sat talking with the girl in Timnah. Coming the same way on the
same errand he passed the dead lion and saw in its carcase a
swarm of bees and their honey. He cupped up the honey in his
hands and stuffed it in his mouth as he went on walking.

Manoah came down to Timnah to arrange the wedding and
the Philistines came out, thirty of them, ready for the party.
During the marriage feast, Samson said to them:

'Here is a riddle, if you can tell me the answer before the
week is up I will give you thirty coats and thirty wedding
garments, if you can't solve it you shall give me thirty such
coats and such wedding garments.'

They agreed to the terms. Samson said: 'Out of the eater
came food. Out of the strong came sweets.'

After three days of thinking and guessing the Philistines had
got nowhere, so they said to Samson's wife: 'Get us the answer
to the riddle or we'll burn you and your father's house. It's no
party if we have to pay.'

So Samson's Philistine wife went weeping and nagging
through their house, and she wore him out with her tears so
that on the seventh day he gave in and told her about the lion
and the honey. And she ran to her countrymen and on the last
evening they came to Samson with the right answer. He was
furious at the trick and went straightway down into the village
and killed thirty of the Philistine men and gave their coats to
those who had answered the riddle. He went back to Manoah's

house, leaving his wife in their home in the village. Her father married her to Samson's best man and thought no more of Samson.

The Israelites told a fierce sequel to this story of their hero.

After a while Samson came back to fetch his wife from Timnah and found her married to the other man. Again the anger was on him. He caught three hundred foxes and tied their tails together so that they were mad with fury and fright; he tied lighted torches to their tails and sent them maddened with pain and running wildly about into the wheat fields of the Philistines. All their harvest was burnt up by the fire of the terrified animals. Then the farmers demanded their revenge and they burnt Samson's wife and her father in their house because they had roused the anger of Samson.

Samson, of course, was angry again that his wife had been murdered, so he slaughtered the farmers in a great fight and went off into the hills. He had had enough.

The Israelites had another story about Samson's marriage difficulties which has become rather more famous than his dalliance with the woman of Timnah. After a whore in Gaza, a girl of Sorek attracted his heart. She was called Delilah. Her story too was concerned with the Philistine woman's dilemma—should she work for her countrymen or her husband?

The Lords of Philistia came to Delilah and persuaded her to ask Samson next time he sat with her to ask him how he came to be so strong and how they could keep him bound. They each promised her a thousand guineas for her trouble. They hid behind a curtain to listen for his answer. So she asked him and he said: 'Seven new bowstrings tied about me would make me as weak as another man.' He went to sleep in her lap: she bound him with seven brand-new bowstrings and the Philistines came out of hiding to hold him. Delilah cried out in pretended fear: 'The Philistines are upon you, Samson!' He woke at the sound, snapped the bowstrings like so many threads and could not be held down. He kept the secret of his strength that time and the Philistines went home with broken heads.

Delilah, of course, was angry with Samson for not trusting her with his secret. She questioned him again to find it out. So he quietened her a second time, pretending that if the Philistines bound him with new ropes, never used before, he would be manageable like other men.

Delilah bound him with new ropes as he slept and sent a message to her countrymen saying that now was the time to seize Samson. But at her warning cry he snapped the ropes at a bound and was free. The Philistines ran all the way home. Delilah pestered him again. And again Samson to gain peace deceived her. 'If you tie my hair in one knot and make it fast I shall be weak.' So she bound his hair in a knot, and made it firm and cried out, 'The Philistines are upon you, Samson,' and he woke and dealt with them as before.

'You don't love me,' Delilah sobbed. 'You don't tell me the truth.' And she nagged him day after day until he could bear it no longer and told her the truth:

'I am a Nazarite, I vowed to Yahweh never to cut my hair and because of this Yahweh has given me strength. If I were shaved then my strength would be gone and I should become weak as any other man.'

Delilah knew that this time he had told her the truth and she sent a messenger to the Philistine lords telling them to come just once more to catch Samson. She had a man shave off Samson's hair as he slept in her lap and then she teased and punched him and he had no strength against her. And she cried out, 'The Philistines are upon thee, Samson', and he got up to defend himself; but he was as weak as any other man and the lords of Philistia took him and gouged out his eyes and put him in a prison in Gaza and set him to work at the mill in the prison.

But his hair began to grow again.

The Philistines had a great celebration (at Samson's capture) in the temple of their God Dagon and sang songs as they drank, songs about Samson. Then they sent for Samson: 'Call Samson, we will mock him again.'

They made him do tricks.

Samson grew tired and said to the boy who led him about like a blind bear: 'Let me rest against the pillars which hold up the building'. The boy led him up to the two great pillars. The great party went on in the temple; all the great men of the country were there to see Samson do his tricks.

Then Samson spoke to Yahweh quietly amid the din: 'Yahweh,

remember me, just this once let me have my strength again that
I may be quits with the Philistines.'

He had a hand on each pillar. Samson said:

'Let me die but let me take the Philistines with me.' Then
he pushed against the pillars with all his renewed strength and
the temple fell down on top of them all, on the lords and ladies
of Philistia and on all their serving people, and on Samson.

The dead he killed there at his own death numbered more than
all he had killed in his life.

This story and many others like it helped the men of Israel to
feel brave and cheerful as they sat in the camp waiting to do battle
with their old enemies, the Philistines, who were still strong. If an
Israelite had beaten them in the past, then they could beat them
tomorrow.

Saul attempts to kill David

After the campaign against the Philistines David came back to
the court and everyone congratulated him on his great slaughter of
the enemy. David put aside his weapons and sat with Saul and
talked with him. Saul fell into a bad mood, thinking that everyone
had deserted him, that even his son Jonathan and his daughter
Michal loved David more than they loved their father.

The king played with a spear in his hand while David strum-
med upon the lyre and in a sudden rage Saul flung the spear
at David to pin him to the wall. But David was too quick for
him and raced out of the palace. Then Saul sent soldiers after
him to surround his house and kill him in the morning as he
came out. Michal saw the soldiers round the house and warned
her husband: 'You must escape tonight or tomorrow you will
be a dead man.' So he climbed out of a window and fled away.
Michal took a statue and wrapped it in blankets and laid it in
David's bed.

In the morning Saul's men came to the house to take David.
Michal met them and said, 'He is sick.' The men returned to
Saul and told him what Michal had said. Saul sent them back
again, saying, 'Bring him here on his bed that I may kill him.'
So they went into the room and went up to the bed and saw
that there was nothing but a statue lying there.

Saul said to his daughter: 'You have deceived me. Why did you let my enemy escape?'

Michal said: 'He threatened to kill me if I did not help him.'

David fled to Jonathan.

'What have I done? Why should your father seek to kill me?'

'I don't believe it. Of course you shall not die. There is nothing secret between me and my father. He has never said anything about this to me. It isn't true.'

'Your father knows that you are my friend. He says to himself, "Jonathan ought not to be told this, he will be too upset." But he does mean to kill me, and at once.'

'How can I help you?'

'Tomorrow is a feast day for the new moon. I should be at the celebrations with your father. But I will hide in the country. If your father notices that I am missing tell him, "He has gone home for a family sacrifice." If he is content then I am still in his favour, but if he is angry about this then certainly he means to destroy me. You have told me you are my friend. Do not let me down now.'

So they walked together into the fields and Jonathan promised to send David news of how the king took David's absence from the feasting, and he said:

'Whatever happens, swear that you will at any rate be my friend as I am yours.'

They swore to be friends for ever. Then Jonathan said: 'When I know my father's mind I will come out to shoot arrows for target-practice at this heap of stones. When the lad goes to fetch the arrows back, if I call to him, "The arrows are near you," come out and be sure of a welcome at the court; but if I call, "The arrows are further away", then go far from here for it is not Yahweh's will for you to stay. But whatever happens we shall be friends.'

So David hid in the field and Jonathan went in to the festival. Saul sat at his table with Abner the counsellor and Jonathan and he noted David's absence.

'Where is the son of Jesse? Why is he not here?'

'He has gone to join his brothers in a family sacrifice at Bethlehem.'

'You are a fool. You have made this man your friend when all he wants is your inheritance. Fetch him here. I'll kill him.'

'What has he done? Why should you kill him?'

Saul would not listen to Jonathan. He took a spear and lunged at his son, and Jonathan rose from the table in a fury, and would not take part in the king's feast.

He went out into the fields with his lad as if to practise archery and sent the lad to retrieve his arrows, calling out as the boy ran 'The arrows are further away, hurry up.' So the lad picked up the arrows and Jonathan gave him his bows and sent him back to his house.

As soon as the boy had gone, David came to the heap of stones and Jonathan hugged him as he wept until David recovered himself.

Then Jonathan said: 'Go in peace and Yahweh be with us and all our descendants for ever, for you are my friend.' So David went away and Jonathan walked back to the city.

David the Rebel

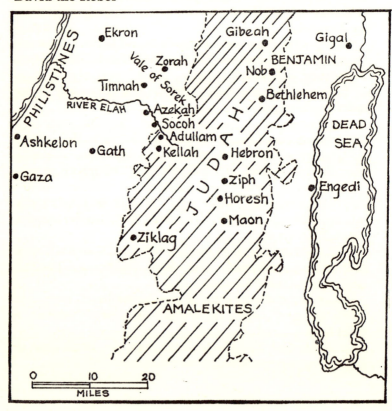

David rode away with his servants to the city of Nob and was met at the gateway by the priest Ahimelech who asked him why he came so poorly attended and with so little provision. 'I am on a secret mission for the king,' said David. 'Give me some food for my men and we will ride on.' Ahimelech had no bread in his house so he asked David whether his bodyguard had defiled themselves with women on their journey; if they had not he would give them the bread laid out before Yahweh. David assured him that on a journey of this urgency he certainly did not allow his men to indulge themselves with women. So the priest gave them the bread of Yahweh.

All the while Doeg the Edomite, the courtier of Saul, watched the business of Ahimelech and David and saw the priest give David Goliath's sword at parting.

David took his men and hid in the cave of Adullam and his brothers joined him and many other members of Jesse's family. When they heard that David was a rebel and an outlaw all the riff-raff of the nation set out for Adullam. The unemployables, the debtors and the malcontents made him their leader. About four hundred of them elected him their captain.

Saul hunted David.

The king sat under a tamarisk tree on the hill at Gibeah, with his spear in his hand, and he glared at his courtiers. He said to them:

'Think for a moment, you Benjaminites. Who gives you your fields and vineyards, who makes you officers and generals, David or Saul? Why, then, do you conspire against me? You tell me nothing of what my own son is doing for this rebel. You keep quiet, traitors.'

Then Doeg the Edomite said: 'I saw David in Nob. The priest Ahimelech gave him shelter and food and the sword of Goliath.'

So Saul sent for Ahimelech and he came with all the priests who were at Nob, and Saul told him: 'You are a traitor, you and the son of Jesse; you have comforted him and given him provisions and weapons, so that his rebellion prospers.'

Ahimelech said: 'Since when has David been a rebel? I know nothing of this. You can't blame me.'

'Off with you to execution, you and all your family. Kill them, guards, for they support the rebel David and are traitors to me.'

But the guards stood still. They did not dare touch the priests of the Lord. Saul turned to Doeg: 'Kill them!'

Doeg killed eighty-five priests that day and went down to Nob and sacked the city. Men and women, children and babies, and all their animals he killed.

Abiathar, one of the sons of Ahimelech, escaped and ran to David's camp to tell him that Saul had murdered the priests of Yahweh. David had guessed while he was with Ahimelech that Doeg would report everything to Saul: 'I am the cause of your father's death and the deaths of all your family. Stay with me. He that would kill me would kill you also. You are safe with me.'

After this David learnt that the Philistines were raiding the village of Keilah during the harvest time and he took his men there and drove off the Philistines from the village. But the villagers were not grateful. They plotted to hand David over to Saul, so he and his men went away into the hill country of Ziph. Saul sent scouts to look for him every day but David was never caught.

One day Jonathan went quietly from the king's camp and rode to David at Horesh to encourage him: 'Don't be afraid, my father will never capture you; you will be king over Israel and I will be your right-hand man. Even Saul recognizes this.' So again they swore their friendship before Yahweh and Jonathan went home.

Then the Ziphites told Saul that David was hiding in their hills and Saul was glad and arranged an expedition to hunt him out.

David therefore moved away ahead of Saul's troops to Maon south of Jeshimon and Saul pursued him. As David was hurrying down one side of a mountain, Saul was climbing up the other side in pursuit. He would have caught him there if he had not had to give up the chase and return to the capital to deal with a Philistine raid. So David made a camp for himself in the rocks of Engedi.

There was in Maon a rich farmer named Nabal who was shearing his sheep. David sent ten young warriors to him with this message: 'Peace be with you. You will observe that we have not molested your shepherds. We have protected them. Send us, therefore, an invitation to your shearing feast.'

The ten warriors stood round Nabal and waited for his answer. Nabal said, 'Who is this David? Where does he come from? There are many rebels about now. I won't have such men to my feast.'

The young men went back to David and told him what Nabal had said.

'Let each man take his sword,' cried David, 'and follow me.' They set out for Nabal's caravan. David swore: 'He has returned evil for good; Yahweh, do so to David, if I do not kill every man in his household by morning.'

One of the shepherds went to Nabal's wife, Abigail, and told her of the way Nabal had refused to have anything to do with David: 'His men were very good to us and protected us while we were in the fields with the sheep. Now he is bound to come against us all because our master railed at them—and our master is so bad-tempered that none of us dare talk to him.'

Abigail got together a great quantity of loaves, and sheep and wine, put them on asses, and set out with the shepherds. She did not tell her husband what she had taken or where she was going. On her way she met David and his men coming towards her husband's house. She got off her ass and knelt in the mud before David: 'My lord, do not pay any attention to my stupid husband, he has always been a fool. If I had known what was going on your men should not have been turned away. Of course you are right to be angry but do not stain your own hands with blood, keep your sword for the enemies of Yahweh and you shall be king. Take, therefore, this present now and when you are king remember your servant, Abigail.'

'Blessed be Yahweh who has sent you to me to keep me from shedding blood in vengeance. For as Yahweh lives, if you had not rushed out here to prevent me I would have killed each man in your husband's house.'

David took the provisions she had brought and sent her back to her husband. When she got back that night her husband was holding his great feast at the end of the shearing. He was drunk. So she told him nothing. In the morning, when he was sober, she told him what she had done. Nabal had a stroke and died ten days later.

David rejoiced that he was avenged without incurring any

guilt by the death of Nabal. He sent a message to Abigail, 'Come, be my wife.'

She came.

David had also married Ahinoam of Jezreel. Saul had already given Michal, David's first wife, to another man.

David among the Philistines

David said to himself: 'If I stay in Israel Saul will catch me one day and have me killed. My only safety is to cross the border into Philistia.'

So he took his men and their families with him and his two wives, Ahinoam of Jezreel and Abigail, the widow of Nabal, and fled to Gath over the Philistine border. A local chieftain let him settle his followers in the village of Ziklag. David had now joined a new feudal society.

Every now and again, David and his men would raid villages in the deep south belonging to the Amalekites, Israel's oldest enemies. His warfare was brutal in the extreme. He killed every man, woman and child in the villages he attacked, so that no one remained alive to say where he had been. Only the cattle were spared as part of the booty. When the chieftain of Gath asked him where he had been he would always say he had made a raid against the Israelites and their friends. Thus he gave the impression that he was making enemies among his own people. The men of Gath trusted him.

So great was their trust that when the Philistines were told to muster against Israel, the men of Gath took David and his troop along to the meeting place to stand in the battle line. But the other Philistines were not so trusting and sent David back to Ziklag.

When David and his men got back to Ziklag they discovered that the Amalekites had made a sudden attack on the village and carted off the Israelites that had been left, women and children mostly, to be their slaves and burnt the houses and ridden away. David said to Abiathar: 'What shall we do? Will Yahweh give us a victory over this band?' He answered: 'Ride after them.' So David and his men set out across the open country in pursuit of the Amalekite raiders. The horsemen who rode ahead of the main body of David's foot-soldiers found a young man lying in the desert almost dead. They brought him to

David and gave him bread to eat and water to drink and a cluster of grapes and he revived. David questioned him:

'To whom do you belong?'

'I am an Egyptian, a soldier in the service of an Amalekite. My master left me behind three days ago because I was sick. We had made a foray on Ziklag and burnt it down.'

'Take me to this band.'

'Swear that you will not kill me, or hand me over to my master, and I will lead you to them.'

The Egyptian led them to the Amalekite encampment. The troopers lay on the ground to eat, or danced and drank, filled with happiness at the thought of all the booty they had taken and the slaves they had captured from Ziklag. David came down suddenly upon them. Those he did not kill fled away leaving their booty and their Israelite captives behind them. David recovered everything his village had lost, and took for himself the herds of the Amalekites and the spoil that the raiders had snatched from other villages.

David sent presents of cattle and the spoil to all those men in Palestine who had helped him earlier as he wandered the country as a fugitive from the anger of Saul.

We can see in David's actions at this time a preparation for the day when the men would choose him for their king. Though he lives among the Philistines he kills not their enemies but the enemies of Israel, and he sends presents not to the five great lords of Philistia but to his supporters in his home country.

The Death of Saul

Meanwhile the Philistine army had met Saul's troops at Mount Gilboa and had won a great victory. They overtook Saul and three of his sons as they fled from the battle. Jonathan and his two brothers were killed.

Saul turned and stood his ground. Only the enemy archers dared attack him and their many arrows pierced his body. He called out to his armour-bearer: 'Draw your sword and thrust it in me lest these uncircumcised men come to torture me and make sport of me.' Saul feared the fate of Samson.

But his armour-bearer would not touch the anointed king, so Saul thrust his own sword into his body and died there. When

his armour-bearer saw that Saul was dead, he too killed himself.
The king of Israel, his sons and his armour-bearer and his men
died on one day and the Philistines occupied the land.

When the Philistines came to strip the slain they picked up
the body of Saul on Mount Gilboa. They cut off his head and
took off his armour and proclaimed a festival in honour of their
gods at the death of the enemy king. They put Saul's armour
in their temple of Ashtaroth and his head in the Temple of
Dagon. They nailed Saul's body and the bodies of his three sons
to the walls of Beth-shan.

When the men of Jabesh-gilead heard of the shameful thing
that the Philistines had done to the princes of the royal house, a
group of daring warriors marched all night to the walls of
Beth-shan and took away the bodies of Saul and his three sons
to bury them.

THE HOUSE OF DAVID

David the King

After the death of Saul at Mount Gilboa an Amalekite snatched up the crown and ran to David at Ziklag.

David said to him: 'Where have you come from?'

'I have run from the battle.'

'Who has won? Tell me quickly, who has won?'

'Saul and his sons are killed, and the people of Israel have fled.'

'How can you be sure that Saul and his sons are dead?'

'I was there. Saul leaning on his spear with the enemy coming about him saw me standing behind him and told me to kill him. So I did. I took the crown from his head, and I have brought it to you, my lord.'

Then David wept for Saul and Jonathan and the dead men of Israel. He said to the Amalekite:

'How dare you raise your hand against the anointed of Yahweh?'

He turned to one of his warriors, 'Kill him.' As the Amalekite lay dying at his feet David said to him: 'Your blood be on your own head for you boasted that you had killed the anointed of Yahweh.'

David made a song for the mourners to sing for Saul and Jonathan:

> The glory of Israel lies dead on the mountain,
> The young men lie dead;
> Keep the news from the men of Gath;
> Silence the crier in the streets of Askelon,
> For the Philistine women will shout
> And the uncircumcised be merry.

In the midst of the battle,
Where the fighting was fierce,
Jonathan stretched his bow-string
And Saul laid on with the sword:
Living together,
Dying together;
Eagles in speed,
Lions in strength;
Dead on the field the strong ones of Israel.

Jonathan lies on the mountain,
My brother Jonathan.
I mourn for my love on the mountain.
Though women love me
I do not hope to have such love again
As I have had of Jonathan.

Then the men of the tribes of Judah came to David and anointed him king.

At the same time Abner, Saul's commander-in-chief, proclaimed Saul's son Ishbaal king in Israel. Two claimed, therefore, to be Yahweh's king. Abner and David's commander, Joab, arranged a meeting at the pool of Gibeon. During the negotiations Abner said to Joab, 'Let our warriors give an exhibition bout of their prowess', and Joab agreed. In the heat of the game they became excited and fell together in earnest and killed each other. Then the other members of the party joined in and Abner and his men had to flee.

Joab had brought with him to Gibeon his two brothers Abishai and Asahel. Asahel was a swift runner and he went in chase of Abner. He ran straight after Abner, paying no attention to anyone else, and Abner called to him, 'Go after some other man'. But still he followed Abner. Abner called to him, 'How shall I face Joab if I kill you?' But he bore down on Abner. Abner halted suddenly and the butt end of his spear went into Asahel's belly and came out at his back and he died there.

Then Joab and Abishai hunted for Abner in the dark but he escaped. Joab buried his brother and marched his men through the night back to David at Hebron.

This was the beginning of a long civil war by which at last David became strongest in Israel.

Abner quarrelled with Ishbaal about a concubine and sent a message to David suggesting that he should hand over Israel to David, but David knew that Yahweh would give him the kingdom and refused to receive it by an act of treachery. He only suggested that Abner should arrange the return of Michal, Saul's daughter, who was his first wife. This Abner did, and while Joab was away on an expedition Abner came to talk with David to suggest that a rebellion be organized against Ishbaal. Again David refused and Abner went back homewards.

When Joab arrived at Hebron he was told of Abner's visit and he hurried to David: 'Why have you let Abner go home free? He is a spy and will deceive you.'

Joab sent men after Abner to call him back, and he came though he had travelled some miles north of Hebron. Joab took him apart from his men as though to talk confidentially with him and smote him in the belly so that he died. Asahel was avenged.

It cannot have escaped Joab's notice that now he was the only experienced general left. David was furious. He was afraid that all the men of Israel would accuse him of tricking Abner and arranging his death. He ordered a solemn funeral for the dead general.

Everyone saw that Abner had been killed against David's will. He said to his men: 'A great prince has been murdered and I can do nothing even though I am king; Joab and his brother rule here. May Yahweh punish them!'

Meanwhile there was chaos and confusion in Israel when news came of the murder of Abner. Ishbaal's courage failed and his government collapsed. Two men of his household by a trick got access to his bedroom and there as he slept in the afternoon smote him in the belly and sliced off his head. They took Ishbaal's head to David:

'Here is the head of Ishbaal, Saul's son, your enemy.'

'When a man came to tell me that he had killed Saul I had him cut down at Ziklag. What less can men who have killed a sleeping prince expect? Kill them.'

David's warriors slew the assassins and cut off their heads and their feet and hung their bodies on the street wall. They buried the head of Ishbaal in the tomb of Abner. Of Saul's house there

Library of
Davidson College

was now left only Mephibosheth, the crippled son of Jonathan, who had been dropped by his nurse when a very young baby. So the great men of Israel came to David at Hebron, and proclaimed him and anointed him king of Israel. David was now king over the whole people. There followed three days of feasting.

David in Jerusalem

David had it in mind to have a city of his own and he chose a well-fortified place set between his new kingdoms, belonging to no tribe. He set out with his own men to take Jerusalem.

The Jebusite men of Jerusalem looked down from their high walls and mocked David for they felt secure in their defences. 'It would need only blind men and lame men to defend this city against David', they declared.

First David captured the stronghold of Zion at one end of the city. He then offered the command of his whole army to the man who would scale the walls of the keep first. Joab was first up the walls and was made commander for this service. David had captured Jerusalem. He set up his house in Zion and began work to make Jerusalem as impregnable as the men of the city had thought it before. Joab took charge of the repair work and the strengthening of the walls.

David, therefore, was king in his own city and all men saw that Yahweh had made him great in the land. The Philistines did not like the look of this at all. They prepared for battle with this too successful man. They sent out an army that filled the plain of Rephaim.

This was an army too great for David to defeat in open field so he went another way about to get the victory. Outflanking them and attacking them out of the cover of a small wood, he so surprised the large force of the enemy that the Philistines ran home along the road from Geba to Gezar.

David saw that he had achieved a breathing-space in his wars and took the opportunity to demonstrate in a valid manner that he was king in Jerusalem by the will of Yahweh. He determined to bring the Ark into his city. Men would then understand that

Yahweh had established David as the guardian of the most sacred sign in Israel.

The Ark of Yahweh

In earlier days, long before Saul was made king, Eli and the young Samuel had guarded the Ark of the covenant at Shiloh.

The men of Israel under the leadership of Eli's sons, Hophni and Phinehas, had gone out to fight with the Philistines. The Philistines put them to rout. The captains of Israel met and discussed the causes of their defeat and one of them suggested that they bring the Ark of the covenant from Shiloh into the camp. 'If Yahweh is with us, we shall have a victory.' So Hophni and Phinehas took the Ark from the shrine and went up to the front line.

On the arrival of the great symbol of Yahweh the whole army of Israel gave an enormous shout. The Philistines heard it across the plain and sent a spy to find out the cause of the commotion. When they were told that the Ark had been brought into the Israelite camp they were afraid and whispered to one another, 'We shall lose. For they have a God in their company.' Then the commander of the Philistines encouraged his men, declaring that they would have to fight all the more keenly because of the Ark. 'Take courage and acquit yourselves like men lest you are taken for slaves.' The Philistines plucked their courage high and went charging into the fight so that the Israelites were scattered. Each man of them that could escape from the field of slaughter ran straight home leaving Hophni and Phinehas dead and the Ark in the hands of the Philistines.

When a survivor came to Shiloh, Eli, who was ninety-eight years old, was sitting on a stool by the roadway; hearing the news of the defeat, of the death of his sons and of the loss of the Ark of Yahweh, he fell backward off his stool for grief and horror, his neck was broken and he died.

The next part of the narrative is evidently written to show the wonder of Yahweh against all other gods.

Meanwhile the Philistines carted the Ark to Ashdod and placed it before the idol of their god Dagon. In the morning when the Philistines came to look at their booty they found Dagon flat on his face before the Ark. Though they set him up again, by next morning the idol had fallen again and smashed into pieces. At the same time bubonic plague broke out in the town and rats ran about everywhere. The men of Ashdod felt that things were going wrong for them and they put it down to the presence of the Ark of Yahweh. They decided to send it on to Gath. But the men of Gath got panicky and came out in rashes and sent

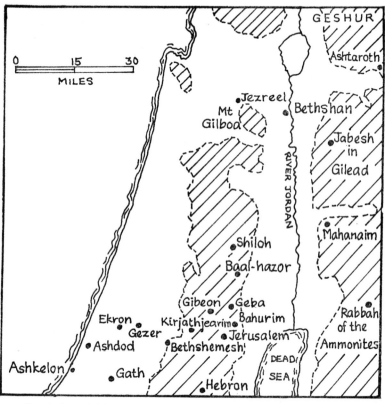

the Ark quickly on to Ekron. When the Ark arrived at Ekron the citizens would have nothing to do with it and sent for the rulers of Philistia at once to take the Ark away. They were scared to death.

So the five great lords of the Philistine cities and their priests arrived at Ekron and resolved to put the Ark on a bullock-wagon and let the animals bear it away. 'For,' as the priests said, 'if it goes back to Israel then we shall know it is the Israelite god who has done this to us and if not we shall know that all these calamities have happened by chance.'

The bullocks set off for Israel and crossed the border at the village of Bethshemesh. The villagers came out and shouted for joy that the Ark was back in Israel again. They chopped up the wooden cart and burnt the bullocks on the wood as a sacrifice to Yahweh. The five lords of Philistia who had followed the cart at a distance saw what had happened and rode back to Ekron. But the men of Bethshemesh were uneasy at the Ark being in their village, they knew what had happened in Philistia, so they sent to the neighbouring town of Kirjath-jearim suggesting that this was a more fitting place for the Ark of Yahweh. The men of Kirjath-jearim came and took the Ark, and it remained there all through the reign of Saul.

The Ark was not taken back to Shiloh because this great national shrine had been destroyed by the Philistines. During the reign of Saul the Ark was forgotten amid the hustle of the civil war and the continuous fight against the Philistines. It became the sacred symbol of the townsmen of Kirjath-jearim rather than of the whole people.

We may see in David's bringing of the Ark to his city of Jerusalem an attempt to show the conservatives that in his kingdom the old sign of the tribal confederation was respected. His action asserted a continuity between the old Judges and the new Kings. Saul's reign was made to appear an unfortunate interlude.

David welcomes the Ark to Jerusalem

It may be that David's plan to remove the Ark from Kirjath-jearim was not welcomed by the men of the city who thought of themselves as particularly protected by Yahweh's presence, but we cannot be certain of this. At any rate it is clear that David's intention was to make his city a national shrine. He was able to colour this by the presence in his household of Abiathar, the last member of the old priesthood of the Ark tradition.

David got his household men together and went to Kirjath-jearim to fetch the Ark away on a new cart, and the guardians of the shrine Uzzah and Zadok guided the cart towards Jerusa-

lem. There was a great procession led by David, singing songs
and leaping before the Ark and bandsmen making a great noise
with cymbals and tambourines and many other loud instruments.

An accident stopped their happiness: at the threshing floor
of Nacon the oxen stumbled and Uzzah thrust out his hand to
steady the Ark, touched the sacred palladium and fell dead.

This incident caused David to lose his temper at the unreason-
ableness of Yahweh who required the ritual ceremonies demanded
of the priests before touching the Ark to be observed at such a
moment, and Uzzah's fate has disturbed most readers of the narrative. It may be that the priestly chronicler meant the story to be
understood as a sign of the sheer power of God's presence which
must infallibly destroy those priests in the temple service who do
not take the proper precautions before approaching the Ark. The
chronicler seems to have had a rather too developed reverence for
rubrics. If it seems a strange way of thinking about Yahweh we
must simply note the strangeness, and be thankful that he has
revealed himself, through Jesus, as our Father.

After this mishap David abandoned his plan to bring the Ark
into Jerusalem and left it on the farm of a neighbouring Philistine (who was, perhaps, press-ganged into accepting this
dangerous charge).

Things now took a different turn. The farmer's wife bore him
a son and his fields grew greater crops than before. David heard
that the man was blessed by Yahweh. He decided that he would,
after all, bring the Ark into his own city. Once again the
bandsmen played and David leapt before the Ark and sacrificed
to Yahweh. David wore a linen loincloth for his dance and, as
he paused under the windows of his own house, his first wife,
Michal, the daughter of Saul, looked out and saw him half-
naked among the shouting peasantry, and she despised him.

The procession moved on and David brought the Ark to the
tent he had pitched for it. There he offered sacrifices and David
blessed the people, giving them meat and cakes and fruit to
keep a feast that day. Then each one went home to his own house.
David returned home and found Michal, the daughter of King
Saul, waiting for him.

'The king of Israel certainly knows how to behave with dignity, dancing half-naked with the servants, like one of the shameless grooms.'

'Your father knew how to be a king and he lost his throne. Yahweh has made me king over all your family.'

Here David sang a snatch of the dancers' song to annoy her:

'Before the Lord I will leap,
Before the Lord I will dance.'

'Anyway,' he continued, 'the servants you despise certainly won't think me less of a king because I humble myself to be Yahweh's juggler, whatever you may think.'

Michal had borne no children and she did not conceive again after that day.

David and Bathsheba

The historian has brought out the important point that at the time when David was working so hard to bring the people to accept his dynasty as the proper authority in Israel all chance of having a line of kings to succeed him seems to be taken away.

The situation was not made any better for David by the next incident that the historian has recorded.

Once David had settled down in Jerusalem and had quietened his enemies and built himself a palace, he thought it was time that he built a house for the Ark of God. He saw very well that the more obviously Yahweh was linked with the monarchy in the eyes of the people the safer was his throne. A palace impressed them and made them respect him, a temple would make them recognize that he ruled 'by divine right'. So he decided to erect a temple in Jerusalem.

Other people saw what David was after and did not care at all for the centralization of authority in the hands of the king. These, led by the conservative religious leader Nathan, opposed the building of the temple on the grounds that they had never had a temple when Yahweh was with them in the desert so why should they have one now. Nathan spoke to the king:

Yahweh of battles has made you king over us, you who were once a shepherd boy, and he has given you victory in all your wars. Now he has given us peace again, we have settled down as we were in the time of the Judges. Peace is enough. He has given you peace and power, and he will give you a long line of kings: be content.

So David dropped the idea of building a temple and went off to the wars to win more treasures for his city and more lands for his kingdom.

At the same time he was worried lest those who were not favourable to his plans might conspire against him to end his rule. They had an obvious pretext in Mephibosheth, the son of Jonathan and grandson of Saul, the surviving member of the previous royal house. So he cleverly shackled Mephibosheth by bringing him to live in his palace at Jerusalem. He could both seem to look after the young cripple and keep an eye on him.

The bringing of the Ark into Jerusalem, the conquest of Zobah and Syria, the surveillance of Saul's grandson, were all measures David took to secure the throne for his son, but his heir still had to be born.

In the spring, the time when kings go forth to battle, David sent his general Joab with an army to subdue the troublesome Ammonites. The army besieged the Ammonites in Rabbah through the long hot summer days.

One afternoon that summer, David went up onto the roof of his palace where it was cooler than in the stuffy rooms below. David walked on his flat roof and looked over Jerusalem. He saw a woman bathing; and the woman was very beautiful. He sent a servant to find out who she was and to bring her to him. Bathsheba, the wife of Uriah, a foreigner, a Hittite, came to David. Her husband was away with the army and she became David's mistress. She conceived a child.

David realized that if his people heard of this his reputation would be ruined, and his throne would become insecure. He thought of a way out of his difficulties. He summoned Uriah back from the army, pretending he wanted news of the siege. He hoped that Uriah would sleep with his wife while he was on leave and that he would think that the child she would bear was really his.

But Uriah did not go to visit his wife that night since a warrior in the 'Holy War' must give up all pleasure; he stayed with the other army officers in the palace. David's plan came to nothing. 'Stay another day', the king said to Uriah, 'and then go back to Rabbah.' Uriah stayed another day and that night David made him drunk, hoping that this would rouse him to go seeking Bathsheba, but he did not go down to his house in the city. David then decided that Uriah was too dangerous to live. He wrote a letter to Joab and told Uriah to take it back to his general. In the letter David wrote: 'Set Uriah in the front line where the fighting is fiercest, and then leave him to fight alone so that he may be struck down and killed.' So Uriah was put with the king's own bodyguard in the front line and was killed.

A messenger was sent back at once to the king and he gave David Joab's account of the engagement: 'The enemy made a sortie from the city but we drove them back to the gates. As we were fighting in the gates their archers shot at us from the walls and some of your own bodyguard are killed; Uriah the Hittite died with them.'

And David said to the messenger: 'Tell Joab that the death of my men is part of the chance of battle, carry on to victory, capture the city.' After a suitable time of mourning David sent for Uriah's widow and made her his wife and she bore his son.

David now had a kingdom and an heir. But it was hardly to be expected that a child born to him in such circumstances would inherit the promise of God's favour. The historian points this out in one of his few comments on the situation he is describing: 'The thing that David had done displeased the Lord.'

Nathan came again to the king and told him a story:

'There were two citizens, one rich and one poor. The rich one was a farmer with huge herds of cows and flocks of sheep. The poor man had nothing but one little ewe lamb. He loved the little lamb and brought it up in his house with the family, it used to eat from his hand and drink from his cup and he sat with it lying on his lap in the evening. It happened one day that the rich man had a guest to supper and he did not want to kill one of his own many animals so he took the poor man's lamb and cooked it for his guest.'

David broke out in fury at this injustice:

'The man who has done this ought to be killed. He shall pay back fourfold what he has taken. Who is he?'

'You are the man. Yahweh chose you as king over Israel when you were a hunted rebel, you have Saul's palace and all his possessions, yet you have murdered an innocent man and taken his wife to be your wife. Yahweh will see to it that trouble comes to you in the midst of your family. Your own wives will be taken from you and publicly given to another. What you have done secretly will be done openly against you.'

'I have sinned.'

'Yahweh will forgive you. But he will also punish you. The child of Bathsheba, your child, shall die.' Nathan went back to his own home.

The baby became ill. David prayed for its life to Yahweh; he fasted; he lay on the ground pleading all night.

His counsellors came to take him up and give him something to eat but David would not listen. After a week the child died. His men were afraid to tell David what had happened. They thought that since he was so upset at its illness he would go mad if he heard that the child was dead. David noticed their whispering in the corner of his room and guessed what it was they were saying:

'Is the child dead?'

'He is dead.'

David rose from the ground, washed and put on a set of clean clothes and went into the tent of Yahweh for a moment to worship him and came back asking his servants for some food. They brought him a meal and one of them dared to ask him: 'When the child was alive you wept and prayed and fasted, now it is dead you wash and change and eat. Why is this?'

'While the child lived,' the king answered, 'I thought Yahweh might give him back his health, but now he is dead there is no need to fast. Can fasting bring him to me from the dead? He will not come again, to me, but I shall go to him.'

That night David comforted Bathsheba for the loss of her baby; and she conceived again and bore a son whom they called Solomon.

David sent a message to Nathan that another son had been given him by Yahweh.

Meanwhile Joab was besieging the royal city of Rabbah, the capital of the Ammonites, and it was about to fall to his army. So he sent word to David: 'Come and be here when the city

collapses so that you may have the glory of its conquest.' David
went to the siege and at the last fight he took the heavy golden
crown off the head of the Ammonite king and put it on his own
brow and wore the golden armour of the dead king. The people
of the city were given saws and picks and axes, and were forced
to work in the brick kilns of David's kingdom.

The Rape of Tamar

The chronicler moves quickly to an account of David's family
difficulties. The prophecy of Nathan is seen to be working itself out
among the king's many children.

Absalom, David's eldest son and the most handsome man in
Israel, had a sister, Tamar, who was very beautiful. Amnon,
another of David's sons—by another wife—fell in love with his
half-sister Tamar—or rather, so lusted for her that he made
himself ill. He told his cousin Jonadab, the son of David's
brother Shimeah, how he desired Tamar. Jonadab thought of
a plan to satisfy Amnon.

'Get into bed and pretend to be very ill and when the king
comes to see you suggest to him that Tamar come to nurse
you.'

So he did and David sent Tamar to look after Amnon. She
cooked him a meal and brought it to him as he lay in bed. Amnon would not touch the food. He told everyone to go out of the
room and said to Tamar: 'Stay and bring me the food again.'
She stayed behind and came up to his bed and he leapt up and
caught hold of her and said, 'Come to bed with me, my sister.'
Tamar struggled, protesting: 'Let me go, do not force me to lie
with you. This is unheard of. I could never hold my head up
again, and your own reputation would be ruined. Ask the king,
he will make me your wife.'

Amnon would not listen to her, he forced her onto the bed and
lay with her. But afterwards he despised her; he had done with
Tamar. He would not look at her. 'Get out', he shouted at her.
Tamar protested: 'This is worse than before; having forced me
you should marry me.' Amnon would not listen to her and called
his servants and had her thrust out of his room. Tamar went
howling down the corridors and Absalom took her into his own
house where she sat desolate. When the king heard what had

happened he was very angry. But he did nothing. Absalom went about the court and refused to speak to Amnon. Absalom neither cursed nor forgave Amnon, he simply waited his opportunity.

It came two years later. Absalom had a fine harvest at his farm in Baal-hazor and planned a party to celebrate. He invited his father and all the king's sons to the feast. David knew that when a king came to a party it cost the host a great deal of money to entertain him, so he refused, but he let his sons go to the farm feast. Absalom poured out flagons of wine till the young men were merry and carefree, then he said to his farm hands. 'Pitch into Amnon. I will take any blame.' So they killed him there and the party at once broke up in confusion. All the king's sons rode away terrified.

A messenger had raced ahead of them as soon as the murder was done and came to David crying out: 'Absalom has slain all the king's sons, they are all dead.' David threw himself on the ground in despair. But Jonadab guessed what had happened and said: 'I am sure that Amnon alone is killed. Absalom had reason enough to kill him after he violated Tamar.' And at that moment the watchman on the tower called out, 'There is a great company of horsemen coming along the Horonaim road.' Jonadab said, 'There, I told you so, the king's sons are returned.' They came in, frightened but alive, and everyone weeping for Amnon.

Absalom fled to Geshur, out of David's reach and after a while the king forgave him. It was no use weeping for Amnon, he was dead and gone. But he exiled Absalom.

Joab saw that David wanted Absalom back with him in the court and he hit on a plan to persuade David to recall his son. Every morning David himself heard the disputes of his people. They came in great numbers to the palace. Joab sent an old village woman to David with a fine tale of woe. She came into the court and cried out to David as he sat on the throne to deal justice to his people:

'Help me, sir.'

'What is the matter with you?'

'I am a widow and I had two sons. They quarrelled with one another and fought in the fields. There was no one around to part them. One killed the other. Now the whole family wants my remaining son killed to avenge the boy he murdered. But if they kill this one I shall have no one left to look after me at all.'

'I will see that everything is set right for you.'

'Swear it, sir, swear that my son shall live.'

'He shall not be touched, I swear.'

'Well then, my lord, can I talk about something else?'

'Carry on.'

'What you say about my son fits your own case, sir. You ought to recall Absalom. Still, I am grateful for all you have done for me and my son, I will not bother you again. Yahweh be with you.'

'Now you answer me a question.'

'I am the servant of the king.'

'Did Joab put you up to this?'

'Oh, you are a clever one, and no mistake, my lord. Yes, I cannot hide it from you. Joab did bring me here to tell the tale.'

'Very well, Joab, have your way. Bring back Absalom.'

So Absalom came back to his farm near Jerusalem, but David would not let his son come to visit him; he told him to stay in his own house. Absalom stayed on his farm for over two years. Then he sent a message to Joab: 'Persuade the king to take me back into favour.'

And Joab did nothing.

Absalom sent the message a second time and still Joab did nothing.

So Absalom determined to stir up Joab. He sent men to set fire to Joab's cornfields. The commander-in-chief came storming to Absalom's farm demanding an explanation and the prince answered him: 'This was the only way to make you take notice of me. It were better I had never come back from exile than to go on like this. I want to go to the king—if he has me killed there will be an end of all this at any rate.'

So Joab told David what Absalom had said and the king summoned the prince and hugged him.

Now that he was able to appear in public, Absalom set about stealing the loyalty of David's people for himself. He used to get up early and stand at the door as the people passed on their way to David's judgment hall. Absalom would hail a man and ask him about his home town, his business and his suit to the king, and would say: 'It is obvious that you have right on your side but the king is too busy to attend to your business. It's a great pity that I am not made the judge, then everything would be set to right at once.'

Whenever a man in the city noticed that he was the prince and made to bow to him, Absalom would put out his hand and treat him as an equal.

Thus Absalom became a popular hero all over Israel.

Absalom rebels

After four years of preparation Absalom was ready to seize the throne. He told David that he was going on a pilgrimage to the shrine of Hebron, and he collected his force there for the rebellion. With him was the crafty counsellor Ahithophel from David's court. Men flocked to Absalom in great numbers.

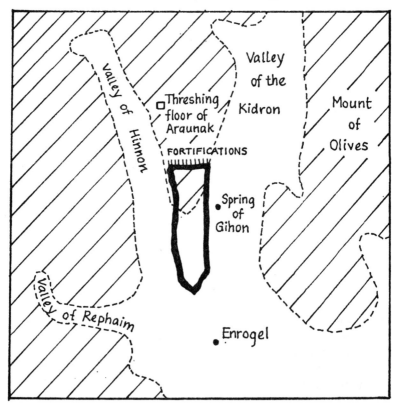

The conspiracy was so successful that David saw that he could not win against his son in a pitched fight. The king had not enough men. He decided to evacuate his court lest Absalom arrive and kill them all. David took only his personal bodyguard with him and left his house in the charge of ten concubines. He walked out of Jerusalem while the citizens wept at the gate. They did not know what would happen to them after the king had left Jerusalem. He crossed the brook Kidron and went on towards the desert. Learning that the king was leaving the city, Abiathar and Zadok the priests took the Ark of the covenant and hurried after David. When they caught up with him the king refused to let them journey on with him: 'Take the Ark of Yahweh back into the city. If Yahweh is good to me I shall return and see the Ark again, but if I have lost his favour then let his will be done. Go back and send me word what happens in the city when Absalom arrives.'

So Abiathar and Zadok took the Ark back to Jerusalem and waited there for the prince. David walked barefoot to the shrine on the Mount of Olives, weeping. A messenger ran up to him with the news that the wise counsellor Ahithophel had joined the rebel forces; David exclaimed, 'May Yahweh turn his wisdom to folly.' He came to the shrine on the hill. There Hushai the Archite, a leading member of the council, met him, determined to share the king's misfortune. David told him: 'If you stay with me you will simply be another mouth to feed, but if you go back to the court and pretend loyalty to Absalom then you can work for me against Ahithophel. Use Zadok and Abiathar as messengers back to me.'

Hushai, David's friend, got back to Jerusalem, just before Absalom arrived in triumph.

David walked on from the shrine and was overtaken by Ziba, the steward of Saul's crippled son Mephibosheth. Ziba brought a couple of asses laden with bread and raisins and a skin of wine. 'Why have you brought these?' asked David.

'Ride the ass, sir, and give your men the food to keep them going on your desert journey.'

'Where is your master?'

'He stayed in Jerusalem thinking that his opportunity had come. "If the house of David quarrels then I may inherit the kingdom of Saul, my father," he said.'

'Then you shall be master instead, and possess all Mephibosheth's wealth.'

'I am your man, for ever.'

David's distrust of the house of Saul seems justified by this incident, it is further strengthened by the next interruption of his journey into the desert. His column of weary men goes along a valley road half-way up the hillside. On the other side of the valley, but within shouting distance, stands Shimei, another member of the fallen royal family of Saul.

Shimei cursed David, vilely abusing him in the presence of his men, throwing stones and mud at the tired king across the valley and shouting: 'Get going, you man of blood, you hoodlum. Yahweh has at last avenged the blood of all our house that you have spilled. Your son hates you. Your kingdom is lost. You are finished; murderer.' And he threw across another clod of earth.

One of the soldiers could not stand this outrage: 'Let me get at him. I'll swing the dead dog's head in the air.'

But David would not let him: 'If Yahweh has put it in his mind to curse me, should I prevent him? If my own son seeks my life may not this man of Saul curse me? I must bear all in patience, then Yahweh may pity me. He may reward my silence today with his favour tomorrow.'

So the column went along the hill road while Shimei flung his stones at them, jeering at the wretched king. They came at last to the Jordan and washed in the river.

Meanwhile Absalom had established himself in Jerusalem and all the people cheered him as he stood in front of David's house leaning on Ahithophel his counsellor. Hushai, the friend of David, was foremost among the cheering men:

'Long live the king! Long live the king!' he cried, and Absalom, surprised at his welcome, asked him:

'Are you, my father's old friend, deserting him now?'

'Yahweh and the people choose you as king, my lord. I serve the king of Israel. As I have been your father's friend, so I will be your friend.'

Hushai was accepted as one of the new king's counsellors. Ahithophel now advised Absalom to pitch a tent on the roof of the palace and let the people see him following his father's concubines into the tent. Then everyone would know that there was no going back. David and Absalom would never be reconciled after such an affront to the king. Absalom's men would therefore be more confident that their prince would not make peace for himself and leave them to the king's pleasure. Absalom's taking of the concubines was tantamount to an announcement that he thought of David as dead. David would seem to have taken Saul's concubines to himself and it may have been the custom. In this instance Absalom was, however, working his own ruin.

The chronicler records Absalom's sense of power and triumph in this act, but in writing it down he must have remembered the story of how Reuben had gone in to his father's concubine and lost the inheritance of the first-born son, keeping only his father's curse.

Ahithophel was thus both furthering the working out of Nathan's prophecy of strife between father and son over the wives and concubines, and bringing about a situation in which Absalom is risking divine vengeance. Ahithophel certainly would remember Nathan's fury at David's snatching of Bathsheba—indeed he must have shared it, for he was Bathsheba's grandfather. He certainly was preparing for the return of Yahweh's favour to David. At a time when David was showing patience in adversity, taking his exile as a penance for his old sins, Ahithophel was encouraging Absalom in an outrage against the law of Yahweh.

Ahithophel next recommended that he take an expeditionary force in pursuit of David and smash him while he was still weary from the long march. Only David need be killed, his men will accept a general amnesty and become servants of Absalom: 'If the people see that you want only one man killed, they will be happy to have you as their king.' Everyone at the council agreed to this. It was a sensible plan. Absalom asked Hushai if he too did not think it a good plan.

'No. It is not a good plan. Remember what a brave fighter your father is, and how courageous the men with him. He will fight like a bear robbed of her cubs. Remember too what experience your father has had in guerilla warfare against Saul. He will come from some hiding place and kill a party of your soldiers in an ambush and lurk in another place for another chance. Then everyone will say that you have lost some men and they

will begin to think how great a warrior David is; they will
waver. An expeditionary force under Ahithophel's command will
not serve your purpose, you yourself, sir, must lead the whole
army of Israel into battle. Then indeed we shall find him out and
kill him and all his followers.' Absalom and the council agreed
that Hushai had given better advice than Ahithophel.

Then Hushai told Zadok and Abiathar how he had defeated
Ahithophel and gained some time for David but that the king
must hurry across the river if he were to be safe.

Zadok and Abiathar sent a servant girl with this message
to their sons, who were waiting at the village of Enrogel just
outside Jerusalem to take the news of the council to David.
As she talked to them one of Absalom's spies saw them and went
off to tell the prince. The priests' sons moved along the road
to the next village and some partisans hid them in a well, so
that when the prince's soldiers came to search the village they
were not discovered. After the soldiers had gone the messengers
ran on to David's camp. On hearing Hushai's warning the king
crossed the Jordan during the night.

Ahithophel saw that Absalom could never win now that he
had let David escape and given the king time to muster his
men. He rode away to his farm, set his affairs in order, and
hanged himself.

The Death of Absalom

David's men, all skilled in this kind of warfare, were now confident of victory, friends brought up provisions and the king was
ready to meet Absalom. The veteran Joab ordered the campaign
and selected the company commanders. It becomes significant
later that he replaced the general Benaiah by Ittai, a young officer.
The old soldier did not forget this relegation.

Then David said to the generals, 'Whatever happens, treat
Absalom well. He is my son.' The whole force heard of this.

The battle was fought at Ephraim among bushes and rocks
and thickets—good ground for David's smaller force of skilled
men but not at all helpful in the deploying of Absalom's large
army of all Israel. Absalom himself, charging down a hill, was
caught in the branches of a tree while his mount went galloping

on from under him. One of Joab's men saw this and ran to tell
the general. Joab cursed him for not killing the prince at once.
'And who would have protected me from the king's anger if I
had? Not you', said the soldier. 'I can't waste time with you,'
said Joab, and ran with his bodyguard to where Absalom hung
struggling in the tree. They hurled their spears at him as he
dangled and killed him. Then Joab had the trumpet blown for
the pursuit of Absalom's men to be halted. Zadok's son Ahimaaz,
who had been a messenger before, asked leave to run with news
of Absalom's death to David. Joab refused: 'This is not a day
for you to carry a message. Another day. Not the day of the
death of the prince.' Joab sent a negro with the news.

'Let me run,' begged Ahimaaz.

'You will have no reward for the news.'

'No matter, I will run.'

'Run, then.'

Ahimaaz took the longer way round but the road was better.
He overtook the negro.

At his headquarters David waited for the news and the
watchman on the high gate of the palisade called to the king
in the yard below: 'There is a runner coming.'

'If there is only one runner he comes with good news, a
defeat can be known by the remnant running away.'

'There is another runner now.'

'Good news again.'

'I think the first is Ahimaaz, he has his stride.'

'He is a good man, it must be good news.'

Ahimaaz cried out at the gate: 'All is well.'

'And Absalom, is he safe?'

'All is well. I don't know the details, sir.' Ahimaaz suddenly
had realized what Joab had been hinting. The man who told
the king of Absalom's death would not be pleasing to David.
The second runner came through the gate blurting out the
news. When the negro told him, David groaned and went into
his own tent and the whole camp heard him crying out. 'O
Absalom, O my son Absalom, my son. If only you were alive
and I were dead. O Absalom, O my son, my son.'

The men stood about, uneasy, unable to take much pleasure
in their victory as the king's cries were heard again and again.
The men came in from the fight and stood silent in the shade

as if they had come from defeat rather than victory. And all
the while the king was heard lamenting:

'O my son Absalom. O Absalom, my son, my son.'

Joab rode home from the battlefield. As he dismounted he
heard the king's wailing, and strode at once into the king's
tent. 'What are you doing? We have all risked our lives for you,
every man here, and you love your enemy more than any of us.
You have made it plain that we, your officers and soldiers, are
nothing to you. You would have us dead and the rebel alive
again. Get up, and look cheerful, speak to the men, praise them
for their courage in today's fight. They will desert you otherwise.'

Then David reviewed his troops as they stood in lines on the
parade ground and celebrated the victory with them. All Israel
came to acknowledge David the king. Absalom was not even a
memory for them that day. David went in triumph back along the
road to Jerusalem.

Shimei came running to meet him as he passed along the
valley road again. The man who had mocked David before the
battle now threw himself at the king's feet. Joab would have
stuck him through with a sword but David held his hand:

'You always want to be killing, Joab, today we will have
peace. You shall live, Shimei, I swear it.'

Mephibosheth, the son of Saul, came down to meet the king:

'Ziba ran away with my asses, sir, and you know I cannot
walk, he tricked me and told you some tale of my wanting to be
king. It is all false, I am your loyal servant, sir.'

'I cannot be bothered now. Ziba helped me; you seem innocent. Divide your wealth with Ziba and be at peace.'

So David came safely home.

In his city of Jerusalem, David determined to build an altar
for Yahweh. He decided to erect his shrine on a great rock plateau
where Araunah, one of the old Jebusite inhabitants of the city,
threshed his corn. The king went up the road with his son
Solomon and bought the site on which he would build his altar.
There he gave the peace offerings to Yahweh; the land of Israel
was at peace for the first time since the people elected a king.

The Accession of Solomon

King David grew old. He was always cold and though his
servants covered him with clothes he never felt warm. All his

vigour left him. Even his new concubine, Abishag the beautiful Shunamite girl, could not rouse him. So his eldest surviving son, Adonijah, prepared to be king. He collected a force of men to assert his right, and found support in the old commander-in-chief Joab and Abiathar the priest who had been with King David in his exile from Saul's court. But Zadok the priest, who had come with the Ark to Jerusalem, Benaiah the general who had been demoted by Joab in the campaign against Absalom, and the old seer Nathan, who had been tutor to Solomon when he was a boy, joined forces to promote the candidacy of Solomon.

Adonijah was a handsome young man, spoilt by his father and popular with the royal officials of Judah, so the opponents of his faction had to work hard for Solomon. Nathan told Bathsheba, Solomon's mother, to speak to the sick king and remind him of his promise to make Solomon king after him. 'While you are talking to him, I will come in and second your efforts,' he told her.

Bathsheba went in to the king as he lay in his bed. Abishag was sitting near him, a watchful nurse for the dying man. The king roused himself a little:

'What do you want?'

'Once you swore to me that Solomon our son should reign after you in Israel, and now Adonijah claims to be king behind your back. He acts as if you were already dead. He has given a feast to the royal officials, to Joab and Abiathar, but he has not even invited Solomon. He hates me and my son and unless you direct otherwise will kill us when you are dead.'

Nathan came hurrying in:

'My lord, have you declared that Adonijah is to be king after you? He is holding a feast and Joab and Adonijah and all the officers are drinking a toast to him, shouting, "Long live King Adonijah". But I and Zadok and Benaiah, all members of your council, have been told nothing of this.'

'As Yahweh lives, he who has delivered me from all my enemies, as I once swore to you, Bathsheba, so I will do today. Call Zadok and Benaiah here at once.'

When all the members of Solomon's party were gathered in his sick-room David said to them:

'Take my bodyguard and set Solomon on my own mount and bring him to Gihon and, Zadok, you anoint him king, the rest

of you shout, "Long live King Solomon", and, Nathan, we will
hope to have a happy oracle from you. Then, Benaiah, escort
Solomon back here and he shall sit on my throne.'

The makeshift coronation was quickly arranged. They took
the prince to Gihon and made him king to the sound of trumpets
and cheers, and all the men of Jerusalem came to greet Solomon
shouting and singing so that the city was full of their noise.
The sound of the celebration was heard in the banquet hall of
Adonijah. Joab sent a servant to find the reason for the tumult,
and at that moment Jonathan, the son of Abiathar, rushed in to
tell them:

'David has made Solomon king! The city is in an uproar
celebrating the anointing of the prince. They have set Solomon
on the king's throne and David watched all this from his bed.'

Then Adonijah's guests one by one left the house until he
was alone. The prince was terrified of what Solomon would do
to him. He ran to the altar David had erected on the old
threshing-floor and flung himself upon it claiming sanctuary.
The royal officials tried to persuade Adonijah to go home again
but he said, 'I will not let go the altar until King Solomon
has sworn that he will not have me killed.'

Solomon sent him a message: 'If you can prove loyal you
shall be safe, but if you are treacherous you shall die.'

Adonijah came and swore loyalty to Solomon and Solomon
put him under arrest in his own house.

As David lay dying he gave his last message to Solomon:

'Joab has always been a murderer, he has blotted my reputation—think of the death of Abner, and there are others. Deal
with him.

'Shimei, who cursed me as I fled from Jerusalem, made me
swear not to kill him, but you can deal with him as well. But
be good to those who have been good to me.'

Then the king died.

Adonijah's Folly

After his father's death, Adonijah determined to make another
bid for the throne. To sound out the possibilities of his success he
thought of a way in which he could make his mind known without
openly proclaiming his ambitions.

Adonijah went to see Bathsheba, the king's mother.

'Do you come in peace?'

'In peace. I want to ask you to do something for me.'

'What is it?'

'Once I thought the kingdom would be mine and the people cheered for me, but things turned out differently. Yahweh has given the throne of Israel to my brother. Now instead of a kingdom I want only one thing.'

'What is it?'

'Abishag the Shunamite to be my wife. Ask the king to give her to me. He will not refuse you.'

'Very well; I will talk to my son about this.'

Bathsheba went to King Solomon. He rose to greet her and had a chair placed for her at his side.

'I have something to ask you. Not a great thing. A little thing.'

'Ask and you shall have it.'

'Give Abishag to Adonijah your brother to be his wife.'

Solomon rose in fury.

'If you ask for the Shunamite woman for my brother you might as well ask for my throne for him as well. Don't you see, mother, Adonijah is my elder brother, he has powerful friends, Joab and Abiathar, and now he wants my father's concubine to show men that he is the true inheritor of my father. He shall die for this. Today.'

Solomon sent for Benaiah the commander of the bodyguard and told him to cut down Adonijah. So the prince died in his house.

Solomon took Adonijah's rash request as a pretext for eliminating all those who had worked for the enthronement of the prince at the critical time of David's illness.

Solomon sent for Abiathar:

'Go to your farm at Anathoth. You deserve death but shall suffer exile only since you were my father's friend.'

Then he sent for Joab, but the old general had already set out for the altar on the threshing-floor and clutched it claiming sanctuary. Solomon then ordered Benaiah to fetch him back to the court, but Joab would not budge from the altar: 'If you mean to have me killed it must be here. Do it here.'

Benaiah knew that the people would not care for such a sacrilege. He reported back to the king. Solomon was determined to rid Jerusalem of all who had worked for Adonijah and sent Benaiah back again: 'Do as he said. Cut him down at the altar.'

Benaiah did as Solomon directed. The king filled Abiathar's place by promoting Zadok and conferred the supreme command of the army, which had been Joab's, on Benaiah. A pretext was found too, to have Shimei killed.

Thus the succession was assured and the Davidic line established.

The narrator has carefully built up to this moment. One by one the possible successors of David have been eliminated; the house of Saul ends with Michal's barrenness and Mephibosheth's discomfiture, Bathsheba's first child dies in infancy, Amnon is murdered, Absalom is slain in battle, Adonijah caught in a politicial net, Solomon emerges in all his glory.

Solomon in his Glory

Solomon set about organizing his government and in particular the fiscal arrangements of the kingdom. He appointed twelve prefects to see to the collection of the taxes. It is to be noted that the districts given to the officers did not correspond with tribal boundaries. Solomon was gradually destroying the traditional social structure of the people in order to strengthen the position of the newly-appearing central government of the king.

The prefects were each responsible for a month's supplies of food for the palace and provender for the royal animals, including the chariot horses of the army. A careful organization of resources characterized the hard practical directions of the king.

At the same time the king found time to engage in natural science and was interested in the different kinds of animals and birds, reptiles and ants, fish and trees.

It was this combination of enormous mercantile flair and shrewd business sense with the inquiring mind of the intellectual that gave Solomon his legendary reputation as the great judge, which has found permanent expression not only in tales of his quick justice, like that of the two harlots and the baby, but has also given his name to books of the Wisdom Literature in our Bible. Later scribes fixed his name to these books as a tribute to the great king. All Israel stood in awe of the king because it seemed that he had been given the gift of wisdom by Yahweh. There grew up this charming tale of Solomon's meeting with Yahweh.

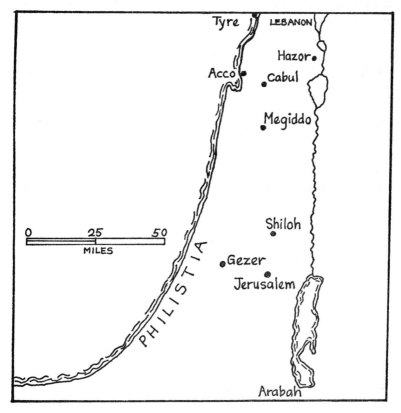

'Ask and I shall give you anything you ask for.'

'I am at a loss to know how to govern your people well. I am like a child in these matters. Give me understanding that I may know the good from the bad and learn to govern well.'

'Good. You ask wisely. I will give you wisdom above all other men. And because you asked for wisdom everything else shall be given you: long life, riches, honour greater than any king has enjoyed before. Go and rule my people Israel.'

Solomon became rich enough to take a part in international diplomacy and balances of power.

6—K.C.

He allied himself with the Pharaoh by making the Egyptian ruler's daughter one of his wives, and made arrangements with Hiram the king of the island city of Tyre for the supply of building materials, architects and workmen, for great building schemes. Both these arrangements are of great significance. They represent a growth in the influence of foreign ideas in Israel.

The alliance with the Pharaoh brought with it the town of Gezer as the Egyptian lady's dowry and this became one of the great monuments of Solomon's reign. By means of the corvée, or forced labour gangs, he conscripted an army of manual workers who were employed to build great forts at Gezer, Megiddo and Hazor and throughout the realm. High walls and turrets were raised to defend the cities which became the centres of manufacture and armament upon which the government was based.

Hiram and Solomon seemed to have engaged not only in trade with each other—when hard bargains were driven—but also to have joined together in mercantile enterprise of vast profit.

Solomon, with the help of Hiram who had skilled seamen in his pay, built a fleet of ships which sailed the Red Sea and the Indian Ocean and carried on a very prosperous trade in the South Arabian area.

It may well be that these enterprises brought to Solomon's court a trade mission which was later elaborated in the 'visit of the queen of Sheba'. The mercantile states of Arabia may have wanted to negotiate trading treaties with the man whose ships sailed in the Red Sea, who controlled Damascus and had occupied the meeting place of the caravan routes at the head of the Gulf of Aqaba. Of these states Sheba seems to have been more powerful than the Minaean and Qatabanian.

The arrangement with Hiram was a necessary preliminary for the great work of Solomon's reign; the building of the Temple in Jerusalem on the site of Araunah's threshing-floor where David, in Solomon's presence, had set up his altar after his restoration in the city.

The Building of the Temple

In the fourth year of his reign King Solomon sent ambassadors to Hiram announcing his intention of fulfilling the desire of his father David and making a house for Yahweh in Jerusalem:

'It is necessary, therefore, that I should obtain from you cedars of Lebanon to make a frame for this great house, and skilled workmen who will direct the building, for we have none so skilled in our country. I will pay whatever you think right.'

Hiram was delighted at the prospect of such economic activity and replied to Solomon's embassy:

'The trees shall be cut and my men shall see to it that the timber arrives and will carry out the building work for you. You, of course, will pay for the materials and all expenses.'

Solomon and Hiram made a treaty to this effect. The Temple was not completed until the eleventh year of Solomon's reign, and then Hiram was paid for his offices by a grant of territory. The district of Cabul near Acco was handed over.

By this act Solomon quietly introduced the pagan notion that the land belonged to the king and was at his disposal. He had, however, long before this piece of business, reorganized the districts of the country according to his own taxation system and this meant ignoring the old system of tribal and family tenure of the land. Regarding the whole land as crown property was a royal attack on the old social arrangements. These were further weakened by Solomon's next step in organization. To secure enough workmen for his great project, Solomon imposed conscription of labour in his kingdom. He formed men into labour-gangs to work in Lebanon and into teams to work as porters and quarrymen in the limestone hills of Palestine. David had conscripted his labour force from foreign prisoners of war, but Solomon enlisted the men of Israel. When built, the Temple was in three divisions—an outer court, a sacred area, and an inner sanctuary for the Ark. On three sides the building was surrounded by storehouses and sacristies in a bungalow construction which was later much enlarged. It is difficult not to imagine some vast building, so enthusiastic and awe-struck are the words of the Hebrew chroniclers when they speak of the Temple of Solomon, but it would seem that the inside measurement of the sacred area of the Temple was about thirty yards by ten yards, to which must, of course, be added the large vestibule or court and the small inner sanctuary; even so it was quite small by modern standards. But the Hebrew conception of the Temple and its importance did not entirely depend upon physical grandeur— though this helped the ordinary man to appreciate the more sophisticated notion—but rather on the significance of the shrine in the life of the nation. The Temple was the house of Yahweh. Once this was accepted matters of size became much less important. The Temple figures largely in the literature of both Hebrew and Christian society because of the divine presence of which it was both the house and the sign.

As the Israelite mounted the steps of the Temple he saw on either side of the entrance two great pillars of bronze surmounted probably by braziers in which fire burned continually. The smoke which rose from them could be seen all over the city, and at night the flame showed in the darkness even more clearly. To the worshipper these fires signified the *presence* of Yahweh in his house.

In the court south-east of the Temple there stood the 'Bronze Sea', a great basin which stood up on twelve bronze bulls. It was far too big and high to be of any practical use and represented Yahweh's *power* by showing that he could put edges to that most elusive and uncontrollable element, water.

These two features later became more significant in Hebrew society and literature than the Ark of the covenant, to house which the Temple was first built. The Ark was placed in the inner sanctuary, the Debir, which was lined with sheets of bright gold, under a canopy formed by two enormous wooden cherubim, plated with gold, which almost filled the sanctuary. The cherubim were winged bulls with human heads. It is difficult perhaps to understand how such creatures and images got into the very central shrine of the Temple when the religion of Israel was so set against any kind of statue, but once foreign artisans were employed by Solomon such things were almost inevitable. The Hebrews adopted these creatures and thought of them as the steeds of Yahweh that drew his chariot.

Within the sacred area, the Hekal, Solomon's artists carved folding doors and panels of cedar with cherubim, palm trees and open flowers and these too were covered with thin gold. Then Solomon brought the famous craftsman Hiram (bronzesmith to King Hiram) from the Lebanese border and he made a vast number of bowls and vessels in bronze for the celebration of the liturgy in the Temple. These were moulded in clay in a foundry at Succoth on the east side of the Jordan. The great amount of metal required for all these utensils, the 'sea' and the pillars came from the escarpments near the Arabah. There was so much metal used that Solomon's foremen did not even attempt to weigh it all.

The Dedication Day

At last all the building was done, the furnishing complete, so Solomon assembled in Jerusalem the leaders of Israel, the tribal chieftains, the elders of the nation, at the New Year feast in the autumn for the dedication of the Temple. They made a great procession as they took the Ark out of the tent at Zion, David's stronghold, to the new shrine. Along the route, as when David first brought the Ark to his city, there were numerous sacrifices of sheep and oxen. The priests carried the Ark into the Temple as the people cheered and set the sacred sign of Yahweh's presence within the Debir. They came out of the Hekal to the people announcing Yahweh's coming into his house.

Then Solomon, standing as an inferior before Yahweh who was seated in his shrine, dedicated himself and the people of his kingdom to the service of Yahweh who had brought them at last to rest in Jerusalem. There followed a great barbecue in the streets when all the people of the city ate and drank in celebration of the presence of Yahweh.

The whole centre court of the Temple became a place of sacrifice so many animals were slaughtered for the feast. So the Temple was finished and dedicated.

Solomon turned next to other building projects: first, the lengthening and restoration of the walls of his own city so that the new Temple on the north-eastern hill and his palace to the south were included in the walled city; then, the enlargement of Hazor, the great fortress commanding the routes from the north; then Megiddo, another fortress on the route from the Euphrates to the Nile where Solomon stabled his cavalry, was strengthened.

It was during the Jerusalem building activity that Solomon met a young man, Jeroboam the son of Nebat, who was to figure prominently in the history of Israel and to undo the work of David and Solomon for the establishment of a centralized monarchical power.

Jeroboam was employed in the Public Works Office and during a walk round the walls to see how the work progressed he met Ahijah, the seer of Shiloh. This ancient shrine of the Ark was now totally abandoned because of the policy of David and Solomon, which was intended to concentrate all religious loyalty in Israel upon the royal sanctuary of Jerusalem. Ahijah longed for a return to the old days of the confederacy of the twelve tribes. He abominated the heavy centralizing authority that was expressed in the forced labour which Jeroboam directed for Solomon. He talked with Jeroboam, urging him to lead a rebellion of the northern tribes against the southern king.

Jeroboam must have talked too widely of Ahijah's idea. Solomon sent his men to kill him but Jeroboam escaped into Egypt and stayed there until Solomon's death.

THE YAHWIST OF SOLOMON'S COURT

IT MUST NOT be imagined that Solomon's reign is a matter of centralizing despotism, grandiose building schemes erected by forced labour, and the accumulation of a harem; it would not be the great period of humanist culture that it is if this were its only glory. With some examples of this civilizing activity we shall be concerned in the next section.

In the following account of the Yahwist's editorial work, nothing is intended to persuade the reader that the patriarchal narratives are to be considered largely useless as sources of history. The Yahwist took great blocks of traditional material, carefully handed down from generation to generation, and with a great respect for his sources, knit and developed his material into a coherent view of the history of Yahweh's promise to Israel. The events of which his narrative speaks may have taken place a long time before the Yahwist wrote, but the continuous oral and written tradition made them available to him in a substantially trustworthy form.

While, therefore, it is not possible to assert that any particular event in the patriarchal history happened 'just so', it is certainly justifiable to claim that the Yahwist's reconstruction gives us a generally valuable account capable of conveying to us a most useful impression of what happened.

What is important in the reading of these histories is coming to understand what the tradition expressed in the Yahwist's framework is saying to both the Israelites of the monarchy and to us. The meaning of the narratives will, I hope, become plain in this retelling. The basic principle of understanding is the realization that these narratives are shaped to bring about faith in Yahweh who has acted in history and gives meaning to our present. If we would ask how much of the story of the patriarchs can be considered today as

established history, answers must vary but a moderate view would
be that we can have confidence in the general outlines of the story.
That the patriarchs were historical figures who belonged to those
semi-nomadic groups which came from Mesopotamia to Palestine
about two thousand years before Christ, seems very likely. Further,
the rise of what was probably a semitic dynasty in Egypt would
suggest that some men of these groups would probably have
migrated to Egypt in the sixteenth century and that the sympathies
of that dynasty might well lead to one of the semitic people
holding high office in the Two Kingdoms of the Pharaoh.

Abraham

When he looked back at the origins of the Davidic kingdom the
Yahwist saw the past as a promise of this present settlement. It may
be that a great deal of our knowledge of the reigns of the first three
kings in Israel depends on the research and writing of the Yahwist,
it is certain that our whole view of the history of the tribes before
Saul is determined by the over-all plan of the Yahwist who erected
a highly sophisticated construction of the promise of Yahweh and
subordinated all the materials of the old cultic sagas and local
histories to this grand design. Taking the credal affirmation of the
old rite as his starting point, 'A wandering Aramean was my father',
the Yahwist set about the demonstration of the pre-history of the
kingdom. He presented the whole patriarchal period as the working
out of Yahweh's promise to Abraham:

> Yahweh said to Abraham:
> 'Leave your homeland, your family and your inheritance
> and go to the country I have chosen for you. I will make you a
> great nation. I will bless you and your power will grow ever
> greater and all the nations of the earth shall enjoy the blessing
> I will give you.'
> So Abraham went from his home town of Haran with his wife
> Sarah and his nephew Lot, and their servants and slaves, and
> they came to the land. But the Canaanites were already in
> possession.

There, at Shechem, Yahweh renewed his promise. This is a
significant detail. The shrine of Shechem was important to the

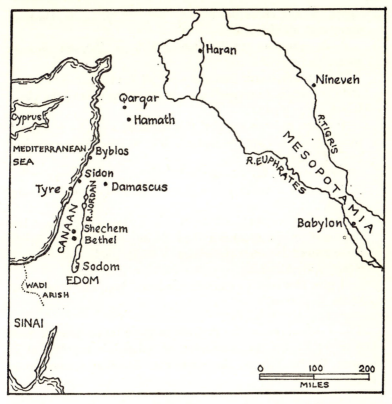

Yahwist as the ancient meeting place of the confederacy. It was at this place that tradition placed the proclamation of the covenant by Joshua and here the great festival of renewal often took place. It seemed to him right, therefore, to point out to his readers that when Abraham first arrived in the promised land Yahweh renewed his covenant at Shechem. It was here that Abraham first worshipped Yahweh in his land.

The shepherds and goatherds of Lot and those of Abraham were for ever quarrelling because the two great herds could not find enough pasture land on which to graze. Therefore Abraham, who hated dissensions in a family, said to his nephew:

'We must separate, choose a place for yourself and I will move on.'

Lot looked across the Jordan valley and saw that it was full of good pasture meadows; it was like Eden or the rich lands of

Egypt. So Lot chose the Jordan valley for his herds. He went down with all his men.

While Abraham stood watching him go, Yahweh came to renew his promise:

'Look north, south, east and west, all this land shall be yours, and your descendants shall be as many as the dust of the earth. It will all be yours.'

Abraham did not see how this could be since he and Sarah were already old and he had no child to inherit the promised land of Yahweh:

'How am I to be sure of this?'

'Bring me a heifer and a goat, a turtle-dove and a young pigeon.'

Abraham brought the animals and cut them in two and laid them out on the ground and as the sun was setting a bright flame moved between the pieces. Yahweh made a covenant, a treaty, with Abraham:

'I give this land to your descendants, from the Wadi Arish to the Euphrates.'

The Yahwist frames the promise in these terms because these two rivers formed the boundaries of Solomon's kingdom at its largest. To the Yahwist the promise to Abraham seemed to be fulfilled in Solomon.

Still Sarah and Abraham had no child so Sarah proposed, according to custom, that her maid Hagar should become Abraham's concubine and that Hagar's child should be counted as Sarah's own offspring. Abraham did as his wife suggested, but Hagar on conceiving a child thought herself one better than Sarah. The women quarrelled all the time.

The Yahwist uses this little piece of the tradition to demonstrate that Yahweh does not, like men, have to adopt such shifts to fulfil his promise. He does not need the child of Hagar for his purposes to be fulfilled.

Yahweh appeared to Abraham as he sat by the door of his tent under the oaks of Mamre. Abraham looked up and there were three men standing in front of him. At once he rushed to offer hospitality to the strangers. Bowls of water for their dusty feet were brought, Sarah was told to take some bread, and a man sent to choose a calf for the meal. After the bustle Abraham waited on the strangers as they ate their meal.

'Where is your wife Sarah?'

'In the tent.'

'By the Spring she will have a son.'

Sarah laughed to herself behind the tent flap as she heard these words.

'Why did your wife laugh? Is anything too difficult for Yahweh? Remember this when I come back again in the Spring.'

Sarah blushed and came out of the tent:

'I didn't laugh.'

'Oh yes, you did.'

Then they all stood up and looked towards Sodom where Lot had taken his herds.

At this point the Yahwist introduces one of his favourite themes —the man chosen by God is able to understand the apparently accidental movements of history for what they are: the hidden workings of Yahweh.

Yahweh said: 'Since I have chosen Abraham to be my man and made a covenant with him I will tell him what I have in my mind. I am going to see for myself whether Sodom is as bad as men say.'

'But if you punish the whole city the good will die with the wicked. It would be terrible to end a city that had even fifty innocent men.'

'If there are fifty innocent men there, I will spare Sodom.'

'I ought not to thrust myself forward like this, but what if there are only forty-five good men?'

'Forty-five will be enough to save the rest.'

'Or perhaps only forty . . .'

And so Abraham beat Yahweh down until he agreed to spare Sodom if there were only ten innocent men in the city.

The Yahwist is not here arguing the case for one city; he takes Sodom as an example of the way any group of men, even Israel, might fail Yahweh. Nor is he arguing that ten individuals are worth the rest getting off unpunished. He is introducing the great concept of the community of men. Abraham argues all the time in order to save the whole population. There is never a question of dealing with the innocent separately from the wicked—all will suffer or be saved together.

Sodom

Two of the strangers came to Sodom in the evening. The preparation of the meal seems to have begun at noon and the city of Sodom was forty miles away on a bad road, so the strangers travelled with more than human speed. As they arrived they were met by Lot who had become a citizen of Sodom and married a wife there.

'Come to my house, sirs, wash your feet and sup with me and rest there. You can go refreshed on your journey at day-break.'

The strangers are persuaded in, and just as they are lying down to sleep a rabble knocks at the door:

'Where are the handsome strangers? Give them to us!'

Lot went out to them, carefully shutting the door behind him:

'Let the men alone, they are not for you. If you must have some excitement, take my daughters and use them for your pleasure, but I cannot surrender my guests to you.'

The rabble thrust themselves against Lot with his back to the door:

'Who is this foreigner to tell us what to do in our own city? We'll soon settle him.'

The strangers dragged Lot inside his house and barred the door against the mob. In the morning they set about their work. Lot, who was still uncertain what to do, they took outside the city with his wife and daughters, forbidding them to look back to the sinful city. Then fire came down on the city and an earthquake swallowed it up.

Lot's wife, looking back, became a pillar of salt. No one can be a mere spectator when Yahweh acts.

Abraham went early in the morning and stood on the spot where he had stood before with the three strangers and he looked to where Sodom had been and saw nothing but the smoke rising over a waste land.

Lot had, in the confused events of the last night of Sodom, offered his daughters to the lust of the rabble because he could think of no other way to protect his guests. His daughters had an ironical revenge.

Lot and his daughters journeyed up to Zoar and found them-selves alone in the wilderness. They sheltered for some weeks in a desolate cave and one night while Lot slept the elder daugh-ter said to the younger:

'Our father is old and there seems to be no other man here at all for us to marry. Let us make him drunk and lie with him so that the family may survive.'

The next evening the elder said: 'Last night I lay with our father, tonight when he is drunk again it will be your turn.'

Thus, unknown to Lot, his daughters conceived his children.

The Yahwist means his readers to learn from Lot that if a man mistrusts Yahweh, or is hesitant in obeying him, or refused to join in the covenant of Yahweh that was offered to Lot as much as to Abraham, then he will succumb to the worst forces in the world. Lot is the drunken victim of incest.

The Child of the Promise

Sarah conceived and a son was born to Abraham; they called him Isaac.

Since the Yahwist is concerned only with the development of the promise until the settlement is reached, he moves directly on to the story of Isaac's marriage for this is a necessary link in the chain of promise. Other men later filled up what they took to be a gap in the Yahwist's account.

Abraham grew old and determined to have his son married so that the line would be secured. He must not be mixed up with the Canaanite women because marrying one of them would let Abraham's estate fall into the hands of the wrong connection, men of a totally different religious attitude. Abraham therefore sent his seneschal with a dowry of rich jewels to find a wife for Isaac among the Aramaic women of Abraham's own clan. The seneschal journeyed to Haran in Mesopotamia and there al-lowed his camels to rest at the edge of the spring. He prayed:

'Yahweh, the protector of my master Abraham, show you care for Abraham this day and show me which girl to take back with

me. Let it be the girl who offers to fetch water to the trough
for my camels.'

While he prayed, Rebekah, a niece of Abraham, came to the
spring with her water jar upon her shoulder. As she came up from
the spring the seneschal asked her:

'Let me drink from your jar.'

'Do, sir, and I will fetch some more for your camels, at the
trough.'

Rebekah went down and up the steps of the spring many times
to stop the thirst of the camels.

'Tell me whose daughter are you, and is there room in your
house for me and my camels to stay for the night.'

'I am Nahor's daughter, and of course you can stay the night
with us.'

Then the seneschal knew he had been led by Yahweh to the
right bride for Isaac. He followed her to her brother Laban's
house and explained to them how it had all happened and Laban
gladly agreed to accept the presents Abraham had sent and to
give Rebekah to Isaac. They set off for Isaac's home.

For the Yahwist the great significance of these events was that
the line of promise would now continue. Rebekah would become
the ancestress of the men of Israel. The promise was working out
through her.

Isaac and his Sons

Rebekah had twin sons, Esau, a hairy, dark-skinned man who
found his food by hunting, and Jacob, the respectable farmer.
Isaac favoured Esau because he brought home tasty game,
Rebekah loved Jacob more.

When he was old and his eyes so weak that he could hardly
see at all, Isaac felt that he was going to die. He wanted to
pass on his blessing to Esau so that the promise would descend
through him. Isaac wanted to be fit when he gave the blessing
so that it should be strong and virile, he therefore told Esau
to prepare a feast. Rebekah overheard this conversation and,
while Esau went out to catch an animal for Isaac, she told
Jacob what had been said:

'Now do as I say. . . . Fetch a couple of kids from the flock
so that I may prepare a savoury dish for your father. I'll do

his favourite; then you can take it into him and get his blessing before Esau comes back.'

'But Esau is a hairy man and my skin is smooth. If father touches me he will know who I am and rather give me a curse than a blessing.'

'Do as I say and I'll take the blame if you're found out.'

So he took the young goats and his mother made the pie and she dressed Jacob in Esau's clothes that smelt of the hunt, and wrapped his arms and neck round with the kids' skins so that he should feel hairy to the touch; and he went in to his father:

'I am Esau, your first-born, with the game pie, come for your blessing.'

'You caught the animal very quickly.'

'Yahweh gave me a quick success.'

'Let me feel your hands.'

Isaac felt the kids' pelts: 'The voice is the voice of Jacob but the hands are the hands of Esau.'

Isaac drew Jacob to him as if to kiss him, and suspiciously sniffed at his clothes.

'You smell of the field and the hunt, my son. May Yahweh bless your fields and grant plentiful harvest every year and may all nations bow before you and all your kinsmen serve you for ever.'

Jacob took the blessing and went out of the room.

The Yahwist thinks of this blessing as fulfilled in the power of Israel at the centre of good agricultural land contrasted with the stony mountain area of Edom that became Esau's portion.

When Esau discovered what had happened he hated Jacob with all his heart and he was ready to kill him. After Isaac's funeral Jacob went away, thinking that it would be only a week or so before Esau's anger lessened, then he could return. He had to keep away twenty years.

Jacob

Jacob journeyed towards his uncle Laban's house in Haran and slept on the road one night at Bethel. He dreamt that Yahweh renewed his promise of a great nation that should come from

Abraham and told him that one day he would be brought back to the land of Canaan again.

Jacob walked on and came to the well head where the seneschal had met his mother. There three shepherds waited with their flocks round the covered well. He greeted them cheerfully, they were almost too lazy to reply:

'Where do you come from?'

'Haran.'

'Do you know Laban, the son of Nahor?'

'Yes.'

'How is he?'

'He is well. There is his daughter Rachel coming with his sheep.'

Jacob wanted to be alone with the girl.

'Well, hurry up. . . . Water your animals, and be gone. This is no time to sit around.'

'We do not water the animals until everyone has brought his flock. We share the well and that is the rule.'

Jacob took the great stone cover off the well and watered Rachel's flock for her as the shepherds worked. Then he kissed the girl and told her who he was. Rachel ran to tell her father that cousin Jacob had come to stay.

Jacob wanted to marry Rachel, but her father's price was high. He was to work seven years without wages and then she would be his wife. Jacob agreed to Laban's terms. He worked for seven years for Rachel and they seemed to him as seven days so dearly did he love the girl.

When the time was up, Laban gathered all his friends and relations for the marriage feast and led the veiled bride to Jacob and he lay with her in the dark. In the morning, when he woke, Jacob discovered that Laban had tricked him, he had given him the elder daughter, Leah, whom he did not love. Laban laughed at this coarse joke and comforted Jacob by offering Rachel as his second wife. If Jacob would serve Laban for another seven years he could have Rachel. Jacob agreed but on condition that this time he was paid in advance.

Jacob made it evident that he did not care for Leah and loved only Rachel. But Leah was consoled by the birth of four fine sons, Reuben, Simeon, Levi and Judah. Rachel was wild with jealousy because she had no children of her own. Then

Leah bore two other sons and two concubines bore children to Jacob. Then at last Rachel whom Jacob loved had a son, Joseph.

All this time Laban's sons were growing jealous of their cousin who prospered while he was with them. In the end Jacob decided that it was not politic for him to go on living with his father-in-law. He took his wives and sons and herds and set out for Canaan.

It was now twenty years since he had tricked Esau. Jacob knew that his only chance of settling peacefully in Canaan was that Esau's mood had changed, but he could not count on it. He sent messengers to Esau to announce his coming and to tell his brother how prosperous he had become at Haran—thus suggesting the possibility of large presents for Esau.

The messengers returned saying that Esau had assembled four hundred men and was coming to meet his brother.

Jacob was terrified and prayed for Yahweh's help:

'God of Abraham, God of Isaac, Yahweh, you told me to come back to Canaan, and promised me a quiet home, now, since you have looked after me up till now, save me from Esau—otherwise how will your promise be fulfilled and my family grow to be as many as the sands of the seashore?'

Jacob was desperate. All through the night he wrestled with Yahweh to exact a promise of peace with Esau in the morning. He was never the same man again after that night of terror and prayer. In Hebrew sagas he was represented as ever after physically limping from the struggle he had with Yahweh.

In the morning Esau arrived. Jacob walked slowly towards his brother but Esau ran up to him and hugged him and greeted Jacob's wives and children and was full of welcome. The past was forgotten. The favour Jacob had won from Yahweh in the night was shining in Esau's welcome: 'Your face is the face of Yahweh to me.'

So the brothers met and were at peace. Esau lived in Seir-Edom in the deep south. Jacob went first to Bethel where he had had his dream of Yahweh. This was the place of the promise. He then journeyed with his wives and sons and slaves and herds to the family settlement in Canaan. It was here that his son Reuben took

7—K.C.

one of his father's concubines for himself and brought his father's curse upon himself. This is the incident that the Yahwist has in mind when he gives the account of Absalom going into David's concubines on the roof of the palace in Jerusalem. Such things always bring disaster upon the doer.

Joseph in Egypt

The Yahwist now turns to the longest piece of patriarchal material that he has inherited from past narration and brings it into the pattern of his general history. This is the story of Joseph the son of Rachel and Jacob; it is important to the Yahwist because it presents two of his main themes. First, despite plots of wickedness, Yahweh's grace still enters the situation to save the good man. Second, through human history, the actions of bad men as much as those of the good, the purpose of Yahweh is worked out and the promise kept. Despite every tack and jib in the course of his life Joseph is at last the man who continues the line of promise.

In his old age Jacob doted on his son Joseph and gave him a long robe with sleeves. Wearing such a coat Joseph of course could not help with work in the house or in the fields with his brothers. He had a lazy time of it. They were all out with the flocks one time, moving with the sheep further and further throught the pasture land, sleeping out at night, and Jacob said to Joseph who remained at home: 'See how your brothers are getting on. Bring me news of them.'

Joseph went off to find the family herds and met them at Dothan. The brothers saw him coming. They grabbed a chance to get even with Joseph for all their father's favouritism and determined to kill him. But Reuben spoke against this, and Judah said: 'There is a caravan coming down the road, let us sell him to the merchants as a slave.'

This they did and when they went home again they told their father that Joseph had been eaten by a wild beast and showed him the long-sleeved robe which they had dipped in goat's blood.

Jacob wept for his son. Joseph was sold in Egypt to be a slave in the house of Potiphar, a great official in the court of Pharaoh.

Jacob who once deceived his father was now deceived by his sons. The Yahwist sees a line of guilt and suffering worked out in this family. And this inheritance of evil is used by God to bring about another phase in the history of the promise and its fulfilment.

Joseph was promoted to be a senior member of Potiphar's household and everything was left to his direction. He was young, handsome and educated and Potiphar's wife lusted for him, but he would not deceive his master. In her fury, Potiphar's wife accused Joseph of the wickedness she had intended: 'This man has tried to rape me, but I cried out and he ran away.'

Potiphar believed his wife and in his anger had Joseph carried away to prison. Here, too, in the royal cells, his breeding caused him to be noticed. The governor of the prison made him his secretary and with his usual efficiency Joseph was soon running the place.

After some further incidents (of which we do not have the Yahwist's account, but only much later versions—for example, his interpretation of the dreams of Pharaoh's servants and that of Pharaoh himself), Joseph is made the vizier of the two kingdoms of Egypt and director of the whole economy. He is given the daughter of the High Priest as his wife and his two sons are born.

Joseph's great achievement was the building of large granaries and storing in them the corn of good harvests. This could be sold at high prices to the people in years when the harvest failed. It was in a year of such failure that Joseph was brought again into contact with his family.

The famine affected most of the Levant and Jacob in Canaan, hearing that the vizier of Egypt was selling grain, though at stiff prices, sent his sons to buy. He kept back the youngest, Benjamin, Joseph's brother, for fear some harm might come to him.

When they arrived and presented themselves to Joseph he recognized them but kept his own identity secret:

'Where do you come from?'

'From Canaan. We have come to buy food.'

'You have come to spy on us.'

'No, my lord, only to buy food. We are honest men, brothers, not spies.'

'I say you are spies.'

'No, we are twelve honest brothers, ten here, one, the youngest, with our father at home, and one dead.'

'You look like spies. We'll soon see if you speak the truth. One of you shall remain my hostage until you bring your youngest brother back.'

The brothers looked at one another and it came into their minds that their present misfortune was somehow a punishment for their maltreatment of Joseph. Simeon was bound and imprisoned and the others were sent home to fetch Benjamin. Before they left Egypt Joseph had their purchase money placed in their sacks of corn. They had been his guests in Egypt. When they discovered their money the brothers thought that some dangerous trick was being played on them. They went home to tell their father the vizier's terms for Simeon's release. Jacob, when he heard the story, was full of fear for the future: 'I have lost Joseph, I have lost Simeon and now you would take Benjamin from me.'

The brothers could not persuade their father to let them take Benjamin to Egypt until the corn that they had brought the first time was all used up and they needed more. Then Jacob reluctantly gave permission for Benjamin to go with them.

They went back laden with gifts for Joseph and with the money he had put in their sacks as well as money for their present buying, and they stood before Joseph.

Joseph on his way to his office told his steward to prepare a great feast, Simeon was set free and Joseph came down at noon to address the men before him:

'How is your father, the old man you spoke of?'

'He is well, sir.'

'And is this your youngest brother? Yahweh be with you, my son.'

Joseph almost gave himself away at this moment but he controlled himself, then pulled himself together in his room and washed and brought them all to his banquet. That evening he told his steward to put a sacred chalice in Benjamin's sack. In the morning Jacob's sons got their caravan together and set off for home. They had not reached the Egyptian border before Joseph's guard rode up to search their bags for the chalice. The cup was, of course, found in Benjamin's bag. They were brought back to Joseph and threw themselves on the ground before him.

'Why have you done this? How did you think you could get away with it?'

'We have no excuse. We are all your slaves.'

'Oh no, I do not punish the innocent, only the one in whose sack the chalice was discovered shall be my slave.'

'But we can't go back without him. He is our father's favourite. Now that Joseph is dead he only lives for Benjamin. He will die if we go home without him.'

Then Joseph could contain his tears no longer. He cried out: 'I am Joseph your brother.'

Then the brothers were astounded—and afraid. They remembered how they had treated him in the past and they knew his present power in Egypt.

'Do not fear. Yahweh has brought me here before you to see to it that you should have grain and should live so that his promise should be kept to the sons of Jacob. Go at once and bring our father here. I will provide for you here. There are five years of famine to come. Tell him what you have seen here, all the marvels of Egypt and bring him quickly.'

When he heard the news, Pharaoh was glad at the happiness of his vizier, and when Jacob came Pharaoh gave him audience and presented him with a fine farm to live on. There at last Jacob died surrounded by his sons. Joseph had his father embalmed as the Egyptian custom was and they buried Jacob's body in Canaan.

The Exodus

In time Joseph himself died and all that generation of Israelites, but their descendants were many.

The Egyptians now regarded the Israelites as poor foreigners liable to be conscripted for the forced labour teams needed in the grandiose building schemes of the Pharaohs. They had forgotten Joseph.

Some explanation has to be found for the sudden reversal of the Israelites' fortunes in Egypt. From being the relatives of the chief minister they seem almost overnight to become the slave population of a bitterly hostile country. We can account for the easy entry that the Israelites had into Egypt by recalling that they came at a time when Egypt was ruled by a family of Pharaohs who were probably of semitic stock, the Hyksos dynasty. The reigning house belonged to the same stock as did the patriarchs. They may have imported a great many of their semitic group to bolster their position in the midst of a predominantly non-semitic population. The promotion of Joseph seems to fit in well with such an explanation.

The fall of the Hyksos dynasty *c.* 1550 and the accession of non-semitic rulers must have been a sudden and unlooked for catastrophe. Under the rule of Sethos I and Ramses II the Israelites (called '*Apiru*' in the Egyptian chronicles, hence 'Hebrews' in our accounts of this period of their history) were conscripted for massive building projects. We may take it that a great many of them were ready to follow any leader who would offer them an escape from such conditions. This slave rabble marched out of Egypt across the wilderness, gradually becoming a comradely community, telling one another stories of their ancestors and merging their traditions until the patriarchal narratives as we now have them were shaped.

Later tradition made of this travelling group the twelve-tribe origin of the Israelite society. We cannot decide with certainty whether members of this or that family came out of Egypt, or whether they came together as one group or, and this does seem more likely, in dribs and drabs over a quite long period. We shall probably never have a precise history of the origins of the tribal system, but we do have an adequate history of the origin of Israel as a people in the stories centred on the Exodus and Sinai events. It is to these stories that we shall now turn, not expecting them to supply much original detail, though they may do this on a surprisingly large number of occasions, but rather a general view of what the pre-history of Israel meant to the men of the kingdom.

The exodus was not written to satisfy a demand for an historical narrative of Israel, at least not for that reason alone, but to show the men of the monarchy what Yahweh is like, how he always acts, and how men should respond in loyalty to Yahweh's providence.

> The Israelite people were set to work in the Egyptian brick kilns for long hours and prayed to Yahweh for deliverance. Yahweh heard their cry.

At this point the Yahwist tells the story of the burning bush as a sign of Yahweh's revealing himself to Moses and giving him the mission of rescuing his people from their slavery in Egypt. Moses said to Yahweh:

'I am a stutterer. I can't put two words together in a sentence. I should be no good as your messenger.' And Yahweh replied: 'Am I not Yahweh? Go and I will teach you what to say.'

Moses then went to the Pharaoh and asked him to release the Hebrews to keep a holy day in the desert. The Pharaoh of course was not impressed by the appeal to the power of Yahweh; he worshipped the great gods of Egypt and in Egyptian cult he was himself one of the gods. He thought that the Hebrews were only trying to get out of doing their work. He took counter measures and ordered that their work was to be increased. This did not make Moses popular with his fellow Hebrews.

Then, since the Pharaoh would not listen to the appeals of Moses for his people, Yahweh inflicted hideous plagues upon the Egyptians. The Yahwist sees in these plagues a demonstration of Yahweh's power and at the same time his care for the Hebrews. The tenth plague was of great significance to them:

> Yahweh said to Moses: 'After this last plague Pharaoh will no longer hesitate, he will let you go. This night I will destroy the first-born of Egypt from Pharaoh's own heir to the first-born of the cattle.'
>
> Moses summoned the elders of Israel and told them to kill a lamb for the celebration of the spring festival of the Passover when the herds were got ready for the move to the summer pasture and to daub their doorways with the lamb's blood as a sign of belonging to Israel. In the night, Yahweh struck the first-born of Egypt and Pharaoh was afraid. He sent quickly for Moses and told him to take his people out of Egypt. The Israelites hurried away, carrying their bundles of food and their babies on their backs and running towards Canaan.

The Journey

At this point we have to consider the meaning of the Yahwist's account of the pillars of cloud and of fire and the miracle at the sea of reeds (not 'Red Sea', which is a popular mistranslation). Since the same principle is to be invoked in speaking of these phenomena they can best be taken together.

At this point too I had better make it plain that I am advancing an opinion which, though I have no doubt of its truth, is not universally accepted.

The Yahwist had to get across to his people the meaning of the old traditional material for their present life. He was only interested in history as a means of understanding the present. When he came to the traditional material of the Exodus journey he shaped it so that it would be immediately available to his contemporaries. He knew that the basic meaning of the old narratives of the Hebrews' journey across the desert from the land of slavery was to be found in two principles: *Yahweh is always with his people* and *Yahweh is all-powerful*. These principles were valid at the time of the Exodus events and at the time of the writing down of those events. They are valid for us now. So the Yahwist, in order to bring close the meaning of his story told it in terms that the people of his own time could easily understand. He told the Exodus story in terms of the Temple architecture with which they were all familiar.

Whatever explanation is advanced for these pillars—and there have been some very odd ones, ranging from a distant volcano to the cloud of dust raised by the marchers in the desert—we have still to answer the question, 'Why are they mentioned here?'

The Yahwist is a man who orders his material for a series of individual purposes subject to the over-all purpose of showing the settlement (as it was in the reign of Solomon) to be the will of Yahweh. It seems to me that the explanation suggested here does at least do justice to the creative purpose of the Yahwist.

It will be remembered that at the time the Yahwist was putting his material together the Temple front was furnished with two pillars at the top of which braziers burned to show that Yahweh was present in the shrine prepared by his people. During the day the cloud of smoke rose in the sky and at night the flames showed against the dark. These were pillars of cloud and fire showing that Yahweh was with them. So too Yahweh was with his people on their exodus journey, and the best way of expressing this idea was to speak in terms of pillars of cloud and fire ever with the people as they marched along. What was true for the contemporaries of the Yahwist had been true for their ancestors.

When we come to talk about the miracle at the sea of reeds we ought to play down the later accretions which describe such melodramatic moments as the wall of water falling in upon the Egyptian cavalry, and think primarily of what is meant by the narrative. Yahweh has used his power to bring his people out of foreign domination. Yahweh's power is in question. Here, therefore, I would suggest we have a story about his control of water because this was thought of as a good indication of how great his power is.

The incident of the reed sea depends for its significance on the same idea as the bronze sea in the Temple. The Yahwist, here, as in the pillars of cloud and fire, is making the past real to the ordinary Temple worshipper of his time by describing the historical event in contemporary images. Once it is granted that the narratives have as their chief aim the demonstration of Yahweh's continual presence and power in Israel, explanations of this kind will not seem difficult to digest.

What of the historical value of such a story as that of the sea of reeds? I think that we ought to accept as an historical core to the story something like this: When one group of the Hebrews fled from their Egyptian masters along the road to Palestine, taking the quickest route rather than that huge detour suggested by the story of the Red Sea, they came to some marshy area, perhaps at the present gulf of *el-'aqaba* on the east side of the Sinai peninsula. At this point, pursued by the heavy Egyptian forces, the Hebrews, with all their belongings packed on their backs, may well have skipped and jumped from tussock to tussock of reeds and arrived dry shod on the other side. The Egyptian forces, on the other hand, if they had attempted to follow the escaping slaves on horseback or in chariots would infallibly have found themselves in a tangle of half-sunken axles and rearing, frightened horses and been compelled to give up the pursuit. Something of this kind is probably behind the story. An explanation such as this does *not*, of course, deny the providential care of Yahweh for his people, quite the reverse. It simply accepts (as in other places the Yahwist has himself taught the reader to accept) that Yahweh works through ordinary events in order to achieve the fulfilment of his promise. It does not make it at all impossible, for example, to accept as primitive the chorus of the song of Miriam, Moses' sister, after the collapse of Pharaoh's force:

> Sing a song for Yahweh and his victory,
> horses and cavalry,
> thrown into the sea.

The Hebrews went on into the wilderness of Shur and set up their camp, grumbling that Moses had led them to such a desolate place.

Yahweh said to Moses:

'I will send down bread from heaven for all the people; each day they may collect enough for the day and on the sixth day they can gather twice the amount.'

There is today, as in patriarchal times, manna in the Sinai peninsula. It is a bubble formed from the secretions of a tree louse's sting in the tamarisk shrub. The stuff is relatively hard in the cool of the evening but dissolves in the day, so the early morning would be a good time to collect it. Quite recently it was, and perhaps still is, the favourite food of the natives thereabouts.

The Yahwist has taken this phenomenon and invested it with new meaning. He again looks to the liturgical structure of the religion of Yahweh in the time of Solomon to give him an interpretation of the past. By speaking of their collecting enough for two days on the Friday, he suggests that the wandering Israelites already kept the sabbath rest in the desert. How far this anachronism was intentional it is perhaps impossible to guess.

When the people had gone without water for some while they again began to grumble at Moses' leadership.

'Why do you always find fault with me?'

'Why did you bring us here to die of thirst?'

Yahweh brought them water from a rock at Meribah.

The available historical evidence points to the Israelites staying in the Kadesh region where there were many springs at which to water their cattle.

At this point the Yahwist inserted a legendary tale of Moses fighting against the old enemy, the Amalekites, who continued to harass the Israelites in the time of David. The legendary character of the story is indicated by the magic gesture of Moses which *of itself* without any prayer to Yahweh is supposed to defeat the hordes of the enemy.

This tale brings in several new characters who have prominence in other sections of the saga of Israel—Aaron, Moses' brother, Hur, one of the elders, and the new general, Joshua.

Then Amalek rode up and attacked Israel and Joshua led the

little band against the enemy, while Moses stood upon a neighbouring hill. While Moses held up his hands the Israelites had the better of the fight but when he let them drop the Amalekites were winning. Since the fight lasted until evening Aaron and Hur came to hold up Moses' hands until the finish. So Israel routed the foe.

Thus began the enmity between Amalek and Israel from generation to generation.

This is, of course, a theme that was noted in the account of Saul's early battles and Samuel's expertise with the axe.

Sinai and the Covenant

The Israelites were encamped at the foot of a mountain and Moses was told by Yahweh to be prepared for a significant revelation there on the third day. On the third day the mountain was enveloped in smoke and Yahweh stood on the mountain top.

Yahweh called to Moses to ascend the mountain to receive the stone tablets on which were written instructions for the conduct of Israel. Moses took Joshua with him, leaving Aaron and Hur to deal with any dispute among the people. Moses went up to Yahweh on the mountain.

There Yahweh renewed his promise to Abraham and gave to Moses the Law of the Covenant. This covenant of Sinai is not described in the terms used in the narratives of the covenant renewal. The other narratives take the form of a recital of past benefits from Yahweh, followed by present conditions of service for the Israelites, the Israelites' acceptance of these conditions and of the curses which will light upon them if they fail to keep the covenant. The Yahwist's description of Sinai contains hardly any trace of these elements. The Yahwist is concerned only with the description of Yahweh's revelation of himself. He is not presented as a helper of the past but as Yahweh who is here now, as Yahweh the holy one, whose mountain is a sanctuary and whose people are members of a sacred community. The Yahwist has moved from the political to the sacral sphere.

In the traditions preserved in the account of Joshua's assembly of the people at Shechem and in Samuel's abdication at Gilgal, the renewal of the covenant was spoken of in terms which echoed those of the covenants between overlord and vassal in the society in which the Israelites lived. In the Yahwist's eyes, however, the original covenant was not a treaty of this kind, but a manifestation of Yahweh's presence to his people. There is no contractual element in his account, the people are not given the terms of a contract but an opportunity to become the sons of Yahweh. The commandments are not understood as the enactments of a legal structure, but as a code of behaviour, a description of the ways of family life with Yahweh, a presentation of the way in which the people of the promise were expected to live. Because Yahweh is good they must be good also.

Joshua

At the giving of the mountain covenant our book of Exodus ends. The Yahwist, however, had not yet brought his history of the promise to a conclusion. In order to show the working out of the promise up to the settlement of the tribes in Canaan he continued the story of Israel under the leadership of Joshua.

It may be that the Yahwist had dealt with the material he possessed which covered this later period before ever he began to tackle the long patriarchal history but we cannot be certain of this and it makes for easier reading if we place this narrative at the end of the great history of the promise.

The story of the conquest is told as if it were a series of sieges and occupations of the Canaanite towns which in turn opposed the progress of the Israelite forces. The narrative is shaped into a history of a long and carefully planned campaign. It would seem that the Yahwist has received an already formed tradition in which the conquest and settlement were described so. The actual events may well have been not exactly of this kind. There is a good deal of evidence to suggest that the various sieges and fights were quite independent events in which various groups of semitic men fought the natives of Canaan. The independent accounts of these individual actions have been brought together to make a coherent story. All this literary activity, however, does not affect the value of the Yahwist's account for us which is more concerned with showing that Yahweh fulfilled his promise than how events moved towards this fulfilment.

In the history of the patriarchs we can see the continuous broadening of the promise. From man, Abraham, in whom all are blessed, the promise opens out towards a family and then into a people. As time passes so the inheritors of the promise increase. The book of Joshua brings the tribes into the land which is given to a people.

Jericho

After the death of Moses, Joshua was given charge of the Israelites. The young general organized the people into companies and led them across a ford of the Jordan into Canaan, having settled a good number on the near side of the river as a base camp.

The people pitched their tents at Gilgal to the east of Jericho. The inhabitants of Jericho shut up their gates for a siege: none could go out and none could come in. Jericho fell. The men of Israel put the whole population, men, women, and children, to the sword and set fire to the pillaged city. They had taken anything of value out of Jericho before they burnt it down. The spoil belonged to the whole people, not to any one Israelite. Joshua had Achan the son of Carmi stoned to death for hiding loot in his tent. News of Joshua's way with the enemies of Israel went quickly round the cities of Canaan.

The Israelites became over-confident and sent only a small force to take the Amorite city of Bethel which lay next along their marching route. They were defeated. Joshua had to become a tactician. He divided his troops for an ambush at Ai. One half he hid under the city walls and the other half he marched openly to the city. When the men of Bethel saw the Israelites coming against them they poured out of their city to do battle. The Israelite force ran from the Amorites who pursued them far from their city walls. At a signal from their general the other section of Joshua's men then came from their hiding places and set the open city alight. The men of Bethel looked back and saw the smoke rising from their city. They were caught between the two divisions of Joshua and died in the ambush. When the Israelites had finished the slaughter of the Amorites in the open plain, they went back to the city to kill those who had stayed there, old men and women and children, and sacked the place.

Joshua hanged the king of Bethel on a tree outside the walls of his town.

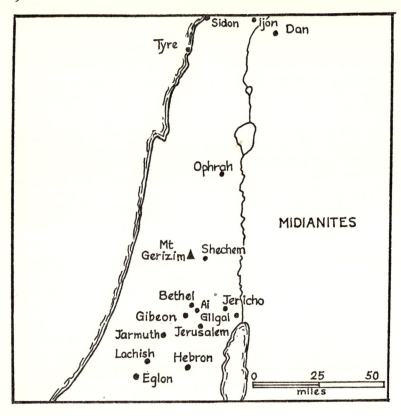

The Men of Gibeon

Hearing the news of Bethel added to that of Jericho, the
Canaanite towns formed a confederation to defend themselves
against Joshua and his men. The men of Gibeon, however,
thought little of the confederation's chances against the Israelites,
and thought up a trick to save themselves from the general destruction. They sent a delegation to Joshua asking for a treaty
with Israel. Joshua was suspicious:

'We cannot make a treaty with you until we are sure that you
do not live in Canaan. Where do you come from?'

'Oh, a long way away, a long way away.'

'Why then do you want a treaty with us? We are not dangerous
to you if you do not live in Canaan. We are going to sack only
Canaanite towns.'

'We have heard of your exploits. Who would not want such men as allies however far away?'

'Prove that you come from such a distance.'

The men of Gibeon had carefully brought stale bread and used-up wineskins and wore patched clothes and tattered sandals as if they had made a long march. These they showed Joshua.

'These are proof of a long journey. See for yourself.'

Taken in by their ruse, Joshua made peace with them and swore a treaty.

Three days later he came with his army along the desert road and reached Gibeon and discovered the trick. But an oath is an oath, and though they were all very angry the Israelites could not kill the Gibeonites. They made them their vassals instead. The men of Gibeon were content with this for at least they had the protection of Israel against any other enemy. They soon needed this protection.

The men of the other Canaanite cities, Jerusalem, Hebron, Jarmuth, Lachish and Eglon, joined together to punish the traitors of Gibeon and in a body they marched towards the city. Gibeon sent a message asking for help from Joshua and Joshua came with his force and defeated the men of the cities—those that escaped from the battle were finished in a storm. The day was long enough for every Canaanite warrior to be killed.

The old sagas proudly boasted that village after village was taken and sacked by Joshua's rough troops. They raided settlements up and down Canaan, leaving a trail of butchered men, hamstrung horses and smouldering hamlet ruins. The Canaanites fought desperately; though they were never defeated totally they could not drive the Israelites back across the Jordan.

The Settlement in Canaan

The evidence of archaeological excavations is certainly in harmony with this account in its general outlines. The sites show that in the second half of the thirteenth century great numbers of semi-barbarous men broke in on the towns of Canaan and established a firm hold on a quite large area of the country. *Joshua* and the remains testify to the extreme horror and bloodiness of the campaign these newcomers waged against the not too well defended townsmen. It must, however, be remembered that the Israelites did

not attempt to depopulate the whole area. Many of the native
population, perhaps from motives like those active in the Gibeonite
story, joined the invaders and fought with them. Many would have
welcomed Joshua and his men because they belonged to the old
semitic stock and were willing to work against the old Canaanite
population. No conquest is without its quislings and collabora-
tors.

Once the land had been occupied and the native population
quietened in one way or another it seems certain that the tribal
pattern grew up quite quickly and that our narratives, though
worked carefully into the scheme of the Yahwist, do reflect the
actual situation after the first decades of the settlement. It is clear
from the old poem that we call the *Song of Deborah*, collected by
the editors of the *Judges* material, that the twelve-tribe system was
in possession by the middle of the twelfth century. From the primitive league of some clans before the conquest, the structure of
Israelite society quickly developed.

The story of the conquest of Palestine is complicated by our
having two separate and not easily reconcilable accounts. The
matter is not made clearer by the archaeological evidence available.
In general we have two main views of the conquest of Canaan—
that of *Joshua*, that it was quick, total, effected by three lightning
campaigns, and that of *Judges*, that it was a protracted and difficult
piecemeal effort. It may be that the *Judges* presentation is more in
accord with historical facts and the *Joshua* account simply the
idealization of the redactor of the tribal traditions. This cannot
however be decisively demonstrated.

At any rate, it is clear that *Joshua* is designed to show how the
promise of Yahweh was at last fulfilled in Canaan. In the second
half of the book there occurs a large number of accounts of the
distribution of the lands to various tribes. These stories have been
shaped by the Yahwist to demonstrate that it is in the rule of the
Davidic line that the true and final settlement has taken place. He
describes the tribal territories not as they were in the cramped
areas available to the people of Joshua's conquering generation but
as they are at the time of his own writing—that is, as the Davidic
line has made them by means of enormous imperialist expansion.
The ancient promise of the land and the laws of division laid out by
Joshua only come to realization in the time of David and Solomon.

That is the Yahwist's thesis—it amounts to a philosophy and vision of history of great sophistication and splendour.

It is all the more impressive because the Yahwist presents his theology of history, not by means of descriptions and visions of the hidden incursions of the glory of Yahweh, but by the quiet account of events as they happen. Yahweh hides his work among the common histories that men direct. It may be that the words of the final summary of the Yahwist's thought are actually the work of a later editor, if so he was an editor who understood the intention of the great writer as he formulated his judgment of the Settlement: "Thus Yahweh gave to Israel the land he had promised them long ago."

The Pre-History of Israel

The Yahwist was evidently a man of great talent, and a man aware of the wide possibilities open to human endeavour. It was with man that Yahweh had made his covenant and therefore man was to be accepted as the first member of creation, the leader of the world. At the same time it was evident to this humanist author that man has somehow blunted the keen edge of his intelligence, somehow led the world awry. Things were not as they ought to be. The covenant had been broken. In order to give an account of the present situation of man the Yahwist produced an account of pre-history. He wrote a preface about the position of man in the world which takes into account both his possibilities and his failures and sets both in relation to the saving will of Yahweh. He wrote, that is, a description of Creation and the Fall.

It is important to realize that while he cast his descriptions in the shape of history, that is, in the shape of a narrative of events which happened long ago, the main intention of the Yahwist was to account for the present. He accepted the principle formulated by Newman in the words, 'the present is a text, the past its interpretation'. He was primarily concerned with his own life at Solomon's court and only very secondarily concerned with life in the dim past of the human race. The stories of Creation and Fall are the Yahwist's considered view of man today; he is saying, 'This is how things are.'

It is noticeable that he begins his narrative of Creation with man. Unlike the author of one of the other Creation narratives, which is

8—K.C.

placed first in our *Genesis*, he is not much concerned with how things began or how they might be but with how they are in his man-centred universe.

Creation

In the day that Yahweh made earth and sky he made man.

Before this there was no rain to make the crops grow and no man to weed the fields.

Yahweh made man out of the dust of the ground and breathed life into him. He placed man in his own great park of happiness.

In the middle of the park was the tree of knowledge:

'Eat any fruit you like but leave this tree alone. If you eat this fruit you will be punished by death.'

To man in his garden Yahweh brought the animals. Man assigned to each animal a place in the life of the garden.

Then Yahweh makes woman. Just as Abraham was put to sleep while the covenant was made, and Moses was not allowed to see Yahweh face to face, so Adam is not allowed to witness Yahweh's act of creation. After this the humanist outlook of the Yahwist is seen in his description of Yahweh as the father of the bride, as Laban had brought Leah to Jacob:

Yahweh brought the bride Eve to the man Adam.

They were happy because they were obedient to Yahweh.

The act of disobedience pictured in the succumbing of Eve to the serpent's suggestion that she eat the fruit of the tree produces a situation in which the human pair are unworthy to come before Yahweh. Throughout the history of Israel great care was taken that no one's flesh should be uncovered unnecessarily during the worship of Yahweh.

The man and his wife hid themselves from Yahweh as he walked in the park in the cool of the evening:

'Where are you?'

'Here in the bushes, for I am naked.'

'Why are you ashamed?'

'I have eaten the fruit of that forbidden tree and know too much.'

At this point we see how the humanism of the Yahweh produces problems that perplex him. Man is evidently the centre of things.

He is the overseer of the world, deployer of the animals, meant to be the friend of Yahweh—and all this is expressed in his ever-increasing knowledge of the world. But at the same time this civilization of which the Yahwist is so proud is a source of doubt to him. Everything seems to go wrong. He does not find happiness simply by growing in knowledge; technology and humane studies do not satisfy him. The Yahwist is not at all sure that the civilization of Solomon's court is the way into Yahweh's favour. He is caught between the satisfaction of exercising his talents and the despair of his failures. The Yahwist comes to the highly sophisticated conclusion that it is because the good of knowing has been achieved through the evil of defiance that things have gone wrong. He does not adopt the easy solution of suggesting that civilization is wrong, he takes the view that life has been spoilt by man's thinking that civilization can be wrenched from Yahweh. He is a serious, questioning humanist.

He also, in passing, rejects any romantic notion that the life of the country man, or alternatively, the life of the nomad, is free from the stresses of urban and courtly life.

To the farmer Yahweh says:
'The soil is cursed because of you. And only by hard labour will it give you food.
'You shall sweat for your livelihood until you too are dug into the soil from which you came';
and to the nomad:
'If you hope for food without work, thorns and thistles are all you shall get and the scrub of the wilderness.

You are dust and you will be dust.'
From this disobedience all frustrations come.
The woman shall long for children
and have them in pain;
she shall long for her husband
and not be satisfied.
Seeking a lover she shall find a master

Man shall long for immortality
and die.

He shall long to be the friend of Yahweh and be forbidden to come near; the cherubim shall fend him from the holy place.

Cain and Abel

When the Yahwist speaks of man eating the fruit of the tree of knowledge of good and evil, he is not speaking primarily of the dawn of moral judgment. 'Good and evil' is for him, as for his contemporaries, a phrase covering 'every thing that is' and 'to know' does not refer to intellectual appreciation only, but to every kind of experience. Thus man is represented as being capable of experiencing a vast range of things. The world has opened out for him. But with this knowledge goes the flaw. It has been won through disobedience and therefore will not work easily in the world Yahweh has made.

This is brought out immediately by the Yahwist's first example of man 'knowing'.

> Adam knew his wife Eve and she conceived and gave birth to a son, whom she called Cain.
> And after him Abel was born.
> Cain grew up to be a farmer. Abel was a shepherd.
> They offered sacrifices to Yahweh and he accepted the sacrifice of Abel and rejected the sacrifice of Cain.
> Cain hated Abel because of this.

Yahweh chooses the sacrifice of blood. He is free to accept and reject. No reason is given. Cain is wrong to expect Yahweh to accept all sacrifices. Yahweh is free.

> Cain said to his brother: 'Let us go out to the field.' There in the field he killed him.
> Then Yahweh asked: 'Where is Abel, your brother?'
> 'How should I know?'
> 'The blood of Abel cries to me from the field. Now you shall be a farmer no longer but a refugee nomad, wandering about the land.'
> This is too much: 'I cannot bear to be cut off from the land and from you. Without your protection every man will fall upon me and seek to kill me.'
> 'Not so. I will tattoo your skin so that men shall know you belong to me.'
> Then Cain went away to the east.

This story needs some explanation. Why did the Yahwist think

of Cain as both cast out by Yahweh and protected by him? And
what was the significance of the tattoo mark? Such questions, and
several others, find their answer quickly enough if, instead of pictu-
ring this odd conversation as taking place in the mythological past,
one considers the contemporary situation that the Yahwist was
attempting to explain.

To the Yahwist Cain was the founder of the Kenites. These were
to him a strange tribe. They were not members of the confederation at any time and yet they worshipped Yahweh and the Yahwist
knew that it was likely that they had in fact worshipped Yahweh long
before the Israelites had come to their faith. The Kenites were not
involved in the Holy War of Israel and yet one of them had been the
father-in-law of Moses and another had smashed a mallet through
the forehead of Sisera, the great enemy of Israel. The Kenites had
joined the Israelites on the march through the wilderness but had
never attempted to settle in the land. The tribe presented a puzzle
to the Yahwist. They seemed somehow to exhibit an arrested existence. Knowing Yahweh and civilization, they had chosen to remain
nomadic plunderers distinguished from other men by their savage
tattoo marks. The Yahwist saw in these men examples of what
would be the fate of one who was cut off from the land. They were
the obvious descendants of a man who, while knowing Yahweh,
had by some act of disobedience cut himself off from the peace of
Yahweh. So the Yahwist adds to his narrative at this point the
traditional family tree of the Kenites, finding historical sources for
the various activities of the desert men of his time.

> Cain knew his wife: she conceived and Enoch was born, the
> builder of cities.
> His son was Irad, his son was Mehujael, his son was Methu-
> shael, his son was Lamech.
> Lamech had two wives, Adah and Zillah. Adah's first son was
> Jabal whose descendants live in tents and look after cattle; her
> second son was Jubal whose descendants play on pipes. Zillah's
> son was Tubalcain, whose descendants are tin and iron smiths.

After this odd list of Kenite ancestors the Yahwist introduces his
own comment before setting out on the flood story.

> Yahweh saw how every man worked evil in the world and let

thoughts of wickedness dwell in his mind. Yahweh was sorry he had ever made man and determined to put an end to the seething world of crime.

But again, without any reason being given, we are told of Yahweh choosing to favour one man. Noah pleased Yahweh.

The Flood Story

We have lost the beginning of the Yahwist's narrative of the flood, during the process of translation and re-editing, we have to begin just before the rain comes down.

Yahweh said to Noah:
'Take your family with you and get into the ark. Take some of each of the animals with you, and the birds so that some will survive in the world.

'In seven days I will send down torrents of rain unceasing and everything that lives on the earth, all that I have made, will be drowned.'

Noah obeyed Yahweh.

He took his wife and his sons and their wives into the ark and all the animals, two of each, as Yahweh had told him. When they were safely aboard Yahweh shut the hatch down. Then the rains came.

While the ark floated up on the water, beneath the floods all living things were drowned. Those in the ark alone escaped.

After a long time the rains ceased and the waters slowly went down.

Noah opened a hatch in the roof and thrust a dove out over the waters, but there was no branch for the bird to land upon, so the dove came back. Noah took it in and shut the hatch. A week or so later he tried again. Again the dove came back but this time with an olive leaf from a tree in its beak. So Noah knew that the waters were going down. He waited another week and sent the dove out a third time. The bird did not come back.

Then Noah himself came up through the hatch and saw that the waters had gone away. The ground was dry. He stepped off the ark and made a sacrifice to Yahweh.

Yahweh then promised that never again would he destroy the world. The seasons should follow one another and day follow night in due order. He would not interrupt life again.

The Ziggurat

The Yahwist connected Noah with his present situation by the simple device of speaking of Noah's sons as the ancestors of the people contemporary with the Yahwist. The ancestor of Canaan turned out to be a bad lot and was cursed by his father. This leads to an explanation of how all the tribes came to be separated. The explanation has its origin in the ruins of a ziggurat, possibly that of Borsippa (modern Birs Nimrud). The ziggurat consisted of a temple at ground level connected by an ascending stepped way to another temple at the top of the artificial mountain thus created. The floors of the ziggurat formed a stairway for the god to move from one temple to the next as he came from heaven or returned thither. Probably this aspect of the architecture suggested the imagery of Jacob's dream of angels at Bethel.

Everyone who lived on the earth at the time spoke the same language. As men spread out across the earth they came to a plain in the land of Shinar and pitched their tents there.

Later they determined to build a city for themselves and set about erecting this sign of their greatness.

'A city is what we need. A great city whose tower shall scrape the sky. Everyone will know how marvellous we are, wherever we go they will praise us.'

Yahweh came down and saw the great tower they were building. He said to himself: 'They are a great people united in one language. And this is only the beginning. There'll be no stopping them once the tower is finished. Let us go down and confuse them. Give them different languages so that when they speak to each other they will not understand what is being said.'

So Yahweh confused them and they left off building their tower and went out in little groups all over the earth. They had only a babel and not a language in common.

In this tale the Yahwist found what he wanted to draw his pre-history towards the great history of the promise to which it was the prologue. The men of Babel tried to form a confederation without Yahweh and by doing so simply found themselves in chaos. When one asked for a hammer he simply got the reply, 'And with your spirit!' The Yahwist got his narrative from some unknown ancient story of Israelite camp-fire sagas, but we can see behind this a reference to the great buildings of Babylon. This great city had been under Hammurabi (1762–1686) the capital of a vast empire and had achieved a legendary fame as the city of wealth and power. The characteristic symbol of this magnificence was the stepped tower or ziggurat. Many of these gigantic artificial mountains had been erected to serve as shrines for the Babylonian gods. The archaeological evidence is conflicting but probably the ruins that the Israelites saw had at one time provided a position from which the pagan star-gazers could watch the heavens. The Babylonians studied the stars in order to find out what the gods were doing. They thought that by seeing which stars were where in the night sky they could tell what was going to happen on this earth. Such things are still popular with pagans today. The essence of the astrologer's work is the belief that one can snatch the secret of the gods by sheer cleverness. In other words, the Babylonians and their ziggurats seemed in the Yahwist's mind to be committing the same sinful folly as the first man at the tree.

They wanted to rule the earth through knowledge gained apart from the will of the creator. Obviously they would be failures. So the ruins of Hammurabi's great empire were signs of the impotence of man when he tried to raid the preserves of Yahweh.

In telling the story of Babel the Yahwist has employed the same mechanism he used in the story of Cain. He has taken a piece of contemporary life as the starting-point for his story and moved out from the local and temporal setting into an account which could be, and was meant to be, applied to all men everywhere.

It is to be noticed that the pre-history that the Yahwist attached to his history of the promise begins with the sin of the whole race. Everyone alive is implicated in the Babel rebellion against Yahweh. The pre-history is a narrative of increasing sin in the world. The Yahwist brings his account to a point at which there is obviously no hope in any human endeavour.

At the same time it is also to be noticed that the Yahwist thinks of men, despite their sin, as being cared for and protected by Yahweh. Adam and Eve are clothed by Yahweh before they face the harsh world outside the park; Cain is tattooed as a sign that he is protected and must not be attacked; Noah is promised that the race of men shall never more be destroyed. There are always indications, that is, that Yahweh will not desert the human race. What then is to happen now? The whole race has rebelled. How will Yahweh show his care for them after this catastrophe? The answer comes immediately in the Yahwist's history. At the end of the pre-history comes history, at the end of the tale of sin comes the promise. The Yahwist tacks his later writing onto his earlier account of the covenant with Abraham in which all men shall be blessed. He has thus shown how Yahweh's purpose of salvation is achieved despite man's sin and how this purpose is first for Israel and then for all men:

'I will make you a great nation. I will bless you and your power will grow ever greater and all the nations of the earth shall enjoy the blessing I will give you.'

The Yahwist has completed his narrative.

ANOTHER VIEW OF THE
MONARCHY

THE YAHWIST must have died before Solomon. The events that followed immediately upon Solomon's death would have shaken, at least, the Yahwist's sense of Israel's history as a promise and its fulfilment, for in a few weeks the whole fabric of the monarchy was rent, the delicate progression from tribal settlement to united kingdom was thrown over, and another interpretation of history given in its place.

How did this come about? Why was the monarchy of the Davidic house rejected by a majority of the Israelite people? The answer to this question is to be found not simply in the events which immediately preceded the rebellion but in the over-all history of the two reigns. The causes of the disaffection described by other writers who dealt with the Yahwist's material must be adverted to if the subsequent history of the people is to be understood. The account that the Yahwist produced of the reigns of David and Solomon was edited later by a writer of distinctly anti-monarchical tendencies. The whole history of the covenant seemed to this writer to be perverted by the action of the kings in seizing the promise which was meant for all members of the old confederation and appropriating it for the new kings of the Davidic line.

We can follow the editorial work of this writer—who evidently did not belong to the inner circle of courtiers, and who is far more representative of the people than the sophisticated and royalist writer with whom we have been so far concerned— through the histories now set down in *Judges*, *Samuel* and *Kings*. This will show his quite different view of the kings and their claims.

Judges

(*a*) *Gideon*

After his victories over the Midianite marauders, Gideon came home to a hero's welcome:

The men of Israel said to Gideon: 'Be our king. We will have you to reign over us, and the kingship shall be hereditary in your family.'

'No, I'll not be a king, nor my son neither. The lord will reign over you.'

Gideon was content with a pile of gold as his booty from the wars. He went back to his city Ophrah, and lived happily with his many wives and his seventy-one sons.

The intention of the chronicler here is to show how a brave man, popular and liberal, would not be king in Israel *because* the Lord is king of his people. There is a blasphemy in the idea of having a man sit upon the divine throne.

(*b*) *Jotham's Parable*

Later an ambitious man named Abimelech tried by employing money and a gang of ruffian bullies to get the Israelites to make him king. His methods had some success:

All the citizens of Shechem came to the shrine and enthroned Abimelech. Then at the northern sanctuary on Mount Gerizim a young soldier, Jotham, stood up to denounce the election of a king. He told this parable:

Once upon a time the trees decided to have their own king. They came in a deputation to the olive tree:

'Reign over us.'

'But I have my own work. Men honour me for my fruit. To reign is not so good as to work.'

The trees then said to the fig-tree:

'Reign over us.'

'But my fruit must be brought forth, I cannot leave my job to reign over you.'

The trees went next to the vine:

'Come now, do be our king.'

'All men love my wine, I am useful here, I do not want to reign over you.'

Then all the trees went in a body to the bramble:
'Be king.'
'If you will be loyal I will shelter you all under my branches
but if you are disloyal you will be put on the log-fire.'

This sarcastic parable is the most savage denunciation of the idea
of monarchy that the Bible contains. Jotham shows firstly that if a
man is any use at anything else he will not want to be a king, and
secondly that a king is full of boasts that he cannot fulfil—the idea
of the bramble sheltering the other trees is nonsensical—and of
threats of violence that he knows only too well how to implement.

Then Jotham ran away from Mount Gerizim out of Abimelech's reach.

The reign of Abimelech is full of violence and war and disaster.
The account closes with this warning for any royalist:

Thus the Lord paid Abimelech for his crime and brought
down punishment on the heads of the men of Shechem as
Jotham had foretold.

II Samuel

Towards the end of his reign David decided to hold a census
of the men of Israel. He said to his generals:
'Make a list of all the men of Israel who are fit for military
service. I want to know the strength of my army.'
Joab, the old commander-in-chief, said to the king:
'You have enormous numbers of men. Why bother to count
them? They have never been numbered before.'
The other generals agreed with Joab but David demanded his
own way.

The next we hear of this proposal is that David realizes that he
has offended against Yahweh in numbering the people. It looks as
if the editor here is suggesting that David was going to reassemble
the levies of soldiers and form an army whose loyalty would be to
the person of the king. David would thus be both limiting the freedom of the men he conscripted and encroaching on the preroga-
tives of Yahweh who was responsible for the conduct of the Holy
War for which the levies were originally intended. Joab and the

generals realize what the king is doing and protest in the name of the old freedoms.

So heinous is the crime against Yahweh that the editor reckons it to be the cause of a great plague in Jerusalem and throughout the kingdom in which seventy thousand men died. Having numbered the people in order to deploy them at his pleasure, David found that he had lost a great part of his force.

I Kings

David's attempt at conscripting the free men of Israel for royal projects was taken as an example to be followed by his successor, Solomon. This king seemed to the editor of the history to be a great despot who managed to achieve his ends by means quite unworthy of Israel. Solomon press-ganged the people to work for him and stifled their protests by pointing to his political successes as justifications of the measures he forced upon them.

Adoram the son of Abda was in charge of the conscription of labour.

Solomon sent forced labour gangs to work in Lebanon cutting down the trees that were to be timber for the new Temple.

And King Solomon levied forced labour from all the tribes of Israel. He had thirty thousand men called-up for the work. He sent them to Lebanon, ten thousand a month in gangs—they had one month in the Lebanon and two months on their own farms, and Adoram was in charge of the gangs.

Solomon got together a force of some thousands of labourers in the quarries, mining and carting great stones for his project. These were in charge of task-masters, some five hundred of them, who saw to it that the people kept at their work.

It was against the forced-labour gangs that the Israelites made their most forceful protest. When Solomon's successor Rehoboam made his appearance before them to receive the popular mandate for his accession it was against the conscription of labour that the elders of the tribes complained bitterly.

There is a short account in the editorial revision of the last events of Solomon's reign of a strange incident, already referred to, involving the young Jeroboam, who was in charge of the forced

labour gangs taken from the clan of Joseph, and Ahijah, a guardian
of the old shrine at Shiloh.

> Ahijah met Jeroboam as he walked alone. Ahijah was wearing
> a new robe and he took it off and tore it into twelve pieces, giving
> ten of them to Jeroboam he said:
> 'Take these, for Yahweh is about to tear the kingdom from the
> king. If you will keep the laws of Yahweh you shall be king of
> Israel and Yahweh will protect you.'

It would seem that we have here a grouping of old themes set up
against the new monarchy.

In the tearing of the robe we have a recollection of the tearing of
Samuel's robe which was a sign of Saul's losing the kingdom. In
tearing the robe into twelve pieces, Ahijah is demonstrating his
adherence to the old idea of the confederation of the twelve tribes.
Although this had become an outworn idea by this time the guardian of the old Ark shrine at Shiloh is certainly suggesting that it
be revived. In the conduct of his successful revolt against Solomon's successor Jeroboam shows that he understood the appeal of
the old confederacy for great numbers of the men of the northern
tribes.

I Samuel

The greatest denunciation of the monarchy inserted into the
history by this editor occurs at the very beginning of the narrative
of the kings. The editor suggests that the last of the Judges, the
wise Samuel, can see that the people in asking for a leader in war
are preparing for themselves a tyrant in peace. It is most unlikely
that Samuel spoke the speech, but it is not the less important for
that. It shows us what one man who had lived under the developed
monarchy thought of the system.

> Yahweh said to Samuel:
> 'This is an ungrateful people. Do not be surprised that they
> are tired of you as their Judge, they have tired of me long ago.
> But do not fret. Warn them, simply, of what they are asking. Tell
> them what a king will be like.'
> So Samuel went out to the people who clamoured for a king:
> 'You want a king? A king will take your sons as conscripts in

his cavalry, he will make them his unpaid servants; a king will appoint overseers to make sure his work is done; a king will take the farmers and make them work on the royal estates, a king will take the blacksmiths for his armament-makers; a king will seize your daughters to be servants in his palaces and work in his kitchens; a king will confiscate your best lands and orchards to reward his courtiers; a king will feed his men with the food you have grown; a king will take your servants and maids and beasts and never pay you anything for them; a king will make you his slaves.'

It was because so many men felt this to be a true summary of Solomon's reign that they were prepared to make a stand against such another reign. When Rehoboam succeeded his father the men of Israel wanted assurances that this sort of thing would not happen again to the chosen ones of Yahweh.

THE TWO KINGDOMS

The Structure of the Davidic Empire

In any account of the reasons for the collapse of the united kingdom three things must be borne in mind. Firstly, the monarchy was a late development in Hebrew history for a reason which persisted even after its establishment—the great distrust of the people of any encroachment on the kingship of Yahweh. They saw how readily the kings of Palestine since the Bronze Age had proclaimed themselves to be divine sons of the Syrian and Canaanite gods and how the Pharaohs of Egypt had been worshipped as the great gods. Even at the height of David's prestige and even in his own city of Jerusalem, where the old tribal traditions were at their weakest, the king was never greeted as anything more than the 'adopted son' of Yahweh. Secondly, the traditions of the tribes were not easily adapted to the notion of hereditary monarchy. The old way of life had known only personal charismatic leadership. Nor for several generations was hereditary succession accepted by the northern tribes. Thirdly, the process by which David had built up his empire was too dependent upon his personal qualities of leadership and courage to move easily into a hereditary succession. It is with this third aspect of the situation that I wish to deal in this section.

David began his career as the leader of a group of professional soldiers employed by Saul. He very soon abandoned his courtly office and formed a band of freebooters who disturbed the royal peace enough to be chased out of Saul's lands. David then accepted the employment offered by the Philistine ruler of Gath and was given Ziglag as his fief in the feudal system of that nation. Upon Saul's defeat and death at the hands of the Philistines, David's chance had come. The men of Judah, disillusioned by the failure of the monarchy to defend them, asked David to be their king and form a separate state in the south. Later chroniclers attempted to provide David with charismatic sanctions by creating the story of Samuel anointing him, but evidently the surprising decision of the men of Judah to have a king was dictated by David's own determination to accept nothing less than royal dignities.

On the murders of Abner and Ishbaal the northern tribes realized that only David could lead them in the fight against the Philistines; only he had the necessary military experience and available troops. Thus David was elected king by the northern elders who came to him at Hebron. David was king of Judah, king of Israel and baron of Ziglag. He removed from Hebron to Jerusalem, a city belonging to neither Judah nor Israel though situated between them. This city became David's personal capital. The only link between his four possessions was their individual allegiance to him.

The Philistines now recognized David as a danger and attacked his combined forces. They lost. They lost to David, not to any state or kingdom. He left them their own separate government on their acceptance of vassalage to his person. Territories other than the five city-states were annexed to Israel and Judah—not, however, to individual tribes. They became new administrative areas in the new kingdom and helped to deprive the tribal boundaries of their remaining reality. The northern militia was then levied for wars against Damascus, Ammon, Edom and Moab. All these territories were conquered for David, who set his governors to administer these new crown lands. The northerners became discontented at being used to further David's political ambitions. Twice they revolted. Judah's loyal troops and David's own mercenaries forced the north to remain in the empire. Absalom and Sheba both failed to break up the system.

It is obvious that the whole structure depends on David. Ziglag and Jerusalem are his own cities, bound to his heirs. His rule over Judah is quite independent of his rule over Israel, the foreign cities and states are his personal vassals and territories. Only the son of David could keep the whole system intact. If the north elected anyone but the son of David, Jerusalem, Ziglag, Judah and the rest would break away. This political reality was recognized in the acceptance of Solomon as ruler of all the empire.

Solomon determined to obtain a firmer grip on the north. He

9—K.C.

built royal fortresses to overawe the peasants and created a chariot force to police the country. In this and in his policy of forced labour camps, he went too far in the direction of absolutist and divine Canaanite monarchy. The forces of independence were kept under only by his ostentatious success in foreign affairs and money-making.

At his death the fascination of David's personality was not so much in the front of the popular mind, and few cared for the auto-cratic imperial government of Solomon. The southern belief that Yahweh wanted a Davidic king to reign in an ever-increasing empire was not shared by the northerners. Rehoboam was rejected by Israel and the whole Davidic structure collapsed.

Rehoboam

Shechem, the old centre of the confederacy of the covenant, seems to have retained a ritual importance, for the new king comes there to be acknowledged by the free men of the northern tribes after the death of his father, Solomon.

Rehoboam came to Shechem where the leaders of Israel had assembled to choose him as their king. Before the acclamation they came to the prince and said:

'Your father made our yoke heavy. We look for a kindlier rule from you after we have made you king.'

'If you make conditions then I must have time to consider your requests. Come back in three days.'

The elders went away and Rehoboam took advice. The old councillors who had been at the court of David and of Solomon said to the young man:

'If you agree to the requests of the people, they will remain loyal to you for ever, give way this once and you can rule for the rest of your life.'

The young men of his own generation said:

'Teach them who is king. Say to these old fellows, "My father's rule will seem kindly when compared with mine. He beat you with the lash, I shall use the cat o' nine tails."'

When the three days were up, the elders of Israel came for the young king's reply. Rehoboam took the advice of the young men. The elders took the king's reply to the men of Israel and there was an uproar.

'Why should we serve David? What is the son of Jesse to us?
To your tents, Israel. Let the house of David look after itself.'

So the old cry of the confederacy was raised and the men of
Israel refused to serve Rehoboam. The young man was acclaimed
king by those who lived in Judah only. The rest looked for
another.

Rehoboam decided that force must be employed against the
rebels. He sent Adoram, the master of the forced-labour gangs,
to deal with the revolt. The men of the northern tribes stoned the
hated minister to death. Then the young king saw that it was too
dangerous for him to stay at Shechem. He got into his chariot
and raced back to Jerusalem. He was king of Judah only. The
men of Israel knew that they needed a leader and determined to
elect a king who would look after their interests against the
Jerusalem court.

When it was learnt that Jeroboam had come back from exile in
Egypt and was living on his farm at Seredah, the elders of Israel
sent for him. He came to them while they were still at Shechem
and there the assembly acclaimed him as king of Israel.

We have now to be somewhat careful in taking our history from
the accounts which survive, for these have all either been written by
scribes of the southern kingdom, servants of Rehoboam and his
successors, or else edited by them when the chronicles of the
northern kingdom were brought south at the fall of the northern
kingdom in 721.

It is evident that we now have two groups, both worshippers of
the one Yahweh, both claiming to inherit the covenant. Rehoboam
obviously appealed to the promise to David. Jeroboam I and his
counsellors thought of themselves as the men who were restoring
the original setting of the covenant. They adopted the old language
of the tribes and thought of the new kingdom as the inheritor of the
promise to the tents of Israel.

What the Yahwist had brought together in his great literary con-
spectus had been sundered politically by the despotism of Solomon,
the folly of Rehoboam and, perhaps, the ambition of Jeroboam.

The Reign of Jeroboam

King Jeroboam was an energetic man and at once took steps to
secure his new country from outsiders and from those who might

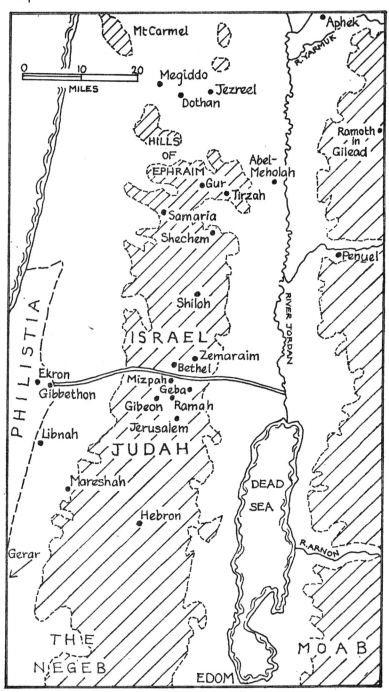

start a rebellion within his borders. He must have remembered
that the men of Gilead had remained faithful to David during the
abortive revolt of Absalom and fortified Penuel against such a
danger to his government.

King Jeroboam fortified Shechem in the hills of Ephraim and
made this city his capital. Then he fortified Penuel. This done,
Jeroboam turned his attention to the worship of Yahweh that
was still centred on Jerusalem and the Davidic Temple: 'If I let
the people go on pilgrimage to the Temple in Jerusalem then the
people will still think of Rehoboam as king and will turn back to
him.'

Jeroboam, therefore, decided to restore the worship of Yahweh in the old shrines of Bethel and Dan to serve instead of
Jerusalem as the religious centres of the kingdom.

Bethel was in the south of Israel directly in the path of the pil-
grims as they went to Jerusalem, Dan was in the far north, and
therefore much easier for the men of Naphtali, Asher, Zebulon and
Issachar to reach than the southern Jerusalem.

At each of the two northern kingdom shrines, Jeroboam had
the priests erect a golden calf as sign of the presence of Yahweh
—rather like the winged cherubim of the Jerusalem Ark. They
were the throne of Yahweh. Jeroboam held a great festival of
dedication at each of the shrines to which great numbers of the
people went and Jeroboam proclaimed the worship of Yahweh:
'This is the sign of Yahweh, Israel, who brought you out of
the land of Egypt.'

And Jeroboam instituted a great feast of the New Year at the
time of the harvest.

This festival became the great royal festival when the rule of the
king was celebrated as the sign of Yahweh's government in the
world. It was designed to outshine, if possible, the attractions of
the New Year festival in Jerusalem and the recent enthronement
ceremonies of Rehoboam. At these the ritual had probably
included songs in which Yahweh had said to the new king:

'I have set my king on the holy hill of Zion.
You are my son, today I have begotten you.

Ask me for the nations
and they will be yours.
The whole world is given to you.
Beat the nations with iron and
dash the foreigner in pieces.'

and

'Sit on my right hand;
your enemies shall be your footstool.'

Jeroboam, therefore, inaugurated a festival to demonstrate to
the people that he also was the chosen king of Yahweh.

The Legend of the Golden Calf

When the northern festival was reported in Jerusalem the royal
scribes took immediate action to produce a piece of effective
counter-propaganda. They decided to show the people that from
the beginning of the covenant with Yahweh what Jeroboam was
doing had been regarded as the worst blasphemy. They took the
old accounts of the exodus and inserted the story of the golden calf.
Jeroboam was breaking the covenant, they argued, so it is right
that this should be easily demonstrable to the people. This is the
tale they put into the narrative; it even includes a quotation from
Jeroboam's speech:

While Moses was on Mount Sinai receiving the law of the
covenant from Yahweh, the people grew weary of waiting. They
were tired of Moses and Yahweh and of their journey. They said
to Aaron, Moses' brother:
'Moses is not coming back. Therefore, make us gods to
worship.'
Aaron took all the golden ornaments of the people, melted
them down and made a golden calf for the people, and presented
it to them:
'This is your god, Israel, who brought you out of the land of
Egypt.'
And Aaron established an altar and arranged a great festival.
The people sang and danced round the golden calf and forgot
Moses.
Then Yahweh was angry at the blasphemy and said to Moses:

'Let me alone with this people for a moment. I shall destroy them all and make my great nation out of you.'

But Moses prayed for the people, reminding Yahweh of his promise to Abraham, Isaac and Jacob that all their descendants should share in the land that he had prepared. So Yahweh relented and did not destroy the people, though they shouted:

'This is your god, Israel, who brought you out of the land of Egypt.'

Moses took the tablets in his hands and went down the mountain to see what the people were doing. The noise was as loud as the noise of war, the festival was so wild.

When Moses came down from Mount Sinai with the tablets on which the law of the covenant was carved and saw the orgy he threw the tablets to the ground in his fury and broke them at the foot of the mountain. This was a sign that the covenant had already been broken by the people. Then he took the golden calf and ground it into a powder and put the powder in water and made the people drink up their own idol. And he had three thousand of them killed for their part in the excesses. Even these deaths were not enough. Yahweh himself sent a plague upon the people because they made the golden calf.

Such an effectively contrived story must have been very useful as a piece of anti-northern propaganda, the calf of Bethel would be associated for ever in the minds of the southerners with the calf of Aaron and so be a sign of Jeroboam's blasphemy. That the calf of Jeroboam served, like their own Ark in the Temple, as a mere throne for the presence of Yahweh, was henceforth hidden from the men of Judah. The hatred of the southern kingdom scribes for Jeroboam comes out in their editing of his history. One example should make this clear.

There came up from Judah a seer loyal to the line of David. He arrived at Bethel just when Jeroboam was standing by the altar ready to offer incense to Yahweh. The seer cried out in the midst of the assembly:

'Behold this altar shall be torn down and the ritual of this shrine brought to an end. The kings of David will destroy it.'

Then Jeroboam pointed to the shouting man to have him arrested, but the people did not dare obey him for fear of the seer's power and the man went back to Judah.

The scribes of Judah took this incident and retold it in a way which emphasized the wickedness of the worship at Bethel and the power of the man of Yahweh when confronted with a mere northern king. Jerusalem is obviously the only place to worship. This is their version of the event:

Hearing the words of the prophet, Jeroboam stretched out his arm and shouted to his guards to arrest the prophet of Yahweh. And immediately his arm was paralysed so that he could not move it.

Then Jeroboam pleaded with the man of Yahweh:

'Pray to Yahweh that my arm may be restored to me.'

So the prophet prayed and Yahweh restored the life of the arm to Jeroboam. Jeroboam was full of thanks and wanted the prophet to come to supper with him but the man of Yahweh would not eat in such a place and set out at once for Jerusalem.

But after all this Jeroboam went on with his old wickedness and set up priests in the shrines of the hill country to keep the people from the worship in Jerusalem. In the end this policy was the ruin of his house.

Abijah, the young son of Jeroboam, fell ill, and the king said to his wife:

'Go in disguise to Shiloh, do not let anyone see that you are my wife, and consult the seer Ahijah who once prophesied I should tear the tribes from David's house and be myself king of this people. Take him something to eat and ask him what will happen to our boy.'

The queen went to Shiloh and found the house of Ahijah, who was blind. But he knew her:

'Come in, Jeroboam's wife, why this disguise? Your journey is useless. As you go in your gates the lad will die.'

And the queen went back to her home, and as she entered the house her son died.

The southern scribes later got hold of this story and put a great speech into the mouth of the blind prophet, denouncing the new kingdom that Jeroboam had set up. Evidently they did not think it odd that the man who had urged Jeroboam to rebel should say:

'Thus says Yahweh of Israel: "Though I gave you the tribes you have not kept my commandments like my servant David.

You have made golden calves and worshipped them, turning your back on me. Therefore I will destroy every man of the house of Jeroboam. I will sweep him away. The servants of Jeroboam will die and be eaten by dogs and become carrion for the wild birds." Thus says Yahweh.

'No. I have not done.

'Yahweh will smite the tribes of Israel and they shall tremble as the reed before the wind and they shall be scattered because they have forsaken Yahweh and turned to idols.'

The Egyptian Menace

The inevitable war between the two kingdoms, for which both sides prepared by fortifying border towns, was postponed by the invasion of the area in 918, that is, five years after the establishment of the division of the tribes, by Shoshenq, the Pharaoh of Egypt. It was this Pharaoh who had given political asylum to Jeroboam in the last years of Solomon. The records at Thebes contain a list of nearly a hundred and fifty towns, more than half of them in Judah, occupied by his vast army. At Megiddo a monument was set up to commemorate his advance. In the Negeb the barley lands were robbed of their fine crop.

At Gibeon Rehoboam paid his tribute to the Pharaoh, and then Shoshenq marched through the northern kingdom destroying the townships. Evidently he did not regard Jeroboam as a loyal vassal.

Rehoboam was forced to give the Pharaoh all the Temple treasures and the palace treasures. The golden shields of Solomon were carted away, and poor substitutes were made to replace them. These had to be used on the state occasions when Rehoboam went in procession to the Temple.

Rehoboam died and was succeeded by his son Abijah, who reigned for under three years in Jerusalem.

Abijah declared war on the northern kingdom and took his army to the hill of Zemaraim in Ephraim. The young king stood on a hillock and called out to the force of Israel facing him:

'Do you not realize that Yahweh gave the kingdom to the house of David for ever? He has sworn a covenant with us. Jeroboam is a rebel. Yahweh is with us. What have you but golden calves? Lay down your arms then and do not hope to fight against Yahweh.'

While he was making this speech, Jeroboam sent his men to come up behind Abijah's rear, so that the men of Judah were surrounded. Seeing this they went vigorously to work to get out of such a position and defeated the army of Israel. Abijah then occupied Bethel.

Abijah seems to have been unable to hold Bethel for long and returned to Jerusalem where he died and was succeeded by his son Asa. In Israel Jeroboam died and was succeeded by his son Nadab. This king's reign was cut short after a few months. While he was directing the attack on the fortifications of a Philistine border town one of his officers, Baasha, killed him and had the army proclaim him king. He remained in power until his death in 877, having had all the members of Jeroboam's family put to death as a security measure.

Baasha moved the northern capital to Tirzah. Asa in his turn had difficulties in the southern kingdom of Judah.

Zerah, a man from Cushan (an adventurer in the pay of Shoshenq of Egypt), made raids from Gerar on the southern towns. Then Asa went out to deal with him and set up his camp in the valley of Zephathah near the frontier fortress of Mareshah.

Asa proclaimed a Holy War, calling on Yahweh to protect his people. The mercenaries of Zerah fell back before the army of Judah. The army pursued them all the way to Gerar and Zerah's men fled before them leaving their baggage by the roadside in their hurry to escape. They left behind their possessions in the tents, their cattle and sheep. All these fell into the hands of Asa.

Seeing how Asa prospered a great many men crossed over the border from Ephraim and Manasseh and Simeon and were given refuge by Asa in Judah. The southern kingdom was therefore on the way to establishing its claim to be the inheritor of the promise to all the tribes. Asa arranged a great festival to proclaim the renewal of the covenant in Jerusalem.

In the northern kingdom of Israel, Baasha saw that he must do something to counteract this southern propaganda. He took an army right into Benjamin and reached Ramah only five miles north of Jerusalem.

Ramah was captured and fortified by the northerners and they controlled the road to Jerusalem. Fearing that his own city might be the next to fall to the northern army, Asa got together all the gold and silver left in the capital and sent it to Benhadad I of Damascus to persuade him to break off his league with Baasha and to enter into a league with Judah. Benhadad agreed and attacked Baasha's northernmost towns in Ijon and Dan and Naphtali. This meant that Baasha had to evacuate Ramah in order to hurry north and deal with Benhadad's invaders. He was caught between his two enemies. Benhadad already had occupied the Transjordan territories north of the Yarmuk and could not be dislodged, while Asa conscripted the whole labour force of Judah to remove the fortifications at Ramah and to use the building materials to build up the walls of Geba and Mizpah.

Asa, therefore, was able to push his frontier a little further north and be more at ease in the security of Jerusalem. At home he was not, however, a popular king.

Hanani the seer came to the king of Judah and denounced his policy of alliance with the Syrians of Damascus:

'Yahweh defeated Zerah for you, he would have defeated your other enemies too, yet you chose to ally yourself with pagans. You are a fool. You do not trust Yahweh. Once you have got yourself mixed up with these foreign powers you will never be free of war.'

Asa had the seer shut up in prison for this effrontery. But the people did not like this policy. When Asa got gout and was in great pain it was taken as a sign from Yahweh that he was not a good king, since he resorted to medicines instead of prayer.

Three years before Asa's death, Baasha died and his son Elah was proclaimed king of Israel. He was king for only a year, then the commander of the household cavalry, Zimri, at the head of an army group, assassinated him as he was at supper with his ministers. The whole of the royal family was murdered and Zimri proclaimed himself the new king.

Within a week, it was obvious that Zimri could not rely on the loyalty of even the army officers, his only possible source of support in the country. The army was in camp at Gibbethon besieging the Philistine inhabitants. The officers held a meeting and decided that they would prefer the commander-in-chief, Omri, to be king in Israel.

Omri, therefore, took the army from Gibbethon and marched

to the capital, Tirzah, where the citizens received him with some show of pleasure. Seeing this, Zimri committed suicide.

At this, to increase the confusion, another general, Tibni, had himself proclaimed king. Civil war followed and it took several years for Omri to establish his claim to the throne.

The House of Omri

Omri was determined to put an end to the history of short reigns, bloodshed and *coups d'état*. He set himself to found a dynasty. For this two things were necessary: an ordered civil government in which the king should be seen as the central and essential overlord and a religious settlement that would indicate Yahweh's pleasure with the monarch.

These two problems were connected. They both derived from the founding principles on which the men who elected Jeroboam had acted. The central government was conceived by these elders as a necessary instrument in the defence of the tribal independence against the centralized forces of Rehoboam. They therefore elected a man to serve the tribal confederation, not to rule a kingdom. They did this on the old conservative grounds of Yahweh's covenant with his people. The relation of the king to Yahweh was a Judah notion and not welcomed by the men responsible for the establishment of Israel as a separate kingdom. To rule, therefore, in the north, was to be confronted with difficulties about political independence and religious sanctions.

Omri settled the first problem by quitting the capital Tirzah, buying a hill in Ephraim for himself, and there building a city which had belonged to no man before. This gave him a royal estate. Samaria was his and he was understood to be asserting his independence of any man in the realm. Omri thus showed that he had real power and meant to be obeyed by every man of Israel. The new king may well have been himself an Israelite and certainly he was not an ardent worshipper of Yahweh. He restored the grandeur of the rituals at Bethel and Dan but in doing so was not averse to incorporating rituals from other religions. It is possible to see in Omri's foreign policy an attempt to curb the power and influence of the old conservatives who still desired a confederation in which Yahweh should be the real king. Omri gave his son Ahab a name of foreign origin, and married him to the princess Jezebel of Sidon. This determined lady brought to Israel both a valuable alliance and a foreign religion.

Ahab himself, as if it were a small thing, took part in the worship of Baal Melqart and he even erected a Temple of Baal Melqart on the royal estate at Samaria. He was less concerned to placate the worshippers of Yahweh than his father. To accept a foreign god was to reject the social order of the covenant and to be free of tribal restraints.

While all the fighting had been going on between the rival factions of Israel, the wily old king of Damascus, Benhadad, annexed more and more of the northern borders of Judah. He strengthened his position by making a treaty with the Phoenician state of Tyre. When Omri became king this alliance was the chief external menace to peace. Hence the marriage arranged for Ahab with Jezebel the Tyrian princess.

At the same time the energetic and cruel master of Assyria, Asshur-nasir-pal II, was increasing his territory further west, and on one campaign he arrived at the coast of the Mediterranean, compelling Tyre to pay him tribute. Tyre, Sidon and Israel faced the same threat.

Naboth's Vineyard

The chronicler now turns to an incident in the reign of Ahab which brings out both Ahab's weak grasping character and Jezebel's determination to rule in the tradition not of Israel but of Tyre.

Next to the winter palace at Jezreel where Ahab and his wife were living was a vineyard owned by Naboth. The king wanted to bring in this area of ground to his own estates and went to bargain with Naboth:

'Let me exchange your vineyard with one of mine. I want to make it into a vegetable garden. Or if you would rather have the money, I'll buy it from you.'

'God forbid that I should give up my ancestral plot and cease to be a free farmer, become one of your dependent courtiers or lose my place in the land altogether.'

Ahab went away and threw himself down on his couch and sulked. Jezebel said to him:

'What's the matter? Why do you sulk all day and eat nothing?'

'Naboth won't exchange his vineyard for another nor let me buy it from him.'

'Is that all? We'll soon see who reigns here. Eat up. Don't worry. You'll have your vineyard quick enough.'

Jezebel took the royal seal and sent letters to the elders of the city telling them to bribe a couple of rogues to accuse Naboth of blasphemy—the punishment for this was to be stoned to death and the dead man's property was confiscated by the state.

It was all arranged and Naboth was stoned. Then Jezebel came to Ahab and told him that Naboth was dead and the vineyard belonged to the king. Ahab walked in the vineyard with his wife. As he walked between the vines he came face to face with Elijah:

'Is the murderer pleased with his orchard? Do you think you can get away with this? Yahweh will see to it that a day shall come when the dogs shall lick up your blood.'

'So, you have found me. You have never been my friend.'

'I have found you. Should I be a friend to such an enemy of Yahweh? Surely you can see that your family will be wiped out just like those of Jeroboam and Baasha, since you have sinned as they sinned? As for the queen, the dogs will fight over her flesh under the city walls.'

Elijah turned away. The king went back quietly into the palace very much afraid. He did not boast of his kingship again.

War with Damascus

Other events occupied the last years of his life. Benhadad II of Damascus came with an army to besiege Samaria. His herald arrived with this message:

'Your silver and gold are mine for the taking; and your fairest daughters shall be my concubines.'

The king replied: 'You are right. All I have is yours. Take me as your prisoner.'

The herald came the next day again: 'No. I do not want you. I will take your daughters as hostages and your goods as tribute. You shall remain as my vassal.'

Then the elders of Israel, who had fled to Samaria when Benhadad II had conquered their towns, advised the king to make a stand. So Ahab returned a refusal to the king of Damascus.

On the third day the herald came again: 'I shall grind Samaria to powder.'

'Boast once you have captured the city, sir.'

On hearing this reply, Benhadad rose from his supper table and ordered the capture of Samaria next day.

Ahab did not wait for the attack. He sent his men down on the camp of the king of Damascus and the Syrians were cut down. Benhadad II only just managed to escape.

By the next spring Benhadad was planning another attack on Samaria. He dismissed the old officers and put in new men, and brought out a new army.

This fared no better than the first force. They were beaten back by Ahab's men into Aphek. There they huddled. And the Israelites mined the walls till they crashed down leaving the garrison defenceless. The Syrians were hunted through the city. Benhadad II himself was forced to run from house to house and at last gave himself up to Ahab:

'Our fathers were allies. What will you do with me?'

'You may go free, but give us back the towns your father took, when my father Omri was dealing with the rebel Tibri and could not fight your father as well.'

It was agreed between the kings. Many of the more conservative members of Israel thought this clemency of Ahab an act of treachery to Yahweh who had given victory in his Holy War and ought to have been given the lives of the prisoners he had won.

The Prophet

With the coming of Elijah to disturb Ahab's complacent possession of Naboth's vineyard we are confronted with the prophet in Israelite society.

1. The prophet was not a fortune-teller and was rarely concerned with the future. The general message of the prophets was that men should turn again to the service of Yahweh. As a corollary of this it would follow that Yahweh would protect them. If they reformed in the present then the future would be happier, but it was on reform in the present that the emphasis was laid.

2. In general the great prophets whose careers fell before the Exile were suspicious of the growing power of the king and hankered after the popular Mosaic tradition of the tribal confederation.

Even after the Exile, when more emphasis was given to the restoration of the united kingdom and the city of Jerusalem, the funda-
mental kingship proclaimed by the prophets was that of Yahweh
himself.

3. The prophets thought of themselves as the messengers of Yahweh the king and often adopted the convention of Near-Eastern
heralds of speaking in the first person of the one who sent the
message: 'Thus says Yahweh: "I . . ." '

4. In the careers of the prophets included in this history three
stages can be recognized in the evolution of the prophetic activity.
Elijah, the earliest dealt with here (apart from Nathan at David's
court), gave formal lectures to his disciples. Amos's hearers understood that his great speeches at the public shrines ought to be preserved—so we have written records of his prophesying, which we
lack for Elijah. In the account of Jeremiah set down by his secretary Baruch, we not only have a record of the prophet's words but a
narrative of his life. The prophet's biography becomes a witness
for Yahweh.

5. Receiving a message for men from Yahweh was the self-authen-
tication of the prophet. The message gave him his job in the community. But there was no single recognized way in which the
message could come. We have no record of the call of Elijah;
Elisha was simply the most faithful of Elijah's followers and carried
on his work; Amos had visions but we do not know if these con-
stituted his call; Hosea simply came to understand his own family
life as a picture of Israel; and, while Isaiah gives a marvellous
account of his call during the Temple liturgy, this is evidently not a
typical case. Perhaps there is no typical case. Perhaps we ought not
to attempt such generalizations and be content with the individual
prophets as they speak to their contemporaries and to us.

Elijah

Of the culture and society of Ahab many monuments remain, including the ruins of some splendid buildings and some delicate
ivories, but the most famous of all the works of that era are the
stories about Elijah the prophet. This great man who had no fear of
the king and who represented the old ways of free Israel was a
challenge to the Tyrian novelties that came into Ahab's court on

his marriage with the energetic and intelligent Jezebel. The story of Naboth's vineyard, which so impressed the minds of the men of Israel that it was used later by one of Ahab's young officers as propaganda in favour of a revolution in Israel, shows the two concepts of society, meeting in head-on collision. Jezebel asserts the autocratic right of the pagan king to total obedience from his subjects; Elijah asserts the inalienable right of the free servants of Yahweh to live free in the land Yahweh has given. On this and other occasions, Elijah is obviously a popular hero. Round such a man stories are bound to grow. The majority of those that are extant were probably set down by Elijah's most prominent disciple, Elisha, during the reigns of Ahab's sons. Since they give an impression of what the men of this period thought a hero and a prophet was like they offer a perfect comparison with such stories as those of the adventures of Gideon or Samson, the heroes of an earlier age in Israel.

Two stories of Elijah belong to this period. Probably they were set down by Elisha quite soon after the events to which they refer. The first is a quiet domestic story of how a good turn was repaid with a better and how Yahweh does not forsake his friends. The second is a busy political incident which reflects the bitter struggle of Jezebel to maintain the worship of Baal and of how Elijah successfully destroyed the Baal Melqart shrine erected on Mount Carmel. How far these stories are to be regarded as historical narratives and how far they have been elaborated to point up their main interests it is probably not now possible to discover. At the least they show us a great prophet of Yahweh cared for by his providence and working for his honour among many enemies.

The Widow of Sarephath

It looks as if there was a great drought at the beginning of Ahab's reign and that the prophet Elijah confronted the king and blamed the economic distress of the nation on the Baal worship of the queen to which Ahab had given a sanction.

The anger of Ahab led to Elijah retiring east of the Jordan into Phoenicia.

Elijah went further and further north until he came into Phoenician territory at Sarephath; as he entered the gates of the

10—K.C.

town he saw a poor widow picking up sticks. Elijah called to her:

'Bring me a cup of water to drink.'

She went to get it at the well and he called after her: 'And a morsel of bread.'

She turned to him: 'Yahweh knows that I have nothing in the house but a small handful of meal and a drop of oil. I am gathering these sticks to make a fire. Then I shall make a small loaf for myself and my boy and then we shall eat it and die.'

'Don't worry. Just make the bread. We'll share it.'

When the cooking was done the three of them ate together and when the widow looked in the bin there was meal enough for another baking. So it continued, a never-failing source of oil and meal throughout the drought and famine.

Later the son of the widow of Sarephath fell ill and he lay lifeless on the bed. Then the widow blamed herself. The boy was lost because of all her sins. Elijah took the boy and carried him to his own room and laid him on the bed:

'Is it fair, Yahweh, that this good woman who has looked after me so well all this time should suffer like this? Let the boy live.'

Elijah stretched the length of his own body three times above the boy's body and the boy breathed again. Elijah raised him up and gave him back to his mother:

'Now I know for certain that you are a man of Yahweh.'

Mount Carmel

After over a year of drought when the rain did not fall in the autumn, nor the moisture condense on the mountains in the summer, Ahab's great worry was to obtain fodder for the horses in the royal stables. He decided that he and his chief minister, Obadiah, should divide the country between them and compel the peasants to give up their last supplies of fodder to the king's servants.

Obadiah was a worshipper of Yahweh and had hidden a great many other worshippers of Yahweh from Queen Jezebel's police who hunted them out in order to establish the worship of the Tyrian god Baal Melqart. He took his half of the country and went searching for hay for the animals. On his journey he was stopped by the great prophet Elijah who had returned to Samaria:

'Go tell your master that I am here.'

'Oh no, sir, I should not risk my life by carrying such a message. For if I go to the king and tell him that you are here he will come down at once to take you—and where will you be? Gone. And I? Well, I will be in the king's prison. It's not fair. I have always served Yahweh and now this happens.'

'I promise you as Yahweh lives, I will stay here to meet the king.'

Obadiah summoned Ahab and the king went to meet Elijah as he stood on the roadway:

'So it is you, you troubler of Israel.'

'You're the troubler of Israel, king. You have deserted Yahweh and run after Baal. But now it is time for all this Baal nonsense to have an end. Tell all your dervishes who worship Baal and are fed fat by Jezebel to meet me at Mount Carmel.'

Ahab summoned Jezebel's dervishes and a great many of the people came to see what was going to happen at Carmel. Elijah stood up and said:

'Men of Israel! How long are you going to hesitate between Baal and Yahweh? Make up your minds and follow the one or the other.'

The people stood silent.

'Well, then, let's try a contest between us. I alone am the prophet of Yahweh and look at these hundreds of priests of Baal. Give us a couple of oxen, and let them choose the better and cut it up and place it ready on the altar, and I will do the same with the other. Let neither set fire to the sacrifice. We will simply ask for fire from heaven, and whoever answers, let him be worshipped.'

The people agreed to the plan.

The priests of Baal Melqart took their ox and dressed it and placed it on the pyre; and from morning until noon they cried to their god: 'O Baal, hear us!'

The god was silent.

Then the men of Baal Melqart danced wildly round the altar still crying to their God: 'O Baal, hear us!'

At noon Elijah began to mock them: 'Cry louder, perhaps he is busy! Gods have a great deal of business. Perhaps he is at an inn, or perhaps he has gone on a journey, or again he may have fallen asleep. Wake him up! Cry louder!'

The men of Baal Melqart cried louder and louder to their god. They took out knives and slashed themselves in a frenzy. Their blood spurted as they danced round the altar. Nothing happened. The god was silent.

The people stood silent.

In the evening Elijah said: 'I have had enough of this. Let us ask Yahweh for his sign.'

He built an altar and put the pieces of meat on it and dug a trench around it. Then he poured gallons of water over the offering and the wood of the pyre and the water ran down and filled the trench about the altar. Then Elijah prayed:

'Yahweh of Abraham, Isaac and Jacob, show us today that you are with Israel, and answer my prayer. Then this people will know that Yahweh is God.'

Fire from Yahweh fell from the sky: it burnt up the offering and altar and licked up the water in the trench.

The people fell on their faces crying: 'Yahweh is God! Yahweh is God!'

Elijah cried: 'Seize the men of Baal. Don't let one escape.'

They lynched them there and slit their throats over the brook Kishon.

Elijah turned to Ahab:

'Let us eat now. The rain is coming.'

Before the meal had ended the sky was black with storm clouds and torrential rain began to fall on Carmel. Elijah sprang up and called to the king: 'I'll race you to Jezebel.'

Ahab harnessed his chariot and took the road, but Elijah ran seventeen miles across country to the city where Jezebel was waiting. Elijah got there first.

When Ahab arrived at the palace he told Jezebel what had happened at Carmel. When she heard of the lynching of four hundred of her priests, she sent a message to Elijah:

'May Baal do as much to me if I do not send you to share their grave before the day is out.'

Elijah left Jezreel in a hurry.

Elijah's Vision

After he had received Jezebel's threatening message Elijah went out into the wilderness and sat down exhausted.

'No, it is too much, Yahweh. Take my life. I cannot go on.'

Half dead with cold and hunger and misery he slept. Nothing was going right.

He woke as he heard the words: 'Get up, eat this.'

Elijah looked. There was a little fire and a pancake cooking on it and a flask of water. He ate and drank and lay down again. A second time the voice came: 'Get up, eat this, you'll never manage the journey unless you do.'

He ate again. He pulled himself together, and on the strength of that meal he walked for days on end until he came to Sinai. There, at the end of his pilgrimage, he slept in a cave of the mountain.

Yahweh said to him: 'What are you doing here, Elijah?'

'I've done my best, Yahweh, but it's no use. The Israelites have forgotten you. They have renounced the covenant, over-turned the altars, and killed the prophets. They have hunted even me.'

'Come out of your cave. Come and be with me on the mountain side.'

A great storm rushed by, but Yahweh was not in the storm; an earthquake shook the mountain, but Yahweh was not in the earthquake; fire burnt the scrub on the mountain sides but Yahweh was not in the fire. Yahweh came in the breath of the breeze and in the silence. Then Elijah understood that Yahweh did not need great melodramatic events to make his presence felt. His will came softly. Yahweh said to Elijah:

'You are old and shall rest. Therefore anoint three men to do my will in the world: Hazael to be king in Damascus; Jehu to be king in Israel and Elisha to be my prophet. Hazael shall kill many of the people, and Jehu many more, but Elisha shall teach those who are left to be my worshippers.'

So Elijah went down to Abel-Meholah in the Jordan valley and took Elisha from his father's farm and made him a prophet in Israel. They walked everywhere together.

It is evident that Elisha's own prestige would be enhanced by this story of Yahweh naming him as Elijah's successor. The next story that Elisha told of Elijah made it all the more obvious that Elisha was to be listened to with great respect. We take this story out of chronological order since it belongs by its subject matter with these others.

The Assumption of Elijah

Elijah walked towards the Jordan, Elisha walked with him. Elijah was now very old and everyone hinted at his death to Elisha but the young man did not want to hear of it. The local dervishes were wondering if Elisha would be the next prophet.

When the two men came to the banks of the Jordan, Elijah turned to Elisha: 'Are you sure you want to be with me?'

'Of course, I'm not going to leave you now.'

Elijah took his cloak and struck the water and a path opened up in the river and, as the dervishes watched, the two of them crossed dry-shod to the other bank.

'What shall I do for you before I am taken from you?'

'Give me your eldest son's inheritance, let me be your true successor.'

'That is not easy. Yahweh must decide that.'

As they went on their way talking together suddenly there was a fiery chariot and horses of flame: Elijah was taken up to heaven. Elisha cried out:

'My father, my father! A regiment of men cannot replace you!'

Then he took up the cloak of Elijah and he smote the water and the river divided for him so that he crossed dry-shod. The dervishes saw that Elisha was now the new prophet of Yahweh.

It is possible to take such a story as this and to say that the writer meant us to think of Elijah as someone who was a good man and therefore went straight to heaven when he died, or, more prosaically, that this is an account of the last prophetic trance of Elijah who died soon afterwards. It is possible, again, to take it as a story to enhance the reputation of Elijah or of the story-teller, Elisha himself. It is possible to take it to be a bald historical narrative of events as they happened. We do not have to choose for each other, only for ourselves.

The handing on of the cloak of Elijah to Elisha is a significant gesture. In Near-Eastern societies of this period and earlier, a man's clothes, being in contact with him and taking the shape of his body, were thought to become part of him. To hand over one's clothes was to hand over control of one's self—so, for example, in Ugarit (whence came Abraham) only sons could wash their fathers' clothes lest a woman got control of a man. In Israelite history David gained power over Saul by cutting off a piece of his cloak.

Ahab's Government

For three years there was peace. Benhadad II was grateful to Ahab for releasing him and would not attack again. Ahab thought Benhadad too strong to be attacked on his home territory. The alliance was at any rate useful in 853, when Shalmaneser III of Assyria advanced on Syria. If Ahab and Benhadad II had attempted to oppose this great empire separately, both their states would have disappeared. They joined forces and, together with King Irhuleni of Hamath in northern Syria, they just managed to stave off defeat and to repulse the invader at the battle of Qarqar. It was four years before the Assyrians tried again.

After this Ahab entered into an alliance with Jehoshaphat, the young king of Judah, who married Athaliah, Ahab's daughter. This brought to an end the petty frontier disputes which distracted Ahab from the larger world of the empires.

Ahab was now ready to attack Benhadad II in Damascus. He persuaded Jehoshaphat of Judah, who was content to act almost as his vassal, to bring his forces to the north for an expedition against Ramoth in Gilead.

Ahab and Jehoshaphat brought their forces to Ramoth. Ahab disguised himself as an ordinary officer and told Jehoshaphat to dress in the robes of the king of Israel. Ahab knew that he was reckoned by the enemy as the ablest soldier in the fight and that he needed to divert their attention from himself if he was to direct the battle. Benhadad II told thirty-two of his officers to seek out only Ahab and kill him. Once the king of Israel was dead the battle would be won. They went out to battle and Benhadad's officers gave chase to Jehoshaphat because they were deceived by his wearing Ahab's robes. But when he was cornered Jehoshaphat told them who he was, so they left him and went off again seeking Ahab. Meanwhile the king of Israel was in the thick of the fight and an archer drew a bow at a venture and it pierced the chain-mail linking the plated cuirass and his leg-armour. Ahab said to his charioteer:

'Turn the chariot about and take me from the thick of the fight, for I am hurt.'

Ahab was driven to the back of the line. Dying there of his wound, he stood propped up in his chariot encouraging his men until night came.

Ahab died in a pool of his own blood on the floor of his chariot. The Israelites drove him back to Samaria and buried him there. While the palace servants were washing down the blood-stained chariot the dogs came and licked up his blood.

Ahaziah and Elijah

After the death of Ahab his elder son Ahaziah became king of Israel. He died after a short reign of about two years having injured himself severely in a fall through a wooden lattice window on the top floor of his palace in Samaria.

The king's accident was the starting-point of one of the crudest of the dervishes' stories of the prophet Elijah.

Ahaziah sent his courtiers to consult the oracle of Baal Zebub, the god of Ekron, to learn whether he would recover from the effects of the heavy fall.

An angel came to Elijah saying: 'Rise up at once and stop the courtiers on their way. Tell them off.'

Elijah went into the road that the courtiers were taking to Ekron and met up with them.

'Away with you, go back to the king and ask him, "Is there no God in Israel that you must send to Ekron?" I can tell you this much. He will only leave his bed for his grave.'

The courtiers went back and told the king what had happened.

'Who was it said all this to you?'

'We do not know his name but he was bearded, with a leather belt to keep his coat of skins about him.'

'That's Elijah all right. Fetch him here.'

A captain of the guard took fifty men and came upon Elijah sitting on a mound by the roadside.

'Come here. The king has sent for you, prophet.'

'Oh yes? Well, if I'm a prophet you're a dead man.'

And fire came down from heaven and devoured the captain and his fifty men.

'Fetch him here,' said the king.

A second captain of the guard took another troop of fifty men and they met Elijah sitting on his mound by the roadside.

'Come here. The king has sent for you, prophet.'

'Oh yes? Well, if I'm a prophet, you're a dead man.'

And fire came down from heaven and devoured the captain and his fifty men.

'Fetch him here,' said the king.

A third captain of the guard took his fifty men and came to Elijah who was still sitting on his mound by the roadside:

'Sir, if I kneel and ask you kindly to come to the king, will you come?—and don't treat me and my men as you did the other captains and men.'

Elijah got up and looked at the angel who stood beside him: 'Go on. Off with you to the king. Don't be afraid at the court.'

Elijah went, therefore, with the captain and his men and came into the king's room where he lay on his bed.

'Now, Elijah, what have you got to say for yourself?'

'Only what I said long ago to your courtiers. You shall only leave your bed to go to your grave.'

Elijah went back home and the king died.

We can readily see in this story a great elaboration of magic and folk tale which hardly endears Elijah to us today. In Elisha's time, however, such legends were told of great men in order that some idea of their greatness should come across in the telling. The king had died and Elijah had not been afraid to tell him that he was dying, so it was necessary to show in vivid pictures how a prophet of Yahweh had faced up to the king and how the king had been worsted.

The Jehorams

Ahaziah's younger brother Jehoram succeeded him just at about the same time as his namesake, Jehoram the son of Jehoshaphat, became king of Jerusalem.

Jehoram of Israel was a man of resource and industry. In the short reign of his brother the Moabites had revolted from Israelite rule. Jehoram of Israel made an alliance with Jehoram of Judah and the two monarchs set out to reduce Moab. Since Mesha of Moab had fortified the villages north of the Arnon, and the southern limit of Moab was naturally secured by the ravine of the Zared, the two kings made a detour to the east to find some weak point at which to make their attack.

It appears that the march round the southern end of the Dead Sea exhausted the troops because the capital of Moab was able to hold out. The two kings were singularly unsuccessful in military matters. It took Israel nearly eight years to secure Ramoth and Judah had to relinquish its hold on Edom and Libnah which revolted and declared themselves to be independent cities. At the same time bands of raiding Arameans came into Israel from Syria and harassed the people. With these Jehoram of Israel determined to deal. The Arameans came down one day into the plain of Dothan and during the night the Israelite chariot force closed the entry. Meanwhile Elisha, the leading disciple of the great prophet Elijah, offered his services to the Arameans as a guide to the most prosperous of the villages. While the charioteers shadowed the Aramean horde Elisha led them southwards to where the main force of Israel waited outside Samaria. At this point, it dawned on the Arameans that they had been tricked. They were caught between the two Israelite forces.

Jehoram of Israel made a pact with the freebooters that they would not molest his territory again, and he would let them go back to their homes. When they had sealed their agreement in a meal, the raiders departed peaceably.

For some time there was peace for Israel and even some friendliness between Syria and Israel.

Naaman, the commander-in-chief of Benhadad II's army, had a disfiguring skin disease. This man's wife had as one of her maids a young Israelite who had been taken from her village by one of the Aramean raiders and sold in the market of Damascus.

This girl said to her mistress: 'If only the general would go to the prophet in Samaria he would be cured of his disease.'

Hearing of this, Naaman asked leave of Benhadad to go to Samaria to seek out this medicine man. Benhadad gave him a letter for Ahab of Israel so that everything would be done for his general. When Naaman presented his credentials to Ahab and the king of Israel read the letter from Benhadad, he was amazed; Benhadad assumed that if there was a man of such marvellous power in Israel it must be the king himself:

'How can I cure diseases? It is a trick of Benhadad. If I say I can't do it he will use this as a pretext for war.'

But Elisha heard what had happened and sent a message to Ahab, telling him to send Naaman to his house. Naaman came in

his chariot and stood at the door of Elisha's house. The prophet
sent a servant to the general with a message:

'Wash seven times in the Jordan and the disease will go from
your flesh.'

Naaman wouldn't stop to hear such stuff, he went off mutter-
ing:

'I thought that at least he would come out to me, after all I am
a great general. He ought to have cried to Yahweh his God and
done some sort of ritual. And why the Jordan? Surely the rivers
of Damascus are better than this stream here.'

He was very angry, but his servants thought he ought to give
the prophet's advice a chance:

'If he had told you to do something terribly difficult you
would have done it at once. Why not do what he says?'

Naaman decided to give it a try. He must have muttered on
the sixth dip when nothing had happened but he went down into
the Jordan water the seventh time and came up healed. Then he
and all his men went back to Elisha's house and stood before it
and Naaman spoke to the prophet:

'Now I know that there is no god but Yahweh. What
present can I give to you, to thank you for your work?'

'No present at all, sir.'

'Nothing?'

'Nothing.'

'Then I will go home to worship Yahweh in my house. Only
let me go with my king into the Temple of Baal when the king my
master goes to worship on state occasions, for this is part of my
profession as a soldier.'

'You may do this. Go in peace.'

When Naaman returned to Damascus he must have talked of
the healing powers of the prophet because when Benhadad II
became ill Elisha was sent for to heal him. The chief minister of
Damascus, Hazael, came to Elisha with camel-loads of presents
for the prophet:

'The king has sent me, saying: "Shall I recover from this
illness?"'

'Tell your majesty that he will certainly recover—though he
will die!'

'Why do you look so terrified? Why do you weep?'

'Because I can see what you, sir, will do to my people; you

will burn our villages, torture our young men, and rip the children from their mothers' wombs with a sword.'

'How shall I do this, I am only an officer of the king, such great events are not for me.'

'You will be king yourself, sir, when Benhadad dies.'

Hazael went back to the sick king:

'Shall I die of this illness?'

'Elisha says that this illness will not kill you.'

Then Hazael took one of the king's blankets, dipped it in water and pressed it down on the sick man's face so that he died. Hazael was made king in his place.

The Rebellion of Jehu

In Judah Jehoram died and his son Ahaziah became king. His mother was Athaliah, the daughter of Ahab. The house of Omri, therefore, with its foreign gods and foreign entanglements, its refusal to accept the limits imposed on the monarchy by the old ideals of the confederation, was in power in both kingdoms.

Jehoram of Israel and Ahaziah of Judah declared war on Hazael in Damascus, intending to have another attempt on Ramoth in Gilead. In the siege, Jehoram was wounded by an arrow and retired to Jezreel. There King Ahaziah visited him.

While the two kings were holidaying in Jezreel, the prophet Elisha determined that the time was ripe for a revolt against the house of Omri. He sent one of his disciples to Ramoth with a flask of oil:

'When you get to the camp of Israel ask to speak to the general Jehu. Take him privately aside and pour this oil on his head as a sign that he is anointed king of Israel. Then come back here at once.'

The man ran to Ramoth where Jehu had set his camp and burst into the tent of the Council of War where Jehu sat with his brother officers.

'I have a word for the general.'

'For which of us?'

'For you, commander.'

Jehu rose from his place and went to his own tent with the messenger. There he was anointed as king of the men of Israel by the servant of the prophet.

When he came back to the other officers, they asked what the man's message had been.

'Nothing of importance.'

'Come on, don't keep it a secret!'

'Well; he came with a message from Elisha and anointed me as king of Israel, there.'

The officers were enthusiastic, they had grown tired of the civil government. They took off their cloaks and made a pathway for him through the camp and as he passed between the soldiers they threw their cloaks on the ground before him and acclaimed him, shouting at the sound of the trumpet:

'Jehu is king.'

So there was a military plot to put Jehu on the throne of Israel. The camp was guarded so that no one could run to Jezreel to warn Jehoram, lying wounded in his palace, that the army was no longer loyal. Jehu got into his chariot and with his personal body-guard drove to Jezreel.

The watchman on the tower of the citadel at Jezreel saw the dust cloud of the chariots and sent word to the king. Jehoram said: 'Send someone to find out who it is that is coming.'

The royal horseman went out onto the road and met Jehu: 'Is all well, commander?'

'What is that to you? Fall in behind me.'

The watchman sent a second message to Jehoram: "The horseman met up with the charioteers but he has not ridden back.'

Jehoram sent another horseman out to meet the troop: 'Is all well, commander?'

'What is that to you? Fall in behind me.'

The watchman reported: 'The horseman reached the charioteers but he does not ride back. I think it must be the general Jehu in the chariot for he drives furiously.'

Then Jehoram commanded his chariot to be got ready and drove out to meet Jehu in the road. Ahaziah came in his chariot with him. The kings met the commander by the vegetable gardens of the palace, where Naboth had had his vineyard once. Jehoram reigned his chariot near that of Jehu and asked: 'Is all well, commander?'

'How can all be well while your evil mother Jezebel lives in the city and worships her false gods.'

Jehoram suddenly realized that Jehu had not come to report some catastrophe from Ramoth, but was in rebellion against him. He turned his chariot in the road and began to race back to Jezreel crying to Ahaziah in the other chariot: 'Treason, Ahaziah, treason!'

Then Jehu reached for his bow, shot an arrow at the back of the retreating Jehoram and pierced his back between the shoulders so that the arrow came out from the king's heart and he fell on his knees in his chariot. Jehu came up and said to Bidqar, the dead king's armour-bearer:

'Throw the body of Jehoram onto the field here. Naboth had a vineyard here. Do you remember? When we were young and drove chariots for Ahab, the prophet Elijah said that blood of the house of Omri should flow at this place. Up now with the body and dump it here.'

Then Ahaziah the king of Judah fled towards Engannim and Jehu shouted to his guards: 'After him!'

They wounded the king of Judah at Gur, eight miles south of Jezreel, as he fled. The wretched king knew that he would be overtaken if he kept to the hill road, so he took the road to Megiddo across the great central plain where his chariot could move as quickly as the horsemen who hunted him. There the charioteers of Jehoram remained loyal to the dead king and took Ahaziah into the town. He died of his wounds. His retainers put his body in his chariot and drove back to Jerusalem.

Jehu, meanwhile, drove to Jezreel. The queen-mother Jezebel came out on her balcony as he drove into the palace courtyard:

'Well, another Zimri, then, another murderer of his master.'

Jehu looked up at the balcony and called to the queen's attendants: 'Whose side are you on?'

They took the hint and, grabbing the queen, threw Jezebel down onto the paving stones beneath. Her blood spattered the wall, and the horses of Jehu's men took fright for a moment and reared up and trampled upon her.

Jehu went into the palace saying: 'See to that woman.'

He showed the councillors of Jezreel that he was their friend by inviting them to dine with him that night. When the feast was over the servants came in to tell Jehu that the dogs had eaten the flesh of Jezebel.

'So,' he said, 'all the words of Elijah come true.'

In order to consolidate his initial success, Jehu saw that he must secure himself against any member of the house of Omri, one of Jehoram's sons, for instance, being acclaimed king. He therefore sent letters to the members of the court at the royal city of Samaria, to the professional soldiers who commanded the king's bodyguard, to the local elders of the people and to the courtiers entrusted with the upbringing of the younger children of the royal family:

'Since you have chariots and horsemen and armour, choose one of Omri's line to be your king and fight for him.'

The senior members of the late king's court were greatly frightened by this sarcastic note:

'Jehoram is dead, Ahaziah is dead, how shall we stand up to this man?'

They sent the grand vizier and the commandant of the city to Jehu as their representatives:

'We will serve you. We will be loyal to you and not the house of Omri. What are we to do?'

'Cut off the heads of all the members of the royal house and bring them to me tomorrow in Jezreel.'

The courtiers took nearly a hundred heads next day in baskets to Jezreel. Jehu was told of their arrival:

'Heap the heads at the gate of the palace.'

The next day he came out and added to the pile the heads of all those who remained loyal to Jehoram in Jezreel:

'Yahweh is taking his vengeance on his enemies.'

Jehu saw that it was necessary for him to show the people that it was zeal for Yahweh and not personal ambition that had prompted his usurpation. Jehu's next two actions were meant to impress the men of Israel with his conservative orthodoxy.

Jehonadab the Rekabite, one of the most rigorous defenders of the worship of Yahweh, an extreme conservative, very ferocious in his zeal for the true religion, came to see Jehu at Jezreel. The new king asked him: 'Are you on my side?'

'I am.'

'Then drive with me in my chariot, here in the city, so that the people will see that you approve my work.'

So they drove together in the royal chariot.

The Reformation in Samaria

Then Jehu drove alone to the free and royal city of Samaria, the centre of Baal worship. He did not want to let the men of Samaria see that he was a friend of the worshippers of Yahweh. He issued a writ there to all the worshippers of Baal Melqart and Baal Zebub: 'All the priests of Baal and all his worshippers are to appear before me for I have a great sacrifice to offer. Whoever stays away shall die. It is to be a solemn assembly.'

The worshippers of the Baals came flocking in great numbers to the temple in Samaria that Ahab had built and put on their robes for the ritual. Then Jehu said to them: 'Be sure that no one who worships Yahweh is here.'

The sacrifice to the Baals began. At a signal Jehu's soldiers marched into the temple and cut down the worshippers with the sword so that none escaped. Jehu had threatened death to any soldier who did not kill as many as came in his way. The soldiers went into the innermost shrine and hauled out the image of Baal Melqart and burnt it. Then they pulled down the whole building and made a dunghill of the place.

Jehu's bloodbath seemed to him justified because it brought to an end, at any rate for the moment, the policy of the house of Omri of alliances with foreign princes and foreign gods, and ushered in a time of peace and harmony within the borders of Israel.

Though later his brutality was to have a terrible backlash he had established a settled reign after the disturbances of the previous reigns.

Jehu's association with Jehonadab gave him the protection of the conservative party, in exchange he gave up the whole foreign commitment of the house of Omri. The alliances with the Phoenician cities were allowed to lapse, the co-operation of Israel and Judah was brought to an end, and when in 841, Shalmaneser III entered Syria for the fourth time Jehu offered no resistance, simply paying the tribute demanded.

It may be that all this was necessary retrenchment and dictated by sound religious principles, but such a set of policies greatly reduced the strength of Israel.

The murder of Jezebel and her Tyrian attendants meant that trade and exchange between Tyre and Israel and the whole economic policy of the Omrides was brought to a sudden end, and with it many of the civilizing influences in the state. The murder of Ahaziah and the discouragement this gave to co-operation between Israel and Judah left Jehu without an ally to the south and produced two small defenceless states. Ahab's policy had made Israel an independent power in the Levant. Jehu destroyed the whole structure of this independence. The murder of the civil servants of Jezreel and Samaria may have given satisfaction to the conservatives for the moment but the country could not afford to lose all its best administrators at one time. The internal economy of the nation suffered from the bloodbath and this naturally encouraged the generality of the people to disassociate themselves from it. A century later Hosea was understood at once when he said that Jehu had brought down Yahweh's wrath on his head by such indiscriminate killing.

It is evident, too, that though the worship of Baal Melqart was stopped, this did not mean that the whole country at once went back to the service of Yahweh. There is a great deal of evidence to show that though the Tyrian god was stopped at the frontier, native deities still flourished in their country shrines.

All this produced a reaction of discontent which was not at all diminished by the success of Hazael of Damascus in his attacks on the borders of Israel. After the withdrawal of the Assyrian armies of Shalmaneser III from the Levant, Hazael saw a chance of aggrandizement in Israel and occupied the Ephraimite settlements east of the Jordan and had soon installed his men in the whole of Transjordan to the Arnon.

The chronicles of Jehu finish at this point and it seems a proper place to describe what was going on in the southern kingdom during Jehu's reign.

The Southern Kingdom and Reform in Jerusalem

When Jehoram had become king on the death of Jehoshaphat he had been confronted by a strong party, led by his younger brothers, demanding that the policy of the dead king be abandoned and a new one adopted. The great matter in dispute was Jehoshaphat's alliance with the house of Omri. The conservatives in both the political and the religious spheres were unhappy about this involvement

11—K.C.

which resulted in both military subjection as a lesser partner in the
northern wars, and the spread of pagan practices among the people
who came in close contact with the northern apostasy to Baal Melqart. Jehoram silenced this opposition by executing the leaders of
the party. A great number of the royal family and the administrative officials died in the first year of the reign.

On the death of Jehoram's son, Ahaziah, at the hands of Jehu's
officers, the southern kingdom was ready to revolt again in favour of
the old ways and the old religion. All this was crushed by the queen-
mother, who, on hearing of the death of the king, her son, had all
the rest of the family put to death and had herself proclaimed
queen. She was Athaliah, the daughter of Ahab and Jezebel of
Israel. A woman of parts. During the night of the murder of all the
royal family, the princess Jehosheba picked up Ahaziah's baby son
Jehoash and ran away from the soldiers of Athaliah. Amongst so
much bloodshed the escape of the princess and the baby was not
noticed.

For six years Athaliah ruled Judah. All this while Jehosheba
and her husband, Jehoiada the priest, kept the young prince
Jehoash among their own children and no one knew what had
happened to him. His grandmother went on with her blood-
thirsty rule, steadily increasing the people's hate of her government. In the seventh year Jehoiada judged the country to be
right for a revolution so he sent for the captains of the royal
guard and, having sworn them to secrecy, showed them the boy
Jehoash, son of the king. He arranged with them to overthrow
the queen:

'You are divided into three companies. Right?'

'Right, sir.'

'The company which comes in on the Sabbath to do guard
duty at the palace is to remain at its post during the revolt. Right?'

'Right, sir.'

'The company which comes to relieve the company on duty at
the Temple is take up its guard. Right?'

'Right, sir.'

'But the third company, which would normally go off-duty, is
to remain at the Temple. Right?'

'Right, sir.'

'Good. When I give the signal the two companies at the

Temple are to take their weapons and form a shield wall round the king and any man who attempts to reach the king is to be killed. Right?'

'Right, sir.'

'Whatever happens, keep the shield wall round the king.'

'Sir.'

The captains did as Jehoiada the priest had commanded them. The guardsmen did not go off duty when their relief came but stayed with the relieving company in the Temple area. Each man had his spear and shield at the ready around the altar. Then Jehoiada brought out the young king and put the diadem upon his head and the scroll of kingship in his hand and anointed him as king of Judah. The guardsmen brought their weapons to the ground with a great noise and shouted: 'Long live the king!'

Hearing the noise of the guardsmen and the people (for they had come running to the Temple and were acclaiming the new king), Athaliah came to the Temple. When she saw Jehoash standing there, with the signs of kingship on his head and in his hand, she shouted: 'Traitors, traitors!'

Jehoiada ordered the guardsmen to make a double file from where Athaliah stood to the entrance of the Temple area. So they made a double line from the altar to the stables and Athaliah was forced to walk between the lines of guardsmen and when she came to the stables and was no longer in the Temple area, they killed her. Then Jehoiada renewed the covenant between Yahweh and his people and they all swore their loyalty to Yahweh and his king. In the rejoicing at the enthronement, the revolutionaries pillaged the altar of Baal and lynched Mattan, the Baal-priest of Athaliah.

Jehoiada brought King Jehoash from the Temple to the palace between the lines of guards officers while the country people, who had come to Jerusalem to take part in the New Year festival of the enthronement of Yahweh and stayed to take part in a great nationalist revolution, danced in the streets.

Then the city was at peace and the whole land of Judah rejoiced.

It would seem likely that Jehoiada could never have brought about his successful *coup d'état* without the goodwill of a large and influential section of the people. It would seem likely also that this favouring section was composed of the small country landowners.

It may be that while the citizens remained quiet and docile and un-
willing to engage in revolution, it was these men of the land of
Judah who rejoiced and by their shouts of acclamation set the boy-
king securely on his throne. Certainly it was this section of Judah
that was most conservative in religious matters and which would
have enjoyed most the upturning of the altar of Baal.

The covenant that Jehoiada pronounced on this occasion would
thus be a declaration that a total break had been made with the
pagan culture of the foreign past. The small country farmers were
voting for a return to the old ideas of the confederacy. Certainly the
young king seems to have accepted as his own policy a programme
of reform in the Temple.

These country squires, who were in many ways the last representatives of all that was good in the days before monarchy, had
now become aware that they could make their influence felt against
the new urban crowds that were often careless of what foreign
practices invaded Israelite society. Having once understood their
power it was unlikely that they would neglect to use it again. They
made at least two more incursions on Israelite political and religious affairs.

An Extract from the Temple History *written by the priests and
kept in the Temple Archives.*

When he was thirty years old, King Jehoash decided to run the
affairs of the kingdom by himself and he began by reforming the
finances of the Temple treasury. He laid it down that all the taxes
and offerings collected by the Temple stewards should be used by
the priests for the upkeep and repair of the fabric. But on inspection
by the royal officers it was noted that the priests had not properly
looked after the building. Then King Jehoash summoned the priest
Jehoiada and the priests of the Temple:

> 'Why are you so careless about the Temple fabric? You will
> have to give up control of the finances if the place is to be kept
> properly. Do you agree to dismissing your stewards and to set-
> ting a great chest, with a slit in the lid for the offerings, by the
> Temple door? You can put all the offerings that come to the
> Temple into this chest. When it is getting full the royal officers
> will come and count it before the priests, there'll be no cheating,

and then the money can be given to the Clerk of the Works to pay the men who are repairing the fabric.'

Jehoiada agreed.

So the money was spent on the repair of the fabric and not on gold and silver cups and candle-snuffers and trinkets for the rituals, as the priests had been spending it. The stonework, the bronze work and iron fittings were all renewed. Only when this was paid for did the royal superintendents permit the buying of new bowls and censers in gold and silver.

All this time Jehoiada had been the chief adviser of the king—he was almost regent while the king was a boy—and the priests had been in power.

On Jehoiada's death, the lay members of the Council persuaded the king to listen more to their advice and to neglect the advice of the Temple priests. Zechariah, the son of Jehoiada, who had become priest in his father's place, came at a festival time to the top of the Temple steps to harangue the people at the way in which secular forces were at work in the government. But the people had been got at by the king's men and they took up the stones from the roadway and flung them at the priest and killed him there. As he was dying he cried out:

'May Yahweh see the king's work and revenge himself.'

The Syrian Menace

In that year, probably 796, Hazael determined to enlarge the territories of his realm. He invaded Israel and the young King Jehoahaz, who had just come to the throne of his father Jehu, was forced to sue for peace terms. These were certainly humiliating. Israel was compelled to accept the cutting down of her army to fifty horsemen and ten chariots and ten thousand infantrymen to police the country. Not so very long before this, Ahab had brought more than two thousand chariots to fight at Qarqar. The men from Damascus then marched further south into Philistia and captured Gath. Thus Israel lost Transjordania, Esdraelon and the coast, while Judah was forced to buy off Hazael with an enormous tribute:

Jehoash took all the royal donations to the Temple of the past three generations, and all the royal treasure in his palace, and

sent it out to the Damascus commander; and the army moved
away from the city.

This humiliation, however, brought about a rapid decline of
Jehoash's popularity. Having antagonized the priests by his strin-
gent overseeing of the Temple funds, and the conservatives in
Judah by his condoning, if not instigating, the murder of the priest
Zechariah, he lost the support of his own court and the generality
of the people by the failure of his government to deal with the
foreign threat.

As king Jehoash went on his tour of inspection in the barracks
of Jerusalem, two of the royal bodyguard struck him down
and killed him, and his son Amaziah was proclaimed king.

The next year Benhadad III, who had just succeeded his father,
moved south and besieged Samaria. The siege was so tight that
the people began to die of famine. The cost of food rose higher
and higher and only the richest could afford anything to eat. One
day during the siege, as Jehoahaz was walking along the walls of
the city, inspecting the defences, a woman called out to him:

'Help me, my lord the king!'

'If Yahweh does not help you, how should I? Can I go to a
threshing-floor and bring you corn or to the wine vat and find
wine there? What is wrong?'

'This woman here said to me, "Let us eat your baby today
and mine tomorrow." So we boiled my baby and ate him. Then
I said to her: " Now we must boil your child," but she has hidden him away.'

Jehoahaz groaned and tore his shirt and the people saw that he
wore sackcloth under his robes. The king was sharing the suffer-
ings of his people. Then he declared:

'Yahweh will make a cannibal's mess of me if the head of
Elisha remains on his shoulders by sunset.'

A man ran to tell Elisha of his danger and found the prophet
sitting with the old men of the city:

'Bar the door! The assassin is just behind me; for the king has
sworn to kill Elisha this day!'

At that moment the king himself strode into the room:

'What worse could Yahweh do if I were to kill his prophet
than he is doing to my people now?'

Elisha was not frightened by the angry king.

'Yahweh is with us. He will save the city. By this time tomorrow bread will be cheap again.'

Then the commander of the bodyguard sneered and laughed in the face of the prophet:

'A likely story, that.'

'It will happen as I said. But you shall not enjoy it, sir.'

What happened next is not clear in the chronicles, but from whatever cause the army of Benhadad III panicked and retired from the siege that night. The most likely explanation is that Elisha sent a dervish into their camp to spread the rumour that the Israelites had hired men from Cilicia to come and attack their rear.

In the night four lepers sitting by the gate of Samaria said to each other:

'What are we sitting here for? If we go into the city we shall die of starvation. If we sit here much longer we shall die. Let us try our luck in the enemy camp. If they kill us, well, we shall simply die quickly.'

They walked into the enemy camp and discovered to their astonishment that it was quite deserted. No soldier to be found. They went into an officer's tent and found there food and wine and the lepers made themselves a great meal and sang songs as they drank. Then they went out and began to loot silver and gold and fine clothes from each tent they entered. One of them suddenly realized that this was a dangerous game:

'We are making a big mistake. We ought to be telling the king the good news, not keep it quiet. For when the citizens find out that the enemy has gone and we did not tell them, they will murder us. Let's go now to the king.'

They ran back to the city walls and called up to the watchman:

'The enemy have deserted their camp. They have all gone. There's no one there, no man there at all.'

The watchman told the guard and the guard told the seneschal and the seneschal told the king. He got up from his bed:

'It's a trick. They have gone to hide somewhere. If we go out there they'll capture the city and we'll be shut out to be killed at their leisure. It's a trick.'

'Well, sir, we have not much to lose. Send five of our few horsemen out to survey the land.'

'Yes. They shall go. Two of them, not five.'

The horsemen went out to discover what had happened to the
besieging army. They saw that the road to Damascus right up to
the Jordan was littered with the baggage the army of Benhadad
had thrown away in the hurry to be back in Damascus. The
horsemen rode back and told Jehoahaz the good news. Then the
people made a mad dash for the gate to plunder the enemy camp,
and as the crowd got out of hand Jehoahaz sent the commander
of the bodyguard to take charge of the gate. There the people
were selling bread as cheap as before the siege and cheaper and as
the commander tried to organize the mob at the gateway struggling to get out to the camp or back into the city with the loot, he
was trampled to death. As Elisha had said, the commander saw
the end of the siege but did not live to enjoy it.

After this it became possible for the men of Israel to live in
open settlements in the plains, and they no longer had to skulk
in the hill places for fear of the invaders.

The old pattern of life, too, began to revive. The people were
able to go on pilgrimage to the national shrine at Gilgal. In this
period of peace king Jehoahaz died and his son Joash became king of
Israel. Just after the accession of the new king the prophet Elisha
himself became ill and knew that he was going to die.

King Joash came to Elisha's house and stood by his bedside,
saying:
'What are we to do without you? My father, my father, a
regiment of men cannot replace you!'
'Take your bow and your arrows. Now, open the window and
shoot.'
The king shot his arrow out of the window, looking towards
the east, towards Damascus. Elisha spoke to him again:
'Take the arrows and beat them on the ground.'
The king did as the prophet told him, three times he beat them
on the ground to please the dying man. But Elisha was angry:
'You should have beaten them again and again. Then you
would have defeated Damascus until they were finished. Now
you will have only three victories.'
Then the prophet died.

The ritual with the arrows seems to have the same significance
as the ceremonial shooting of arrows to the four cardinal points
by the newly enthroned Pharaoh in the temple of Horus. The

god gives the new Pharaoh power to defeat all his enemies in warfare. Elisha is using a device which later came to be very popular
with the prophets. He acts out in mime the lesson he wishes the
king to learn. It ought not to be too readily assumed that Elisha
believed in the magic properties of the mime. He believed in the
mime as an image of the reality of Yahweh's divine power.

The Assyrian Menace

At this moment Israel and Judah were freed from all fear of
Damascus. Benhadad III found himself faced with a much more
formidable force than Joash and Amaziah presented.

Adad-nirari III took over power in Assyria and following the old
policy of Shalmaneser III made an expedition into the Aramean
states. They were all destroyed and even Damascus was forced to
pay an enormous tribute which crippled the country for many
years. Israel also had to pay tribute but evidently only a token sum
to signify submission to the Assyrian. When Adad-nirari retired
to Assyria, Joash seized the opportunity of attacking the very
weakened Damascus.

Joash had his victories. They were enough to get him back all the
border towns that Benhadad III had captured from his father
Jehoahaz.

He was then surprised by a challenge from Amaziah of Judah.

This young king, as soon as he was safe on the throne, had set
about reordering his father's realm with great energy. He had his
father's murderers, who were responsible for his being king so
suddenly, executed. Then he determined to extend his territory in
the direction of Edom. The Edomites had unwisely assumed that
Hazael's occupation of Gath meant that they could with impunity
grab control of the western end of the trade route from Arabia.

Amaziah, now that Damascus had been dealt with by the Assyrians, set out on an expedition to teach the Edomites a lesson. He
conscripted a great force of young men from Judah and then hired
some thousands of mercenaries from Israel. At the last moment he
decided that he did not need the mercenaries and sent them back.
The disgruntled old soldiers pillaged the Judah townships on their
road home to compensate themselves for their trouble.

Amaziah had a successful campaign against the Edomites and

felt fit for any fight. When he discovered, on his return to Jerusalem, what the mercenaries from Israel had done while he was
away in Edom he declared war on Israel.

The War of North and South

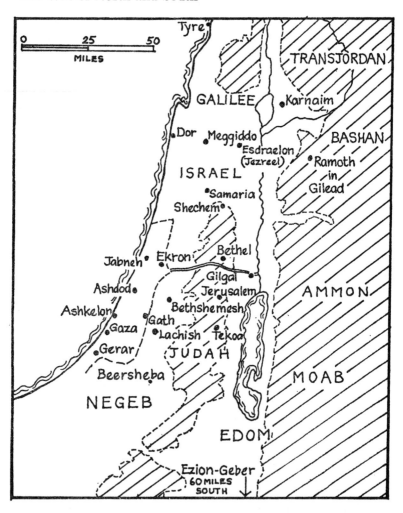

Joash of Israel tried to keep the peace between the two countries and warned him that treading on the thistle of Edom did
not mean he could step over the cedar of Israel. Amaziah would

not listen. So the battle line was drawn up at Bethshemesh on the Judah side of the border. There Judah was totally defeated. Joash marched down the coastal plain and then to Jerusalem with Amaziah as a hostage in his army. Joash broke down the north wall of Jerusalem and entered the city. He removed what treasures he could find in the Temple and the palace and marched back. These treasures were not enough to satisfy him, for the treasury of Judah had been greatly depleted by the exactions of Damascus not so long before. Joash, therefore, took hostages to be ransomed by the payment of further sums in the future. Amaziah he released.

The king of Judah now had to face his angry subjects. He had declared war on Israel for no cause at all and had been heavily defeated. The treasures of the Temple were now totally gone from Jerusalem, so the priests were bitterly opposed to him.

They stirred up a revolt in Jerusalem, and the king rode to Lachish, the second city of the realm, which was a large army centre. But the officers were disgusted by a policy which had ended in the total destruction of the fighting force and the humiliation of the professional soldiers. They killed him at Lachish.

His son, Uzziah of Judah, who had been made co-regent when he was sixteen years old, was proclaimed king. He was then in his early forties.

The Golden Kings

By this time Joash had died in Israel and been succeeded by his son Jeroboam II. Uzziah and Jeroboam II both reigned for many years and their able government brought about an almost 'golden age' in the history of the two kingdoms.

During the reign of these two astute and long-lived kings the combined territory of the kingdoms amounted very nearly to that of Solomon at the height of his power. Uzziah took over his father's Edomite policy and managed to subdue the towns there completely and then made himself more sure of the Arabian trade route by expeditions against the tribesmen on his frontier. The economic possibilities of these conquests were supplemented by development of the post of Ezion-geber, the control of the Negeb and the capture of Gath, Jabneh and Ashdod. These successes combined with some of equal importance in Israel so that by 750 the main trade routes were in the hands of the two kings. Adopting the tolls and taxes of Solomon's financial system the kings maintained a highly prosperous peace.

The people of the two kingdoms found themselves enjoying an economic miracle and a financial boom. Peace between Israel and Judah allowed everyone to get on with the business of making money. The merchants imported all kinds of bright new commodities and sold them to a population eager to spend. Of course this was the case with the aristocratic and merchant sections of society only. There were still large numbers of the very poor and the oppressed—men left over from previous wars with wounds which made it impossible for them to work, men who had little business acumen and who fell victim to the slick talk of the townsmen, men who found that they had borrowed at inordinate rates of interest, all these are attested for this period too, while the rich men bought their ivory ornaments from Phoenicia and rebuilt their houses in new and costlier styles.

One result of this peacetime luxury was the enormous and sudden increase in the population of the kingdoms. Not only did the established townships burst their walls, but new settlements were made in the Negeb and new industries promoted to employ this great labour force.

The reign of Jeroboam II was, thus, one of the most important economically and politically in the history of Israel. It is surprising that the official chroniclers of *Kings* dismiss it in a few sentences and these are mainly of condemnation. We have to rely on the descriptions of the reign given by the prophets Amos and Hosea and the modern archaeologists to discover what went on in the mid-eighth-century boom. These unite in telling a tale of extremes of wealth and poverty. The very existence of such extremes shows us that the old confederacy outlook had been supplanted by competitive bargaining. It was no longer a primary responsibility of one member of the confederation to see that another was provided with at least the necessities of life. Of course it had not been so for a long time—the history of the settlement shows each tribe fighting for itself and rather careless of what happened to the others—but never before had the whole theory of the confederacy been abandoned. The social structure of Israel was a denial of all that the old men of the covenant had worked for.

This was perhaps inevitable with the rise of an efficient and mercantile monarchy. The law of the covenant was replaced by the law of the king, the Holy War by the king's military commitments, and loyalty to Yahweh by good citizenship—by which was meant acquiescence in the policy of the governing class.

With the rise of the secular monarchic power went an increasing secularization of the worship of Yahweh, and a shift away from the old covenant. It is not at all surprising that the priests did not do anything to resist this creeping apostasy. After all they were themselves men who had grown up in the service of country shrines that had never been wholly of the religion of Yahweh. The local cults and legends may have changed their names with the coming of Yahweh's men to conquer the Canaanites and their gods, but the old pagan ideas survived in the hill shrines of the country folk. Nor had there ever been any systematic attempt to suppress those aspects of the cults which were incompatible with the pure religion of Yahweh. Even Jehu in his fervour was only concerned with uprooting the foreign devil Baal Melqart. He did not make any move against the native cults of the kingdom. Besides, the priests of these shrines shared in the enthusiasm of the two kings and deployed their rituals to keep Yahweh in the same frame of mind. 'Yahweh, keep us rich and happy' was their theme.

This was even more obviously the attitude of the priests who were employed to perform the rituals in the royal shrines of Bethel and Dan and Samaria and who were dedicated to keeping the established order secure in Israel. The fury of the priest of Bethel when Amos denounced social injustices must be taken as typical of the priests' attitudes. Having got rid of Baal by the force of the royal power they were unlikely to make much further effort, particularly if it seemed that they would be involved in opposition to the king. The covenant had been long ago tamed to something much more comfortable to live with than the Law of a demanding Yahweh. The dominant theme of the priests' preaching was that the covenant was a binding of Yahweh to protect his people for ever until the great Day of Yahweh came when the men of the covenant would rule the world. The religious demands of Yahweh were thought by the ruling class to be fulfilled by contributions to the expenses of the elaborate ritual festivals in which Yahweh's everlasting favour was proclaimed.

Amos

Into this complacent situation stepped the herdsman and farmer
Amos from Tekoa, a garrison town on the edge of the wilderness in
Judea. His message was a simple one: Yahweh demands obedience
to his covenant and this means not merely worship in the shrine but
justice in the courts and honesty in the bazaar. His concern is for
the *morality* of the covenant as can be seen from these extracts from
his preaching:

> 'The aristocrats have great chests full of violence and robbery;
> they buy up the poor man for the price of a pair of shoes;
> lolling upon their ivory beds of luxury as they lap up wine by
> the bowlful.'

Amos comes to the northern shrine of Bethel and offers the
people an alternative. They must choose Yahweh and his covenant
at the renewal ceremony in the New Year festival, or they must
acknowledge to themselves that they have rejected him. He speaks
to the people just as Joshua spoke to the people at Shechem:
'Choose whether you will worship Yahweh or not.' The covenant
festival is seen as a time of real decision not as a great ceremony of
spectacle and music: 'Seek me and live.' They must give up their
unholy complacency which attributes their prosperity to their own
efforts and their peace to their own victories: 'Have we not by our
own power taken the city of Karnaim?'

They have ignored Yahweh in ordinary life, thinking it enough
to sing him hymns at the festival.

It would seem that one of the great ideas of the Israelites at this
period was belief in the coming glory. The present prosperity
seemed to them a promise of greater things yet. They adapted the
notion of promise that the Yahwist had elaborated and made of it a
triumph for Israel and a humiliation for all the nations. One day
Yahweh would come and make the other peoples the slaves of the
Israelites. They prayed for the coming of that day quite unaware of
the horror they were seeking. Amos proclaimed that the Day of
Yahweh would be something very different from the kind of celebration they imagined, on that Day the sins of the country against
the Law of the covenant would be trumpeted to all men and Israel
be shamed into sorrow:

> 'All the while they say to themselves complacently:

"We offer sacrifices and tithes, thank-offerings and free-will offerings; surely Yahweh will defend us against every enemy."

They come to the New Year festival and bawl out their hymns.

Surely Yahweh will come and destroy them; the day of Yahweh will be a day of mourning for them, the revels at the shrine shall cease and the palace musicians lay down their instruments.'

The southern character of Amos's view of Israel under Jeroboam II comes out plainly in his denunciation of the shrines of Bethel and Gilgal and Beersheba set up in impious rivalry to the holy city of Jerusalem:

'Yahweh is sick of your songs, he has no pleasure in your offerings;

he will destroy your sanctuaries and overturn your altars.'

All this and much more Amos shouted to the 'cows of Bashan' and their husbands as they passed in their holiday clothes to the ceremonies of the shrine.

Then Amaziah the priest of Bethel came out to Amos and told him to go back to his own country:

'We are deafened by your shouts, you fill the whole land with noise; prophesy somewhere else. This is the royal sanctuary and no place for you.'

'I am not one of your professional seers or mad dervishes, I am a free man of Judah and I speak out plainly for the rights of Yahweh.'

'Go away, go back to Judah.'

'Yahweh has seen the injustice here and will not shut his eyes to the abuses of you and your princes and your king.'

The priest sent a message to the king that Amos was preaching treason in the royal shrine. It is not known what Jeroboam II did but we do not hear any more of Amos.

Amos is a representative of the old traditions before David, he insists on the kingship of Yahweh among the Israelites and detests all human usurpation of this divine royalty. It is therefore likely that among both southerners and northerners there remained groups of men to whom the call of the confederacy was still strong and to whom the covenant was a reality. It is these traditionalists who were able after the total collapse of the monarchy of both king-doms to bring about a revival of the worship of Yahweh. Amos is to be understood as the successor of all those earlier prophets, Nathan, Elijah, Elisha, for example, who saw in the old covenant tradition the only safeguard of the rights of Yahweh and the rights of the free men of Israel in a monarchy that tended always to tyranny.

Hosea

At roughly the same time a native northerner, Hosea, got up to denounce the society in which he lived. He did this in ways strik-ingly different from those of Amos. Amos denounced the religious activity of the effete aristocracy as a betrayal of the covenant. Hosea, perhaps because he knew the whole business from the inside, casti-gated his contemporaries for 'going a-whoring after Baal'. Hosea, that is, sees what Amos did not see, that the religion of Yahweh has been totally abandoned by the majority of the Israelites. At the same time, while accusing the people of a worse crime, he regards them with a greater tenderness than Amos did. For Amos the Israelites had become worse than Gentiles, for Hosea this was un-thinkable, for him they were still the chosen people whom Yahweh loved. While both prophets expected a calamity of huge propor-tions Amos thought that *a remnant of Israel* would survive—rather as the family of Joseph had survived when everyone else died of famine in Canaan—and Hosea looked forward to a time when, sorrowful and chastised, *the whole people* would be brought home by Yahweh. These were two different ways of thinking about the promise which were later developed in the differences between the thought of Isaiah and Ezekiel.

For Hosea the relationship between Yahweh and Israel was best expressed by the relation of husband and wife. He found in his own bitter experience a hint of how the history of Israel was to be inter-preted. Hosea had married the woman he loved, only to discover that she was unfaithful to him and went off with other men, leaving him to look after her children. Though he punished her when she came back to him he went on loving her all through her deceits and runnings away. This situation seemed to him to be very like that between Yahweh and Israel. While Yahweh remained true and steadfastly loving, Israel went after false gods and sinned with them,

now and again returning in penitence but never faithful for long.
Hosea thought that at least Yahweh would punish Israel and then
accept the people back.

For Hosea the events which immediately followed the death of
Jeroboam seemed to be the beginning of the punishment.

Hosea describes the effect that these quick changes of government by the most violent means had on the country. He pictures
the palace revolutions and faction intrigues which lead up to
abortive anointings:

> 'In their wickedness they anoint kings,
> and set up princes by their treachery;
> They have prostituted
> the day of coronation;
> after the murder of kings comes the carousing.
> All their kings are dead,
> and not one of them called on Yahweh.'

Even their partisans are disloyal to the new kings:

> 'They say "We have no king
> and we have no god;
> we are free and have no need of a king."
> They make promises,
> swear oaths, and care nothing at all.'

As each king came to power in Samaria the government's attitude
changed towards Assyria, the people were turned like a spinning
top from one side to another:

> 'Israel went to Assyria,
> hoping for help from the great king,
> and then came home:
> like a silly dove
> flying from Egypt to Assyria,
> from one to the other,
> and never a bit of peace.'

He called Israel's policy, 'herding the wind', as if one might shepherd the elements with a crook and a dog.

Meanwhile the people were the prey of outlaws and bandits,
since the guards were used by the noblemen to kill the newest king:

> 'There is no loyalty, no kindness,
> no love of Yahweh here:

only false oaths and deceit,
murder and theft and adultery.
Nothing is left for us
But mourning, sickness and death.'

The shrines are polluted and debaucheries shoulder aside the
worship of Yahweh:

'The men at the shrine are drunk,
slobbering before a thing of wood,
gawking at oracles,
leering at prostitutes in the garlands
of Baal.'

Hosea then thinks of Yahweh, who sees every orgy and smells
every stench:

'Woe to them!
I shall leave them to the slaughterers
and love them no more;
look to your kings to save you,
cry to your princes for help,
where are they now?'

Yet Yahweh has sworn his covenant and will in the end bring
peace to a sorry nation. Hosea thinks of this peace as symbolized
by the old life of the exodus and the confederacy:

'I will bring Israel into the desert
and speak only love;
I will give vineyards to my people
in the valley of Achor;
and all shall be as again in the old days
when Israel came out of Egypt.'

and

'I am Yahweh
who has been with you from the land of Egypt;
I will give you tents again to live in,
like the day of the feast.'

After all the bloodshed, the civil war, the jealousy of ambitious
princes, after all Yahweh's punishments there will be a new thing
in Israel. It is surprising that Hosea, caught in the horrors of his

time when kings were five a decade and tribes went warring with tribes, could yet be optimistic and look beyond the disasters to a new kingdom and a new covenant.

Assyria again

The death of Jeroboam II had removed the one man who was able to make the society of eighth-century Israel viable. The tension between the prosperous secular life and the rootless immorality that it concealed gave way to an open display of murderous decadence, and this just at the moment when a strong and determined society was essential if Israel were to survive. For at this time Assyria was again ready and willing to conquer the Levant in order to gain control of the woodlands and the sea ports. The brilliant army commander who ruled Assyria, Tiglath-Pileser III, settled on his accession all disputes with his neighbours in Babylon, destroyed his most dangerous rival Sardur II of Urartu, and turned his attention to the Levant. In Israel he found bloody chaos. Jeroboam's son, Zachariah, was assassinated after a six-month reign by Shallum of Yasib as the new king went on a tour of Jezreel. He died quite near the place where the dynasty had begun by Jehu's butchery of the kings. Shallum proclaimed himself king, held the throne for four weeks and was in turn killed by Menahem in the palace at Samaria.

Menahem was then proclaimed king by his faction which was pro-Assyrian. At this point the men of Yasib revolted against the new king and Menahem came down with his guards and murdered all the men of the district in a pogrom of extreme ferocity. In order to ensure that the town would never recover from his visit he had all the pregnant women ripped open and their babies chopped. He then felt secure on his Israelite throne. The Assyrians, in return for their support of his *coup d'état*, were paid a thousand talents of silver. This was raised by taxing all the men of property fifty silver shekels each.

These bloody events were followed closely by another revolution. Menahem died within two years and was succeeded by his son, Pekaiah. Within a very short time Pekah, the commander-in-chief, murdered Pekaiah and his household in their rooms in the palace at Samaria, and took over the government.

It would appear that in these terrible incidents after the death of Jeroboam, we have another aspect of the demand by some Israelites that a return should be made to the customs of the confederacy. The attempt was made to throw over the principle of hereditary monarchy and revert to the election of tribal leaders. Shallum appears to have been an Ephraimite and to have been supplanted by Menahem the Manassite candidate.

At the same time, it had now become normal for the Assyrians to interfere in the affairs of the kingdom. The accession of Menahem may have been achieved by the Assyrians actually coming down to occupy the country while he installed himself. Certainly when Pekah had himself proclaimed king after the assassination, this was regarded by the Assyrians as a hostile act. Tiglath-Pileser III made Assyria a power in the Levant. He set out on a march into the area.

Against him, Uzziah of Judah made a stand of great courage and little practical wisdom. He arranged a coalition of the small city states who accepted his leadership because after the death of Jeroboam II he was one of the few dependable men in the area. Uzziah was very old, and incapacitated by some dreadful skin disease, and ruled through his son Jotham, but he had spirit enough to stand up to the might of Tiglath-Pileser III. His efforts came to nothing. The Assyrians swept on through the tiny states and received tribute from Hamath, Tyre, Byblos, Damascus and Israel. Judah seems to have escaped this time for when Tiglath-Pileser's armies came up through Israel in 738 Uzziah was already dead and resistance at an end in Judah.

The kings, meanwhile, seemed driven to procure disaster. Pekah, realizing that the Assyrians would have him removed if he did not act with speedy determination, arranged an anti-Assyrian league with Rezin, king of Damascus.

These two leaders tried to persuade Jotham of Judah to join them against Tiglath-Pileser III. The king of Judah, however, was wary enough to see that this was a dangerous proposal and he refused to be drawn. Thereupon, the kings of Israel and Damascus turned the forces they were preparing against Assyria on Judah, and marched on the southern king. Jotham died as they came towards his country and his son Ahaz was confronted with this crisis on the day of his accession.

Ahaz was terrified and sought immediate help from Moloch, the

Phoenician god whom he had made his patron. He took his first-born son, then still a small child, outside the city to the valley of Himnon and threw him into a fire before the god as a sacrifice imploring rescue. This horrible practice was resorted to at several other times by kings in Jerusalem. It had no effect this time on the march of events. Rezin of Damascus and Pekah of Israel invaded Judah and threatened to take Jerusalem. In a pitched fight a great many of the courtiers and members of the royal house of Judah were killed. Vast numbers of the people of Judah were deported by the conquering armies. At the same time, the Edomites rebelled at Ezion-geber and drove Ahaz' troops out of their territory and the Philistines raided the Negeb and occupied the border towns.

All this news may well have come in to Ahaz in Jerusalem on the morning of the day in which he offered his son to Moloch. As he returned in the evening from the grisly business, he was met outside the city at the conduit of the Jerusalem reservoir by Isaiah. This man was to dominate the country for many years and become not simply the leader of the conservative nobility, but the spokesman of the ordinary men of Judah before the king. He stopped the king on the road:

'Do not fret. There is no cause for worry. Israel and Damascus are not gods. Pekah and Rezin are but men. They will die soon enough. Shall I give you a sign from Yahweh?'

'I want nothing to do with your signs and your Yahweh.'

'You try my patience, sir, you try the patience of Yahweh. But you shall have a sign.'

Here, perhaps, he looked at poor Queen Abi who had seen her baby burnt before the god:

'A young woman can conceive now and before her son can grow to tell good from bad the lands of these kings will be deserted and Yahweh will bring such things on Judah as you can scarcely guess now.'

Ahaz would not listen. Isaiah was warning him that in a few years Assyria would control the whole of the Levant. Ahaz hurried things along. He sent a message to Tiglath-Pileser III:

'Save me from Damascus and from Israel and I will be your subject.'

The message was accompanied by a great deal of treasure. Tiglath-Pileser came.

The Assyrian army swept down the coast in 734 through Israel and Philistine and then Tiglath-Pileser III established a border guard to prevent Egyptian forces surprising him as he mopped up the Levant. He occupied Galilee and Transjordan and deported the leading citizens of the area in order to obtain a compliant population. Pekah's court realized that Israel would be totally destroyed if resistance continued so they assassinated the king, placed the more acceptable Hoshea on the throne and immediately sought peace. They paid for it.

The Assyrians were then free to deal with Damascus. In 732 Tiglath-Pileser sacked the great city and hanged Rezin. The whole territory of the once-great city was divided into four counties and these were administered by Assyrian governors. Three similar officials were assigned to the newly acquired provinces of Gilead, Megiddo and Dor. Pekah's policy had been a disaster for Israel, all the gains of Jeroboam II had been lost and Hoshea came to the throne as an Assyrian vassal, king in name of a tiny state not very much larger than that belonging to Ephraim in the tribal days of the confederacy. Judah, however, was not in a much better position than Israel. After the execution of Rezin, Ahaz was summoned by Tiglath-Pileser and went hurriedly to the Assyrian at Damascus. There he paid homage to his new overlord and was forced to worship the Assyrian gods at a bronze altar that Tiglath-Pileser III had had erected there. The usual demands of overlordship were asserted by the Assyrians. Ahaz was told to set up in the Jerusalem Temple an altar to the gods like that in Damascus. Workmen were sent to Jerusalem to build it and Uriah the priest was given instructions in the new liturgy which was to be practised in the Temple— not as a substitute for the worship of Yahweh but as an additional ritual.

When Ahaz got back from Damascus he went through a service of dedication of the new altar and offered sacrifice to the foreign gods. The old altar of Yahweh was brought from its central position and placed next to the altar of the Assyrians. The king then performed divination rites with the entrails of animals on the altar of Yahweh. Strangely the king was filled with enthusiasm for this Assyrian superstition. The complacent priests officiated at the new altar.

Because the Temple in Jerusalem was built with royal money, it was in many ways thought of by the ordinary folk as the king's chapel. The Assyrians thought that it would be expedient to remove their vassal from a position of authority in the cult of the gods. They therefore required Ahaz to wall up the door connecting the palace and the Temple which had been built to give the king free access to the rites.

The Last Days of Israel

Shalmaneser V, the successor of Tiglath-Pileser III, continued the policy of his predecessor and took a close look at the doings of Israel and Judah. Hoshea, who had accepted him as his overlord, was conspiring with the Egyptian court in an effort to regain his independence. Hoshea refused to pay the tribute to Shalmaneser V and then discovered that Egypt was in no position to save him from Assyria. In 724 Shalmaneser V arrived to deal with Israel, Hoshea went out to him in order to arrange peace terms and was taken prisoner. The country then made a last desperate effort to resist the imperial power of Assyria. For two years the city of Samaria held out behind the walls of Omri and Ahab—towards the end of the siege Shalmaneser V died and was succeeded by his brother Sargon II—but at last Samaria was forced to surrender. In 721 therefore, with the deportation of nearly thirty thousand citizens from the capital to Mesopotamia, Israel came to an end.

Sargon II repopulated the area with men from another revolted colony in southern Mesopotamia. These intermarried with the northern population and were the ancestors of the Samaritans.

JUDAH ALONE

Micah

If we would understand the society of Ahaz' Judah we can get a view of it from the prophet Micah. This prophet was certainly pessimistic in his judgment on the southern kingdom. For him there was little difference between the corrupt state of Israel which had been punished by Yahweh and the corrupt state of Judah which must in the future be punished. Yahweh of the Temple will come from his holy mountain and put an end to every transgression:

> All this is for the evils of Israel
> and the sins of Judah;
> the disease of Samaria has come to Jerusalem,
> it has reached the gate of my people.

What will happen in Judah is told as the final act of the great history of the people, an act which recalls other moments in the long story. Micah is thinking of the corruptions of Israel as lepers sitting at the gate of Jerusalem—as the lepers sat at the gates of Samaria where Jehoahaz was besieged by Benhadad's army.

> Keep the news from the men of Gath,
> do not dare to weep.

The prophet is remembering the line of David's lament for Saul and Jonathan, when he told the people not to let the Philistines know what a loss they had sustained lest the enemy be spurred to greater attacks on the enfeebled army of Israel. Micah thinks of the Assyrians as second Philistines who will bring many defeats on the corrupted men of Jerusalem.

Micah's reasons for thinking of Judah as no better than Israel were similar to those which prompted Amos' sayings of doom.

The landed gentry were totally careless of the peasantry who worked their farms. There was an evil system of enclosure which deprived the poor husbandman of his plot in order to enlarge the estates of the lord of the manor: he thinks of these exploiters of the poor as similar to Ahab in his robbery of the farmer Naboth:

> They plan evil on their couches
> and are up at dawn to perform it,
> needing only might to make it right,
> they are jealous of other men's fields
> and seize them for themselves.

He thinks their punishment will fit their crime when the Assyrians make them their prisoners:

> They will be yoked together, like oxen,
> and their fields will be given to another.

The great landowners of the kingdom have paid the judges to wrest the law to their ends and there is no redress for the dispossessed. This is the end to which the Fall story pointed:

> You have juggled good with evil
> and will tear the skin off the backs of the poor.

The Judges are bribed, the priests are fat with drinking fine wines with the landlord, the people have abandoned Yahweh, therefore, Micah says, in tones very like those of Amos, the Day of Yahweh will come with terrors:

> It shall be like night when no man can see,
> you will not be able to search the secrets
> from the guts of a beast that day,
> there will be no glimmer of light
> and all false seers shall be put to silence.

Assyria was ready to fulfil these signs.

That Micah was not simply shouting against the wind and unregarded by those in power can be seen from an incident in the life of a later prophet, Jeremiah. When the members of the ruling class were tired of Jeremiah's continual activity against them, they considered having him executed. The argument used to dissuade them from this policy was that when Micah was attacking abuses in an earlier reign he had not been stopped but his advice had been followed. This refers to the reign of king Hezekiah, the son of Ahaz, and, unlike him, a religious reformer on behalf of Yahweh. Some of his reforms, it would seem, were begun after hearing Micah's denunciation of injustice.

The Coronation Ritual

The accession of Hezekiah is a convenient point to say something of the coronation rite of the kings in Jerusalem. The importance of the king in Israelite society led to the elaboration of a great ritual when one king succeeded another. The enthronement ceremony of the kings of Judah can be reconstructed from the evidence of the writings of the period of the monarchy.

It seems most likely that the king was first anointed at the spring Gihon outside Jerusalem. There is a reference to this in the account of Solomon's accession—though this, it must be kept in mind, was a hurried affair:

> The priest Zadok and the prophet Nathan and the captain of the guard, Benaiah, took Solomon to Gihon and there Zadok took the holy oil and anointed Solomon.

After the anointing at the spring by the priests the king probably drank from the sacred spring—perhaps the water was a symbol of vitality and this ceremony had the same significance as the traditional cry, 'Long live the King'.

The anointing at the spring may have been omitted in the enthronement ceremonies after the division of the kingdom and the whole complex of ceremonies have been performed within the Temple area.

The anointing of the king marked him out as the adopted son of Yahweh, ruling the promised land of Yahweh as his delegate. In the psalms composed for the anointing ceremony Yahweh is represented as saying:

> I have placed my king
> on Zion, on my holy hill,

and the king says to the people:

> I will announce the decree of Yahweh:
> He said to me: You are my son,
> today I have made you my heir.

And the people accept the will of Yahweh in their loyalty to the new king:

> Yahweh gives you power in Zion,
> you can crush your enemies;
> we shall be your men
> following you into battle
> and on the holy mountains.

This psalm gives us an indication of what the people expected of a king. Evidently he was to be victorious in battle. The first king, Saul, had been chosen by the tribesmen because he looked capable of leading an army in war and of winning the war. This demand remained throughout the period of the kings—the new monarch was to crush his enemies by leading the whole people to the fight. The king was to engage in the Holy War of Yahweh against all other nations.

The king, therefore, had taken on some of the characteristics of the early Judge. He was the leader in the Holy War chosen by Yahweh. He was also the man who had been given wisdom to act as a Judge of the people: to see that honesty flourishes in the kingdom. This is brought out in another psalm in which, after his anointing, the king promises to keep the Law of Yahweh during his reign and to see that others may live honestly and securely within the rule of justice:

> I have received goodwill and righteousness
> from Yahweh.

> I will walk the path of integrity,
> keeping my eye fixed on justice
> and not on baseness.

> I will not give my favour to the deceitful
> and the proud;
> I will give no heed to sorcerers.

> The faithful man in the land
> shall live in my house;
> the honest man
> shall be my courtier.

> Each dawn shall see the deaths
> of the wicked,
> cutting off the bad men
> from the life in the city of Yahweh.

The king is accepting the Law of Yahweh as the framework of all his actions. He is not to be a despotic tyrant like the kings of other nations but a man who knows that he must further the rule of Yahweh, seeing to it that by his government good men are encouraged and bad men deprived of their power in society.

We have some evidence of how this worked in the reigns of David and Solomon, both of whom were described in terms used previously of the Judges. For example, the old woman of Tekoa whom Joab put up to show David the unwisdom of his treatment of Absalom greeted the king as: 'The angel of Yahweh who can tell good from evil' and as one who, 'knows all about everything in the world'.

It was because David failed to live up to his judicial responsibilities that Absalom was later able to win men's loyalty from the king to himself: 'If I were Judge things would not be like this.'

On the other hand, Solomon was thought by his chroniclers to be the best Judge that there had ever been and this was accounted for on the supposition that he had been specially endowed with wisdom by Yahweh on his accession. The story of how he found the true mother of a child was told as the best proof of this gift to the king. The king, therefore, was seen, by at least some of his subjects, as exercising his power in rather the same way as the Judges had exercised their power in the old days. This must have been a more popular notion in Israel than in Judah. In the northern kingdom no dynasty lasted long enough to establish the notion of hereditary government. Revolution was the ordinary way of changing the king. In such a situation the 'great man' called by Yahweh to rule was more easily accepted than in the southern kingdom where the family of David had undisputed tenure of the throne. The northern kings, Jehu for instance, were like the Judges in that Yahweh designated them for a particular task at one time in the country's history without in any way sanctioning the establishment of a dynastic tradition of hereditary right.

At the same time, the Davidic kings of Judah made every effort to preserve the appearances of continuity with the pre-monarchical past. The ceremonial of their enthronement was tied into the old way of life. All this is to be understood within the context of the covenant the people and their king had with Yahweh. When the newly anointed ruler announced the *decree of Yahweh*, he was telling the people that in setting him on the throne Yahweh was appointing him the leader of the covenant community. In the writings of this period *decree* and *covenant* meant the same thing. The king had, by this ritual, taken over the covenant from the people. They had to accept him as their representative to Yahweh, and as Yahweh's representative to them. The reality of the confederation of the tribes round Yahweh was certainly a thing of the past as far as the kings were concerned.

After the anointing the king was escorted into the city by the leaders of the council and surrounded by the people: Adonijah saw from his window Solomon coming into the city:

> They have come from Gihon, shouting and singing, so that the whole city is in an uproar.

On his arrival in the Temple area, the trumpets sounded and the king was conducted to his throne. There the king was proclaimed as the favoured one of Yahweh:

> Solomon sat on the royal throne . . .
> Then they blew the trumpet, and everyone shouted:
> 'Long live King Solomon,'

and again, on the accession of Jehoash:

> The priest brought out the king's son and put the crown on his head and handed him the protocol of the kingdom and they proclaimed him king and anointed him. The people clapped their hands and shouted:
> 'Long live the King!'

The accession of Jehoash was like that of Solomon, a matter of quick arrangements and unusual happenings—that is why they both are recorded in detail while the peaceful enthronements of all other kings are passed over by the chroniclers as of no interest to the reader. However, the same ceremonies seem to have been observed, and that these were done each time is borne out by the description of what the queen-mother Athaliah saw when she came to the Temple: . . . the king, standing on his dais, *as the custom is,* and the heralds round the king with their trumpets and all the people cheering.

The protocol, or list of the king's titles, was read out by the herald and then handed to him as a sign of his power. We have an example

of such lists in the proclamation of the future messianic king—
something like this was announced to the people:

> A child is born for us,
> we have a son
> to rule us; he shall be called:
> Wonderful Counsellor, Mighty God,
> Everlasting Father, Prince of Peace.
> His kingdom shall grow always greater
> and we shall be at peace for ever,
> while he sits on the throne of David
> and rules the kingdom.

Then the whole population held a feast at the renewal of the covenant of Yahweh with his people, for the accession of another king
showed that Yahweh was taking care that the rule of his Law should
continue in Jerusalem. The people of Judah were obviously more
amenable than the people of Israel to the growing power of the king
and his claim to rule by 'divine right'.

Hezekiah and Solomon

The court of Solomon was one where literature, particularly
poetry and proverbs, flourished. The king himself has the reputation of composing 'three thousand proverbs' and 'a thousand and
five songs'. Whence such a reputation? Not certainly from the
Gibeon dream narrative which is concerned with the king's capacity to administer justice.

It may be that Solomon made an art of wisdom, and its succinct
expression in proverbs, in imitation of the customs of the Egyptian
Pharaohs—he had married an Egyptian princess, and set up an
administrative structure on the lines of the Egyptian court. The
story of Joseph shows how interested the men of the early monarchy
were in things Egyptian, particularly in the wisdom of Egypt. But
this is not evidence enough to show that Solomon was in fact copy-
ing the Egyptians. The chroniclers certainly thought that their king's
wisdom was not a copy of any other: 'Solomon's wisdom was
greater than all the wisdom of the East and all the wisdom of Egypt.
He was wiser than any other man, even wiser than Ethan and
Heman the sages of Edom'; and the story of the queen of Sheba
also is designed to show the surpassing wonder of Solomon's

wisdom—and the emphasis is always on other nations marvelling at Israel's king, not the other way about: 'Men came from every nation to listen to Solomon's wisdom, and envoys arrived from every king because of his great reputation as a wise man.'

The chroniclers also note that the wisdom of Solomon brought great material prosperity for his kingdom: 'Thus King Solomon was wiser and richer than any other king in the world.'

The queen of Sheba declares: 'I had not heard the half of it; your wisdom and your riches are far greater than any report suggested.'

Solomon's wisdom and his great political prestige and his enormous wealth all belong to the same tradition. It seems likely that the tradition of a king of the past who was wise and therefore rich took on its present fully developed form at a time when the Israelites were trying hard to make themselves once more a great nation and the government wanted some illustration of what had been done once and could be achieved again. Such a time was the reign of Hezekiah.

Hezekiah determined to bring back the glories of the old Israel. He saw himself as the new Solomon and was indeed the first king since Solomon's time to be the only claimant to Israel's civil loyalty. There was no king of Israel. He took every measure in his power to revive the old magnificence. Some of his subjects seem to have credited him with such a Solomonic revival in reality:

> Many men came with tribute to Jerusalem, to Hezekiah king of Judah, so that men wondered at the glory of the king above all nations. Hezekiah had very great treasuries of money and was held in high honour. He built storehouses for silver and gold and precious stones and spices, he built a great armoury and warehouses for grain, and wine and oil, and huge stables and stalls for his animals. Yahweh gave him great wealth.

Of Hezekiah's reformation the Chronicler writes: 'There was great joy in Jerusalem, for since the time of Solomon, the son of David, king of Israel, there had been nothing like this in Jerusalem.'

Hezekiah was like Solomon, too, in his interest in Egyptian customs—as Isaiah noted with fierce disapproval, his love of chariots as a sign of royal splendour and his encouragement of wisdom at his court. He was so like Solomon that he was said to have written songs himself and to have composed pieces of literary wisdom.

Hezekiah's scribes set about collecting the literature and traditions of the Hebrews in a great effort to give permanent form to a culture that the fall of the northern kingdom had shown was in danger. They took as their models in setting down the traditional wisdom of their people the already highly developed styles of the Egyptian court scribes. They did not, however, merely indulge in literary imitation, they invested the foreign forms with the traditional themes of Israel's Law and presented afresh the old world view of the age of Solomon.

In this way a foreign literary form and a narrative of the past were brought together in order to further the designs of Israel's present king.

By such means the scribes of Hezekiah demonstrated to the people that they had a glorious past and by the wisdom of their king they could themselves enjoy a new glory. Hezekiah indirectly proclaimed himself as the new Solomon and there is evidence that some of his subjects warned him severely not to follow too slavishly in the footsteps of the king who, though building the Temple and exhibiting to the world a grandeur and luxury before unknown in Palestine, later became himself the slave of foreign women and foreign gods.

Hezekiah's Government

Ahaz had restrained his people and adopted a policy of subservience to Assyria. His son Hezekiah on his accession set about a total reversal of this policy. In this he had the complete support of the men of Judah. Everyone was tired of belonging to a vassal kingdom in the power of a great military empire. Those who remained loyal to Yahweh had a further grievance against Ahaz' eagerness to placate the Assyrians. To them Hezekiah's determination to achieve an independent kingdom shone with a religious light. The whole people therefore was in favour of a reform of the religious life of the nation as a real step in the throwing-over of Assyrian domination.

The failure of the monarchy of Ahaz to live up to the expectation of the patriots and the worshippers of Yahweh made many think of an ideal king who would restore the Davidic glory in a renewal of the covenant. At this time, therefore, there was much talk of a Messiah who would lead his people into a kingdom of happiness round the holy hill of Zion. To make peace with Assyria was simply to put off a great moment.

At the same time the courtiers of Judah knew that Sargon II was not so firmly secure in Assyria as his predecessor. Coming home from his conquest of Israel, he was greeted by news of a rebellion in Babylon led by the Chaldean prince Marduk-apal-iddina. The rebels retained control of Babylon for more than a decade. This trouble and the wars with Urartu distracted Sargon II from his Palestine concerns. It seemed to Hezekiah the moment for freeing his kingdom from its vassalage.

At the same time there was a revolution in Egypt and the effete Pharaohs of the Twenty-Third Dynasty who had looked on helpless at the fall of Samaria were ousted by a vigorous Ethiopian, Piankhi, in 715, who set about reasserting the old foreign policies of the Two Kingdoms of Egypt. Piankhi made it one of his first tasks to remove the power of Assyria from his borderlands. This meant freeing Judah from Sargon's overlordship. As a first step in this direction, Piankhi encouraged the city state of Ashdod to revolt against Assyria and sent ambassadors to Hezekiah urging him to support the rebellion when it should take place. Isaiah, who was present when the ambassadors came, describes their embassy: 'They came from a land of swarming insects, in papyrus boats sailing the Nile, tall men with glossy skins, a mighty nation.'

Piankhi also tried to enlist the goodwill of Edom and Moab for his counter-moves against Sargon. After the ambassadors had stated their case the council of Hezekiah was divided, all wanting to be free of Sargon but not all thinking that the plan of Piankhi would work. Isaiah led those opposed to the Egyptian alliance. He staged a strikingly dramatic sign of his view, he came dressed to the council as he thought the rulers of Egypt would dress in a few years' time—barefoot and in a loincloth: 'So shall the king of Assyria lead away the captive Egyptians, naked and barefoot and ashamed.' And, he continued: 'If this happens to Egypt what will happen to us if we have allied ourselves with Egypt?'

Isaiah won the day, and Judah refused to join the conspiracy against Assyria. The wisdom of his advice became obvious to all

13—K.C.

when in 711 Sargon marched into Ashdod and made it an Assyrian province. The rebel leader ran for cover to Egypt, seeking political asylum. The value of Egyptian support was revealed when the Pharaoh handed the refugee over to the Assyrians at the first time of asking.

The success of Isaiah in matters of foreign policy led to his advice being taken in the home affairs of Judah.

National pride in Judah was a suitable context for Isaiah's work on reform of the worship. King and people were convinced that zeal for the nation's independence and zeal for Yahweh were almost synonymous.

The Reform in Jerusalem: I

Hezekiah removed one by one the foreign nonsenses that Ahaz had introduced to the Temple worship and then set about reform of the local shrines where popular pagan rituals and superstitions flourished under the name of Yahwism. Of course the country people did not care for these sudden changes introduced in the liturgy by the power of the central government in the name of some theoretical view of 'the people of Yahweh'. Although the reforms were passively accepted during Hezekiah's lifetime they were soon dropped in the time of his successors.

Hezekiah then moved to the reformation of the Temple liturgy by a thorough examination of the credentials and meaning of the rites that existed before the recent sacrileges of his father. One of the most prominent victims of this stage of the reform was the Nehushtan—a bronze serpent said to date from the exodus times and to have been made by Moses himself. On the morning of the great clearance Hezekiah lectured all the priests in Jerusalem on the way in which they must approach the worship of Yahweh:

> Be holy yourselves so that the Temple service may be holy, and bundle out all the rubbish of paganism that litters this place from the times that are past. How can we expect Yahweh to protect us if we abuse his Temple with such stuff? Look what happened to Israel! Let us, therefore, renew the covenant of this people with Yahweh, and you, sirs, must see that the covenant is kept from now on.

Then the priests cleared out the holy place and dumped the pagan oddments over the wall of Jerusalem. After about two weeks' work they went back to the king and told him that the Temple was ready. Then the king and the nobles and the people came and held a great feast in honour of Yahweh and celebrated the Passover. To this festival Hezekiah invited refugees from the old northern king. He wanted everyone to understand that Jerusalem was always the place of worship for Yahweh, whatever the divisions of the people.

Few of the northerners responded to the invitation Hezekiah sent them. Their freedom for travel was limited by the Assyrians and at their own shrine at Bethel the occupying forces had restored the worship of Yahweh on the principle that one ought to sacrifice to a country's gods otherwise they would take their revenge. The Assyrians were confirmed in their notion by the number of lions who roamed the country after they had come to occupy it. No doubt these beasts were simply taking advantage of the piles of Israelite corpses that provided easy meat immediately after the advance of Sargon's troops. At any rate the lions went away about the same time as the worship of Yahweh was begun again at Bethel. Since Bethel had returned to the true religion the northerners were less likely to make the pilgrimage to Jerusalem.

Hezekiah's Illness

In the middle of all this good work, Hezekiah became very ill. He knew he was dying. Isaiah, who was a much older man and seems to have got some comfort from the sight of a younger man dying, told him: 'Arrange all your affairs, put your papers in order for you cannot recover.'

Hezekiah had appointed his son Manasseh as regent already; he took one look at Isaiah and turned his face to the wall: 'Yahweh, I have tried to be your servant all my life. Look kindly now.'

Isaiah left the king in the roof-chamber where the sick man lay because he could not bear the stuffy palace, and walked down the arched staircase into the court that separated the palace from the Temple. Then Isaiah stopped. He felt sorry for Hezekiah. He went back to the king, knowing that Yahweh had heard Hezekiah's prayer.

'Sir, Yahweh has heard your prayer. You will recover, you will live years yet.'

'How can I be sure of this?'

'Can the shadow go back as evening comes? Yahweh does not desert his friends.'

While he was convalescing, Hezekiah was visited by am-bassadors from Marduk-apal-iddina, the Chaldean prince of Babylon.

This prince was a great soldier. He had very nearly defeated Sargon II and on the accession of Sargon's son Sennacherib he saw a chance of reasserting Babylon's independence. He had en-listed the help of Elam and wanted to create a diversion in Pales-tine to keep Sennacherib busy on more than one front. His proposal was that Hezekiah, in league with the governors of Ashkelon and Ekron in Philistia, and the men of Moab, Edom and Ammon, and above all with Shabako, the newly enthroned Pharaoh, should arrange a great revolt through Sennacherib's empire at precisely the time when Babylon would declare its independence. Sennacherib's forces would be divided and so both Babylon and the Levantine states should achieve their freedom.

Hezekiah was very much interested in this proposal and en-tertained the embassy. He went into the economics of the situa-tion and showed the Babylonians his armaments and treasury. After the departure of the ambassadors, Isaiah came to see the king:

'What were you talking about to those men? Where did they come from?'

'From ever so far away, from Babylon. To see how I was.'

'What did you show them?'

'Everything. All my armaments, all my treasures.'

'You are asking for trouble. Babylon is not our friend, soon it will be our enemy—an enemy who knows just precisely how long we can hold out.'

'Well, this won't be in my time. I'm all right.'

Hezekiah did not follow Isaiah's advice on this occasion. To him it seemed as if everything were coming together to secure the downfall of Assyria. He decided to take his chance with the rebel coalition. Ambassadors were despatched to Shabako in Egypt and a treaty of offensive signed against Assyria. Isaiah saw that all this must end in the destruction of the kingdom and de-nounced the whole proceedings:

'There is no sense in asking Egypt for protection, no sense in relying on the Pharaoh. Of course he is sending ambassadors everywhere but it will all come to nothing. Egypt is useless and yet they are sending asses and camels laden with presents for the Pharaoh. It is all a nonsense.'

'But think of the lines of Egyptian cavalry, think of their chariots and their knights.'

'The Egyptians are but men and they ride on horseflesh, they are not Yahweh. Seek your help from him.'

So the debate continued. Hezekiah came out openly in defiance of Assyria in the affair of the kingdom of Ekron. Padi, the ruler of Ekron, when approached about the coalition against Assyria, remained loyal to his overlord and refused to co-operate. At this his patriotic subjects arrested him and sent him under guard to Jerusalem. There Hezekiah threw him into prison. It would seem that Hezekiah adopted military measures to compel several Philistine cities to join him. All this anti-Assyrian activity made it obvious that Sennacherib would attack Judah. In anticipation of this Hezekiah constructed the celebrated tunnel of Siloam. He ordered his men to dig a tunnel from the spring of Gihon to a pool within the battlements of Jerusalem. Great haste was required so the tunnel was built from both ends through the rock. It is impressive that when the two teams were about to meet the overlap was very small. Hezekiah had now secured the water-supply necessary for withstanding a long siege.

The Coming of Sennacherib

(In the next paragraphs the view is taken that Sennacherib conducted two campaigns in Palestine. It may be that there was only one, and many historians support this interpretation of the evidence, but there are so many difficulties against the theory of one single offensive that it seems safer at the moment to speak of two separate campaigns.)

In 701, Sennacherib, having dealt with Babylonian affairs, turned his attention to the other members of the alliance. His army took the coast road south and began by occupying the kingdom of Tyre, where a puppet government was installed. At this the little states suddenly lost their nerve. Byblos, Arvad, Ashdod, Moab, Edom

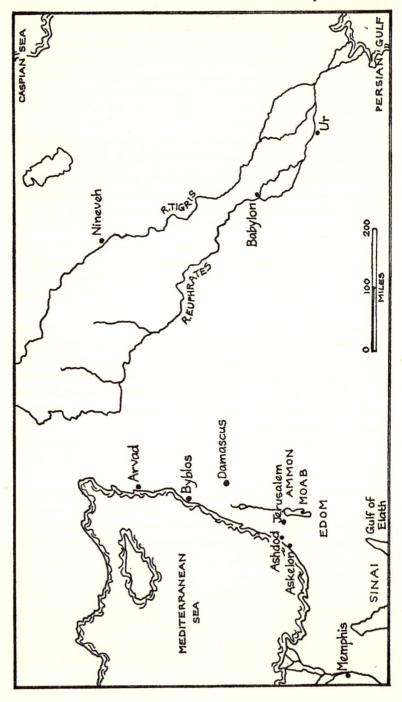

and Ammon at once sent messengers to Sennacherib asking him to accept them as tribute-paying states of his empire. Ashkelon and Edom, having been in the conspiracy from the beginning and not hoping to gain much by submission, remained loyal to Judah and Egypt. Sennacherib advanced through the towns of Ashkelon towards Ekron. Shabako's army hurrying to defend his ally was totally defeated near Ekron. Sennacherib was then free to kill, exile or imprison any of his opponents in the areas and did so with much ferocity. He marched his army through Judah, sacking the towns, pulling down the fortifications and deporting the population. A great number of men died on this progress through Judah. At Lachish 1,500 were dumped in a common grave.

Isaiah urged Hezekiah to submit while the people of Jerusalem were still alive. The army officers deserted the king and he took Isaiah's advice. Messengers were sent to Sennacherib amid the siege-engines and blood of Lachish and announced the king's submission to Assyria: 'I have been a fool. Leave my land and I will pay whatever you demand.'

The Assyrian demands ruined the economy. Three hundred talents of silver and thirty talents of gold had to be found. Everything of silver or gold in the capital, even the decorations in the palace and the Temple, had to be put in the balance to make up the enormous sum. In addition Sennacherib sliced off pieces of Judah to reward Ashdod and Gaza who had been more loyal than the other states of the empire. The king of Ekron was put back on his throne and set to deal with the subjects who had rejected him. Hezekiah had also to send some of his daughters to be concubines in the imperial harem at Nineveh.

The catastrophe of 701 had one other long-lasting effect. Since his mercenaries had surrendered to Sennacherib and his treasury had been emptied, Hezekiah was unable to build up an army on the previous pattern. He had to find troops that would not demand high salaries. There was only one way to do this. Hezekiah restored the militia. The free property-owning men of the land were called-up. The squires, their tenants and farm labourers formed the new army. The new army had old ideas. The men who were brought into service were precisely those who held the old view of Israel and the covenant. The men of the land looked for a return to the old days of the confederation. They had been organized by the king, but they were to become the forceful proponents of a return to the days of the confederacy.

Sennacherib had then to go back to settle Babylonian matters. The affair dragged on, one abortive rising after another being quelled by Assyria, but each sapped some of the strength of the empire. Eventually, in 691, Sennacherib was defeated. Hezekiah joined forces with the young Pharaoh Tirhakah and took back the lands he had lost in the submission terms ten years before. Sennacherib was not then in a position to do anything about this new act of revolt.

In 688, however, things were different. Babylon had at last been crushed and a savage occupation force brought disaster and misery into every home in the land. Sennacherib again turned to Levantine matters. He again reduced Lachish and marched to Jerusalem. Hezekiah appealed to Egypt to honour Tirhakah's promise of support. This time Egypt was ready to help. A large army was sent to relieve Hezekiah in Jerusalem. Hearing of its approach Sennacherib wanted the siege quickly ended and sent envoys to Hezekiah.

The Assyrians stood by the conduit where Isaiah had once met Ahaz as he came back from his terrible worship of Moloch, and called for the king to speak to them.

Hezekiah sent three senior officials to negotiate from the walls of Jerusalem. They stood listening to the loud words of the Assyrian:

'Do not try to beat us with speeches, just submit now. Who is there left to help you? Egypt? You might as well lean on a broken reed. Yahweh? Well, is he pleased with Hezekiah when the king has broken up his shrines and left him only one shrine and that in Jerusalem?

'If you want to fight we will lend you two thousand horses, if you can find enough horsemen to sit astride their backs. Come on, try it.'

The officials said to the Assyrian:

'Talk to us in Aramaic, we understand it; do not talk in Hebrew for all the men to hear and understand.'

'But it is to them I must speak, they are the men who have been brought to this disaster by their king.'

He shouted up to the men on the ramparts:

'Hear the message of Assyria: Do not let Hezekiah deceive

you. Do not let him fix your hopes on Yahweh. Listen to my king. He says to you, "Make your peace with me and each one of you shall sit under his orchard tree and drink the water from his own well until I come to take you into a beautiful land of corn-fields and vineyards, olive trees and honey, so that you may take your ease." '

This was a fine way of describing deportation to another part of the empire to become part of the great rootless proleteriat.

'Hezekiah says Yahweh will deliver you. Which god has delivered his nation from the king of Assyria before this? What makes you think that you and your God are so different?'

The people on the walls stood still and silent. Hezekiah had forbidden them to say anything to the Assyrians. The officials of Hezekiah turned away and reported to the king what the emissaries had said.

Then Hezekiah proclaimed a national fast for all the people; he himself put sackcloth on his body and went from the palace into the Temple. There he stood before the shrine of the Ark:

'Yahweh, you are the ruler of all, heaven and earth are yours, everything is possible to you. Help us now, then. You have heard the words of the king of Assyria, how he has mocked you, the living God. Save us now and show Sennacherib that there is no God like Yahweh.'

By the king's side was the aged Isaiah, and this time he knew things were different:

'Yahweh has heard our prayer, the Assyrians shall not plunder Jerusalem, sir. They shall go back the way they came.'

In fact, it seems that a plague brought by rats broke out in the besiegers' camp, so they loaded their battering rams and packed their bows and arrows and went quickly away from the city. The men of Jerusalem did not kill one of the many that died.

Sennacherib did not return. A little while after returning home he was assassinated by one of his sons as he bowed his head in the temple of his god. About the same time Hezekiah died peacefully in his bed and Manasseh, his son, was proclaimed king of Judah.

The Reaction in Jerusalem

Manasseh sent at once to Assyria assuring the great Power that he would not continue his father's policies. Even if Manasseh had

been an enthusiastic worshipper of Yahweh and a violent nationalist he would probably have been forced to accept the harsh realities
of Assyrian domination. Manasseh seems to have accepted them
willingly enough. The young Esarhaddon of Assyria quickly restored civil peace after the murder of his father and set about
quietening the Babylonians. After this he decided to deal with
Egypt. In 671 the Egyptian troops were put to flight, Memphis
occupied and the royal family captured. The country was then put
under a group of Assyrian provincial governors. Esarhaddon took
his army back to Assyria and the Pharaoh Tirhakah, who had
escaped his captors, rallied the Egyptians again and drove out the
Assyrian administrators. Esarhaddon marched his army back towards Egypt and though he died of disease on the way, his son
Ashurbanipal put an end to the Egyptian trouble.

One by one the Egyptian princes were brought in to Nineveh and
executed, and to render Egyptian resistance totally impossible,
Ashurbanipal's troops went up the Nile as far as Thebes and
sacked this centre of the old nationalism. Assyrian records show
that Manasseh had judged the situation rightly and had assisted
Ashurbanipal in his march on Egypt. Manasseh reigned for more
than half a century as an Assyrian vassal.

The religious policy of his reign also witnesses to the ascendancy
of the Assyrian influence. All the debris of the Assyrian cult that
Hezekiah had thrown out of the Temple seems to have been brought
back by his son. Things were as they had been in the days of Ahaz.
The altar of the Assyrian gods was restored in the Temple and the
king engaged in the rituals of the foreign worship of the stars.
Astrology flourished. Deliberately Manasseh undermined the worship of Yahweh in Jerusalem by re-opening the old local shrines on
the hills and under the green tree groves where the muddled worship of pagan deities under the name of Yahweh was resumed.
Everywhere men resorted to the entrails of animals to discover the
future and to magic to influence events.

Manasseh himself was fond of such fooleries and even sacrificed
his own child to Moloch in an attempt to win the god's favour.

The mists of paganism covered the land and Yahweh was almost
forgotten. He had become merely the lord of the stars, and men had
made the stars their immediate gods and patrons. In foreign
fashions they took up foreign gods and the king ruled in the auto-

cratic manner of foreign kings so that injustice was done in the
courts of the once-free people of Israel. Those who spoke against
all this were silenced.

Even these pro-Assyrian attitudes did not suffice to protect
Manasseh from Ashurbanipal's suspicions when in 652 a general
revolt took place in the conquered territories of the empire. From
Babylon to Egypt a concerted effort was made to overthrow the
power of Assyria. Manasseh was taken as a prisoner to Nineveh
suspected of aiding the Egyptian rebels who had successfully re-
gained independence. Ashurbanipal may not have believed
Manasseh's protestations of innocence but he decided that he
needed a strong vassal on the Egyptian border and sent the king
home with instructions to fortify his country.

In 642 Manasseh at last died and his son Amon became king of
Judah. The young man remained faithful to the Assyrian overlords
and worshipped their gods. After he had reigned for two years an
anti-Assyrian faction assassinated Amon and attempted to proclaim
an independent government. The general opinion of the country
squires of Judah, however, was that the Assyrians were still strong
enough to destroy Judah if they proved disloyal and so the con-
spirators were executed and the Council put Josiah, the eight-year-
old son of Amon, on the throne. Then the men of Judah waited for
the collapse of the Assyrian power in the face of the combined
menace of the Babylonians and the hordes of Median barbarians
waiting to rush upon the effete luxury of Nineveh.

The events present us with another situation in which the free
country farmers of Judah took a decisive part in the history of the
country. As in their acclamation of the boy-king Jehoash, they secured
the kingdom for a prince who represented the 'legitimate line of the
royal house' and by so doing brought about an opportunity for the
country to return to the religion of Yahweh in its monarchist form.
The policy of Josiah is simply the policy of Jehoash writ large. Both
kings accepted the mandate given them by the conservative elements of the country population and withstood the humanist
paganism of the city dwellers of Jerusalem.

The countrymen were not, however, interested exclusively in
religious worship. They had a foreign policy as well. The kings
they sponsored embarked on a cautious programme of independent
action in the world of the great Powers. The men of the land of

Judah had a sense of national integrity which was not so strong in the more cosmopolitan citizens of Jerusalem. At the same time the policy of independent action was pursued with a caution that is characteristic of every farming community—they had no intention of employing the revolutionary methods of the mob. Everything must be done gradually.

This caution accounts for the preponderance of cultic matters in the history of Jehoash and Josiah. The general policy of their supporters was to reform internally so that the nation could be strong enough to exercise freedom in foreign affairs. Religious reformation was a prerequisite of political independence.

Zephaniah

At this period the call to restore the true worship of Yahweh was taken up by the leading men of the court. It was probably in this circle that Zephaniah wrote. It seems possible that this prophet was a member of the royal house, a grandson of Hezekiah. He was a gloomy man who saw so much evil in the world about him that the only solution was for Yahweh to come as a conquering commander and plunder the world:

> 'I will sweep the world away,'
> says Yahweh,
> 'I will sweep away man and beast,
> the birds of the air
> and the fish of the sea.'

The destructive power of Yahweh will be felt first in Jerusalem:

> 'I will strike the men of Judah,
> the citizens of Jerusalem;
> for they have turned to Baal
> and their priests have bowed
> to the stars.
>
> 'I have prepared my sacrifice,'
> says Yahweh,
> 'and invited the guests
> for the feast.

'I have noted the councillors
and the courtiers
In their foreign fashions
swearing foreign oaths.

'When I come,
the merchants shall cry out
in the market;
the chink of money shall not be heard
above their cries.

'I shall take my lamp
and search out the rich
who suppose I do not care
what they do.
Their houses shall fall.'

Just as Amos warned the men who came to the sanctuary of Bethel that they had nothing to look forward to on the Day of Yahweh, so Zephaniah warns his contemporaries that for them chaos will come again.

The trumpet shall sound:

Day of wrath that day shall be,
Day of terror and of fear,
Day of chaos and despair,
Day of darkness and of gloom,
Day of trumpets blasting hope
for those who sit within the walls
or walk the battlements.

If such things were to be avoided Jerusalem must reform and turn back to Yahweh immediately.

The words of the prophet gave an impetus to the movement for reform. The ruling classes and the city crowds were ready to return to the worship of Yahweh. The international situation also gave hope that an opportunity might soon be found to set about ordering Jerusalem according to the Law of Yahweh. The overlord seemed too much troubled by other matters to take much care for the worship of the foreign gods in Jerusalem. Everything was coming together for a renewal of life among the people of Yahweh.

The Reform in Jerusalem: II

By 630 it was apparent that Assyria was much too much engaged in protecting her own borders to interfere in the affairs of Judah. The king, who was a worshipper of Yahweh, began to repair the Temple fabric which had been neglected in the previous two reigns and to prune the worship in Jerusalem of foreign pagan accretions. First the Assyrian astral deities were expelled from the Temple. These were the most unpopular of all because they represented the power of the hated Assyrian overlord, and with them went the astrologers. The idols and the calendars of star movements were burnt in limekilns outside the city. The priests of these cults and the women who served them were put to death. The horses that pulled the chariot of the sun-god were removed from the Temple stables and set to work on the farms and the chariot burned on a rubbish heap.

Then Josiah turned his attention to the native cults that had been practised under the cover of the worship of Yahweh but which were pagan in belief and action. The local shrines were closed and as the king's power increased and he could take the old northern territory of Israel under his control, one shrine after another was broken up and its superstitions mocked. Josiah accomplished the dream of Hezekiah and concentrated the worship of Yahweh in the one Temple in Jerusalem. The priests who had served in these shrines were offered places in the Temple. Of course, the priests of the central shrine did not care for this but the offer was certainly made.

This grand reform was given impetus and direction by the discovery of the *Book of the Law*. This was an early version of our book of *Deuteronomy* probably written by zealous Yahwists during the reign of Manasseh, and perhaps incorporating the writings of refugees from the north since some of its traditions seem to be northern in origin. The priest Hilkiah somehow got hold of a copy of this book, written some fifty years before by the silent Yahwists of the apostate's reign, and presented it to Josiah as a proper programme for their reform. The king received it with enthusiasm and ordered that it should be read to the people in order that they would understand what he was doing. The *Book of the Law* was taken as a description of the proper service of Yahweh.

The people of Jerusalem were assembled in the Temple area for a great service of dedication to Yahweh. The whole Book of the Law was read out to them by the king himself.

The Book of the Law

It is not possible to reconstruct this document exactly for our *Deuteronomy* is the result of several editors' work, but certain features of the Book can be confidently pointed out.

(a) The Freemen of Yahweh

The old view of Israel as the community of men chosen by Yahweh is asserted against the growing tyranny of the royal administration and the greed of the ruling classes. This is brought out in the restoration of the law about slavery and the law about debts:

> If your brother, a Hebrew, a man or woman, is sold to you, you may keep him for six years but on the seventh year you shall set him free. On his release you shall set him up with cattle, grain and wine, for we all live upon Yahweh. Remember that we were all of us slaves in Egypt and Yahweh redeemed us . . . do not grudge him his freedom and Yahweh will bless you.

and

> Every seventh year you shall cancel all debts among you. You can claim a debt from a foreigner but not of a brother Hebrew. Listen to Yahweh's commands and he will bless you.

and

> Do not let your brother Hebrew live in poverty in the land, open your hand and heart to him, for Yahweh has given us the land—if you are generous Yahweh will love you and bless you.

The old Law has become a call to be kind and friendly. It is a summons to live as mature men of Yahweh's community.

(b) The Holy War

In the days of the old confederation of Shechem the community had recognized itself in the battle against the enemies of Yahweh. The restoration of the sense of community and the nearness of Yahweh brought about a new enthusiasm for the Holy War:

> When you set out for the battle and see how many the enemy

are and how few the forces of Israel, do not be afraid: Yahweh is with you.

and

> When you set out for battle see that you are a holy people. The officers shall see that no one takes part in Yahweh's fighting line who has not dedicated his home to Yahweh or left unfulfilled his duties in the community, and no one who is afraid and does not trust Yahweh shall remain for the fight.

The Book of the Law is here reminding the men of Yahweh of the old customs of the fighting men—Uriah the Hittite, for example, had consecrated himself for battle and therefore to David's great annoyance would not lie with his wife Bathsheba; Gideon had impressed upon his men that it was not numbers of troops nor the clash of weapons that would bring the victory but only Yahweh.

(c) The Presence of Yahweh

All this depended upon the choice of Israel by Yahweh and his promise to be with them. The men who produced the Book of the Law were not ignorant of the sad history of Israel's apostasies since the old days of Joshua and the confederacy, but this did not haunt them in their confidence that Yahweh was with them in their day as much as in the past. The opportunity was open for men of Israel to inherit the promise if only they would take it now, this very day:

> This day Yahweh commands you to obey all his statutes. Take care to keep his law with all your heart. This day you have sworn your loyalty to Yahweh and your readiness to obey his law.
>
> This day Yahweh has declared that you are his people, inheritors of his promise, obeying his law, and chosen by him to be above all the nations.

(d) Blessings and Cursings

After the proclamation of the covenant of Yahweh and the people comes the ritual of blessings on those who keep the new law of Yahweh and curses on those who prove disloyal.

The shape of the Book of the Law is taken from the ritual of the old ceremonies at the renewal of the covenant by the confederacy at Shechem. The plan of the Book of the Law is itself a pointer to the past, reminding the men who take part in the renewal of the covenant in Josiah's day what it is what they are renewing, the covenant of Joshua.

A small but significant indication of this Shechem tradition in the Book of Law is to be found in the introduction to the section of curses and blessings. The curses are prefaced by a direction that they are to be pronounced at Mount Ebal—that is, the mountain on the northern side of the pass of Shechem that had to be crossed by the settlers as they came into the promised land—while the blessings are uttered on Mount Gerizim—on the southern side of the pass which is in the land. The Book of the Law deliberately places its picture of the covenant renewal in the setting of the old covenant-making by Joshua at Shechem.

After the reading of the Book of the Law Josiah took his place in the Temple and where he had been crowned he formally renewed the covenant of Israel with Yahweh and all the people shouted their willingness to serve Yahweh. The covenant was again at work in Israel.

It is noticeable that the northern view of Yahweh making a covenant with the whole people seems to overshadow in this ceremony the southern belief in the covenant being made between Yahweh and the royal family of David. This is one instance of the increasing influence of the intellectuals of Israel who had fled south at the fall of Samaria, and of the conservative farmers, the men of the land.

Josiah certainly thought of himself as the king of the two kingdoms. His reform was active in the north as well as the south. The local shrines were demolished and the altar of Jeroboam I at Bethel was broken. These priests of the northern shrines who resisted the progress of the reform were promptly executed. In all this the king seems to have been taking the advice not simply of Hilkiah but also of Zephaniah, the prophet, and perhaps of the young Jeremiah as well. The king was seeking with the help of such men to bring back to the people a sense of their election by Yahweh which was not simply a promise that he would look after them but a demand for a faithful response. In many ways Josiah was a second Joshua. This is brought out in the account of the first celebration of the Passover after the reform:

The king issued a proclamation to the people ordering them to
14—K.C.

keep the Passover to Yahweh as it is set down in the book of the
covenant. The Passover has not been celebrated like this since
the days of the Judges who governed Israel. We had to look back
beyond the kings of Israel and the kings of Judah to find a time
when the Passover rite was performed as it was in the reign of
King Josiah in Jerusalem.

At this festival the Passover was established as a great occasion of
pilgrimage to Jerusalem, it became a national holiday. The nation
was reminded of that time when the whole tribal confederacy had
kept this festival together—when the men of Joshua's army had
crossed the Jordan and proclaimed the covenant.

The Jericho Narrative

The renewal of the covenant led to a new interest in the old
narratives of the conquest of Canaan by the first settlers. The men
of Josiah's time saw in the destruction of the old pagan cities a perfect example of the Holy War. It was at this time that our present
version of the siege of Jericho was set down. The old traditions have
been shaped for recitation at the festival and demonstrate the way
in which Yahweh takes his part in the Holy War:

The people of Israel kept the passover on the fourteenth day of
Nisan in the evening while they were encamped on the plain of
Jericho. The next day the manna ceased and the people ate for
the first time the produce of the land.

Joshua looked towards Jericho and saw a man with a sword
drawn standing before him:

'Are you for or against us?'

'I am a commander of the army of Yahweh, the God of Battles.'

Joshua knelt before him: 'What am I to do, Lord?'

'Take off your shoes for this is holy ground. I have given this
city to you and all the brave men in it. Take it when you will.'

So Joshua called the people together and they formed a great
procession of the people of Yahweh. The seven priests blew the
sacred trumpets and marched forwards and others carried the
Ark between a guard of warriors. They all marched round the
city in silence as the priests blew the trumpets.

They did this for six days.

On the seventh day they marched round the walls of Jericho

seven times and at the last, when the priests had blown their trumpets for the seventh time, Joshua called to the people:

'Shout, for Yahweh has given you this city.'

So the people shouted and the trumpets blared and the wall of Jericho fell down flat. Then the people marched forward and destroyed everything that was in the city.

The bronze and silver and gold of the city was taken and placed in the house of Yahweh.

This account is evidently composed not as a description of an actual campaign like those against Ai or the five kings, it is much more a symbolic narrative of Yahweh's action in the Holy War. The story tells how Yahweh alone took the first city of Canaan for his people, and that the people's part was to share in the liturgical procession of Yahweh. The design of the narrative is to demonstrate that it is not by siege engines or large armies that the Holy War is won, but by the service of Yahweh in the rituals of worship.

Thus the story makes it plain to the contemporaries of Josiah that the vitality of the nation and its political prestige depend upon the faithful adherence to the demands of the covenant renewal. The Reform proceeded by such means. There was a great revival of interest in the liturgy of the Temple.

The Temple of Yahweh and the Covenant of Yahweh

The worship of Yahweh in his Temple at Jerusalem impressed the ordinary Israelite labourer and the sophisticated priest alike as a revelation of Yahweh. We can understand something of the magnificence of the liturgy and its capacity to show Yahweh to his worshippers in the autobiographical fragment describing the moment when Isaiah knew that he had to go out and tell everybody about Yahweh:

> In the year king Azariah died I went into the Temple and it seemed to me that Yahweh sat upon his throne with the seraphim about him calling out: 'Holy, holy, holy is the Lord of hosts; the whole earth is full of his glory.' I could not stand the sight of so great a wonder. All men should know of it. I called out, 'Make me your spokesman.'

Isaiah was caught up in the splendour of light and incense, gold and music, and the chants of the Temple singers and knew that Yahweh was present.

His experience cannot have been unique. Men of all classes must have learnt something of who Yahweh was and how he acted by taking part in the liturgy. One of these, it seems, was asked to write an account of the first time that the community experienced the presence of Yahweh—the giving of the Ten Commandments. The scribe looked about him for images and signs that would be understood by his fellow worshippers in the Temple. He found them.

1. He remembered the periodic renewal of the covenant in the Temple festivals. How the Law was proclaimed and how Israel took on the obligation of obedience: 'I will be their God and they shall be my people,' and asked for Yahweh's protection: 'Take us for your inheritance'.

2. He remembered how Hezekiah had acted as the ambassador of Yahweh to the people and of the people to Yahweh when they had renewed his covenant oath in his time.

3. He remembered how at the ceremony of the covenant every Israelite present knew that Yahweh was present to the assembly and took part in the covenant.

4. He remembered the incense going up in clouds as the name of Yahweh was solemnly announced.

5. He remembered the blaring trumpets at the festival, symbols of the voice of Yahweh.

6. He remembered the fierce denunciations of those who worshipped other gods, especially those who went to the northern shrines with the golden calves.

He sat down and wrote his wonderful account of the coming of Yahweh to set up his covenant with Israel at Mount Sinai. He did not know much about that distant event except that the Yahweh who came to his people then was still coming in the liturgy of the covenant. It seemed, therefore, appropriate to him to set forth the wonder of the covenant by means of the images and signs his people knew in their liturgy:

(i) At Sinai the Law was proclaimed: ' So Moses gathered the elders of the people about him and told them all that Yahweh had commanded', and the people accepted the Law. They were offered protection: 'If you will obey my word and keep my covenant you shall be my own people'.

(ii) which was offered them in the covenant mediated by Moses: 'he wrote the covenant down, the ten commandments'.

(iii) Yahweh came to his people, saying: 'My presence will be with you wherever you go and I will give you peace . . . I make a covenant with you and all the people shall see the work of the Lord.'

(iv) 'Behold I am coming to you in a cloud of smoke.'

(v) 'And on the morning of the third day thunder crashed and lightning darted in the sky and there was a sound of trumpets blaring and the people in the camp were afraid.'

(vi) And after the covenant had been proclaimed in Sinai, Moses came down from the mountain to find the orgies of the golden calf and Yahweh was angry: 'Let me deal with this people who have turned from me. I will burn them up.' But Moses persuaded Yahweh to forgive them and to give them another chance to live according to the covenant.

The writer has found a way of making the past alive for his contemporaries without distorting the event. He has spoken of the reality of the covenant with which their society began in the terms which they understand now. It is a brilliant piece of writing.

The activity of the reforming king, the revitalization of the worship in the Temple, the growth of a new nationalist spirit produced a sense of freedom and release in the city.

Nahum

All this was possible in Jerusalem because of the weakness of the overlord in Nineveh. Many men must have seen the end coming for Assyria, few can have interpreted its meaning so magnificently as the prophet Nahum.

Nahum sees in the coming downfall of Nineveh the manifestation of the power of Yahweh. The prophet belonged to the Temple clergy and probably composed his two great hymns for the Temple liturgy of the New Year festival. At this autumn celebration the Israelites had particularly in mind the mighty power of Yahweh who was king of the universe. They remembered how he had separated the dry land from the waters and set up his kingdom in the world. This thought of the creating, powerful king dominates Nahum's hymns. He speaks of Yahweh coming to rule all lands:

'He comes on the whirlwind and the storm,
striding the clouds.
He makes the sea run back in fear,
the rivers dry up,
the mountains shake at his anger,
the hills crumble
and the world is afraid.'

Yahweh comes with a fierce threat for Nineveh:

'I shall hit you hard
and will not need to hit you again!
Your temple and its gods
shall tumble down
into the grave
that I am digging now.'

and a promise of help for Jerusalem:

'Assyria's yoke shall be lifted
from your shoulder
and his shackles fall
from your hands'

Nahum thinks of Yahweh as a marching conqueror through enemy
territories coming at last to the walls of Nineveh:

'He sets up his engines
for a siege.
He guards the roads
against escape.

His troops carry the red shields
to war, and wear the scarlet coat;
his chariots flash past aflame;
his horses prance in the field,
eager for battle.

The walls are down,
the chariots race through the streets;
the squares are occupied;
the Temple swept away
by the rising rivers of Yahweh.

The goddess of Nineveh
is led captive, her harlots
moan in the streets.

The men of Yahweh take up the spoil,
silver and gold they take
in their arms,
they stagger under the weight.
. . . .

King of Assyria,
your generals sleep in death,
your councillors are led away
and all your people scattered
over the hills.

And nobody cares.'

The Respite

In 626 Babylon achieved independence and in 612 the Babylonians in alliance with the wild Medes of the north sacked Nineveh
itself. As a side-effect of these great changes in the world Judah was
suddenly independent again. The last Assyrian king died at the
siege of Harran in 610.

At this moment the Pharaoh Necho II, seeing the collapse of
Assyria and fearing that the Babylonians might take over Syria and
Palestine, organized an expedition to grab them for Egypt. Necho II
had determined to fight on other men's land and set out for the
Euphrates. Josiah saw this move as a menace to his newly united
kingdom and raised an army which met the Egyptians at the pass of
Megiddo. The Pharaoh asked for a free passage to the north which
Josiah, knowing he would never be free of Egyptian and Babylonian
interference if he allowed this, refused. In the pitched fight which
took place at Megiddo in the early summer of 609 Josiah was badly
wounded. His men put him on a chariot-floor and raced for Jerusalem where he very soon died.

In many ways Josiah was one of the greatest of the kings.
Obviously he was regarded by the worshippers of Yahweh as the
man who had brought back the true religion, as such his epitaph is
written in the Second Book of Kings:

There was no king like him, a man who was loyal to Yahweh in every way, with all his will, with all his mind, with all his strength, following the Law of Moses. No king matched up to him.

But the restoration of the worship of Yahweh is not Josiah's only claim to be regarded as a great king. By his policy of cautious pushing back of the borders of Judah he came at last to govern a great deal of the old kingdom of Israel and even some Philistine territory that had never before been included in the Davidic state.

Gradually the governors of the Assyrian provinces were forced to accept new boundary lines, until the whole of the province of Samaria and part of the province of Galilee and Megiddo were under Josiah's rule. His death removed any possibility of extension of Judah's territory. The march of the Pharaoh Necho II through Palestine destroyed the structure of Josiah's kingdom.

After the burial of Josiah, the men of the land made a desperate effort to secure the accession of a king who would continue their policies. They had Shallum, the second son of Josiah, anointed king in Jerusalem, passing over as unsuitable the elder son, Eliakim. Shallum was dedicated to the policy of national independence for Judah. This action was pregnant with difficulties. The unfortunate young king was to pay heavily for the support that the conservative farmers gave him. The Pharaoh had noted his accession with displeasure.

This was the last time that representatives of the men of the land secured the throne for their candidate.

The Egyptian Occupation

Shallum reigned for three months, not even long enough to take part in the enthronement ceremonies of the New Year festival—he was to have taken the name Jehoahaz at this festival and, as a courtly gesture, the chroniclers call him by his name. Necho II marched across Palestine into northern Mesopotamia in June and returned to Judah in 609. The Egyptian army camped at Riblah in central Syria and Necho ordered Jehoahaz to present himself there. On his coming Jehoahaz was put in chains and imprisoned in Egypt. Necho then appointed Eliakim to be king in Judah since this elder brother had offered to collaborate with the Egyptian overlord. The first act of the new king was to collect the enormous tribute demanded by the Pharaoh. All the gains of Josiah's reign were lost. The frontiers of Judah were again reduced to what they had been on Josiah's accession, a rather cut-down version of the old kingdom of Judah. Independence was a thing of only twenty years and the new overlord was nearer at hand than the Assyrian and therefore more forceful. For the people of Israel the new régime's pagan might was symbolized in Necho II's changing Eliakim's name to Jehoiakim. The kings had always been given new names at the enthronement ceremony. These had been names given by Yahweh. This king's name had been given him by the Pharaoh. This king was obviously a vassal of a foreigner who impiously claimed to be divine. Jehoahaz was not forgotten. The story of the last independent king of Judah became part of the nation's lore, he was mourned in tales and songs and in small personal poems like this one by Jeremiah:

> Do not cry for the dead,
> do not weep for them;
> keep your sorrow for the exile,
> the prisoner who shall never see
> his home again.

Jehoahaz died in the prison of Necho II and was buried, not with his family in Jerusalem, but in an unknown grave in Egypt.

The contrast between the half-brothers Jehoahaz and Jehoiakim was seen by the prophet Jeremiah in the latter's extravagance in building a new palace as if his father's were not grand enough, his tyranny in erecting this great house by the forced-labour of the men of Judah, and his irreligious refusal to keep up the movement for reform. Jeremiah led the opposition in Jerusalem. He spoke out against the government wherever the people gathered.

Jehoiakim was twenty-five years old when he was put on the throne by Necho II in 609. For the first few years of his reign he was occupied with collecting the tribute money and pleasing his Egyptian patron. In 605, however, the whole political situation changed. The Babylonians, having got firm control of the southern half of the old Assyrian empire—the north had been given to the Medes—decided to take over Syria and Palestine. They sent out an army under the crown prince Nebuchadnezzar which defeated the

15—K.C.

Egyptians and occupied large areas of Syria and Palestine. Tribute
was now sent from Judah not to Egypt but to Babylon.

Jeremiah

In the fifth year of Jehoiakim's reign the Egyptians were routed
at Carchemish. On the arrival of this news, Jeremiah decided upon
the preparation of his most melodramatic activity against the
régime. He made a final effort to show the people how useless it was
to resist the Babylonians and how foolish their plans to work under
Egyptian patronage seemed to Yahweh. It seems likely, also, that,
in the dark days of 604, when a national feast had been proclaimed
by the king, Jeremiah prepared the scroll, so that there should be
some permanent record of his advice to Jerusalem. His secretary,
Baruch, took down all he dictated.

Jeremiah hoped that the king might read the scroll and be warned
before the country rebelled and brought down the Babylonian
power on its head.

By this time Jeremiah had been excommunicated by the priests.
He was not allowed to go into the Temple because he had made
such a disturbance when the royalist lackey Hananiah prophesied
peace. So he told Baruch to go into the Temple and read aloud from
the scroll so that all the worshippers should be able to stand round
and listen to the warnings of Jeremiah. Baruch did as he was told.
The young courtier Micaiah, whose grandfather had been the chief
secretary of state, took Baruch into his room in the Temple area
and Baruch sat down among the men who crowded in and read the
scroll of Jeremiah. When Micaiah heard all that the prophet had
dictated he went to the office of the chief secretary where several
members of the Council were in committee and told them what was
going on. The councillors sent for Baruch. He came down and read
it to them. When they had heard it all they decided that this was
too important a matter for them to deal with. The king had to be
told. First they asked Baruch who was responsible for the document:

'Jeremiah dictated it to me.'

'Well, before we go to the king, it might be a good idea if you
and Jeremiah went into hiding. The king will not be pleased.'

The courtiers then went into the palace leaving the scroll in the chief secretary's office. On hearing their report, King Jehoiakim sent for the scroll in order that it could be read to him.

It was winter and the king was sitting in his room with his hands to the brazier trying to keep warm. As the courtier read column by column of writing, Jehoiakim took his pen-knife and cut them off the scroll and threw them into the fire. The whole scroll was burnt to ashes. Jehoiakim did not worry at all that he was destroying the word of Yahweh. Even when the courtiers remonstrated with him and asked him not to burn the scroll he paid no attention to them. He simply ordered the captain of the guard to arrest Jeremiah and Baruch. But they were already in hiding and could not be found.

Jeremiah's book was a retrospective exhibition of all his prophecies. He meant it to be a sign to the people that he knew the end to be near. Babylon was going to destroy the faithless people. He ended the work with these words:

Since the thirteenth year of the reign of Josiah, son of Amon, king of Judah, until now—twenty-three years in all—I have taken every opportunity to urge you to turn from evil and wickedness and to serve Yahweh who gave you this land. But you have never paid any attention, you have played deaf to Yahweh. You cannot then expect to escape the northern menace. The land is ready for invasion and sack and desolation. There will be an end to your laughter and your wedding feasts. The mill wheel shall stand still and the lighted lamp be snuffed out. All my prophecies collected in this book shall be fulfilled.

It is not surprising that the king destroyed such a collection, nor surprising that the indefatigable Jeremiah should have set Baruch at once to work making a second copy. To this second version was added Jeremiah's curse of the king who had burned the word of Yahweh:

Disasters wait for this man,
for Jehoiakim;
no man shall follow his funeral,
no lament be made at his death,
no one cry 'Alas, for the Lord',
or 'Alas, for the king'.
He shall be buried like a dead donkey,
flung over the walls
beyond the gate of Jerusalem.

The Babylonian Occupation

The tribute money was paid to Babylon for six years. Then Jehoiakim in 597 made the mistake of withholding the money from Nebuchadnezzar who had now become king in Babylon. The Babylonians immediately sent an army to collect the tribute. They laid siege to Jerusalem. At this moment Jehoiakim died and left his eighteen-year-old son, Jehoiachin to deal with the disaster. The young king opened the gates of the city and surrendered to Nebuchadnezzar. His troops took their plunder from every house and palace and, digging up the corpse of Jehoiakim, flung it over the walls of Jerusalem.

Jehoiachin was deported and his uncle, newly named Zedekiah by Nebuchadnezzar, was appointed king in his place in March, 597.

The Babylonian deported to his capital not the king alone but also the royal family and the chief officers of the kingdom, collecting also any artisan of promise who might be employed in the decoration of his city. The territory of Judah was again diminished, the Negeb being taken away from Jerusalem's jurisdiction and given to the Edomites, who had supported the new Babylonian ruler in his attack on Judah.

It would seem that in Jerusalem it was confidently expected that Jehoiachin would be sent back to reign in an independent state. Jeremiah would not let the people cherish such an illusion:

> Set this man down as childless,
>   unhappy all his life;
> no child of his shall reign
>   from David's throne
> in the land of Judah.

From the moment of the deportations of 597, the Jews were split into two unfriendly groupings. Those who were deported included most of the liberal statesmen who had protected Jeremiah from the understandable angers of Jehoiakim and the mob. Those who remained were happy to find for themselves the empty offices and houses of the exiled aristocracy. Between these two sets there grew bitter animosity.

Jeremiah was left in Jerusalem and began by thinking highly of his exiled protectors but he soon became disillusioned about these angry aristocrats. They had made the mistake of thinking that their exile would be short—so they took no trouble to settle into their new conditions which were not very uncomfortable. They deluded themselves into thinking their exile could be made shorter —so they intrigued against the government of Nebuchadnezzar with such disaffected persons as they could find in Babylon. These activities, as Jeremiah warned them, were too dangerous to be tackled by such an insecure minority dependent for life and freedom on the good pleasure of the tolerant but not enfeebled government of Nebuchadnezzar.

Zedekiah's Rebellion

In 594 there was an unsuccessful army revolt in Babylon which somehow involved some of the more prominent of the deported Jews. Nebuchadnezzar had the leaders executed but this did not put an end to Jewish plotting. In 593 the agents of Edom, Moab, Ammon, Tyre and Sidon were in Jerusalem attempting to make arrangements for a concerted attack on the occupying forces. This came to nothing, probably because the Egyptians wisely refused to take part. Zedekiah therefore went to Babylon to assure Nebuchadnezzar of his loyalty.

The forces in Jerusalem in favour of revolt were very strong, however. Zedekiah found it increasingly difficult to withstand their pressures on him. He had several private conversations with Jeremiah, trying to work out a way of keeping his authority at the court while at the same time not getting caught up in the war with Nebuchadnezzar. But every time Jeremiah gave him cold comfort: 'The Babylonians will take this city and set fire to it and there shall be an end to Jerusalem'. Advice like this did not help the king, it gave him no hope for the future.

Zedekiah was continually urged by his counsellors to rebel against Babylon and retrieve Judah's independence. Prophets got up in the Temple demanding revolt in the name of Yahweh. Hananiah, the prophet from Gibeon, spoke to the priests and the people:

'Yahweh has broken the yoke of Babylon; in two years he will set things in order again, the exiled king and all the officers shall be brought back and Babylon defeated.'

Jeremiah, who was present on this occasion, knew that Hananiah was talking nonsense:

'Well, let us hope Yahweh will do this, and the exiles are brought back. But remember that all the prophets who spoke in the past told us of war, famine and disease, they did not talk glibly of a slick peace.'

Jeremiah had come into the Temple wearing a wooden yoke round his neck as a sign of the subjection of Judah to Babylon.

Hananiah went across to him and took the wooden yoke off Jeremiah's neck and broke it in two:

'Thus will Yahweh break the yoke of Nebuchadnezzar of Babylon within these two years.'

'You have broken the yoke of wood but Babylon is preparing a yoke of iron for the nation. Do not deceive this people with your lies.'

Then Jeremiah turned to the priests and the people:

'Do not listen to him and the false prophets like him. Worse is to come. Let us pray that we shall be spared from that rather than trust in vain promises of relief.'

Zedekiah was a cautious man but in the end he stupidly allowed himself to be persuaded by the hot-headed nationalists that the time had come for resistance to Babylon. In 589 he renounced his allegiance to the overlord who had made him king on his nephew's throne. The Babylonian army arrived in a few weeks to besiege the capital, having taken every other town in Judah except Lachish and Azekiah. Zedekiah appealed for help to Babylon's old enemy, Egypt.

A letter from one outpost of Lachish to the commander there has survived, scratched on a potsherd:

'We have received your signal. There is no sign of life from Azekah. . . . In Jerusalem there are men who weaken the city's will to resist.'

This letter may well refer to the gloomy speeches of Jeremiah.

Jerusalem betrays the Covenant

An Egyptian army crossed the border and the Babylonians left the siege of Jerusalem to deal with this expeditionary force. Everyone in Jerusalem, except Jeremiah, thought they had seen the last of the enemy. They forgot Yahweh to whom they had prayed in their anxiety, they broke the oath they had made to Yahweh in their fear. During the siege the rich masters of Hebrew slaves had repented that they had enslaved members of the old confederation of free men. They had set their brethren at liberty, binding themselves with an oath to Yahweh of the covenant. When the Babylonian generals took their army away the masters took their brethren back into slavery.

Jeremiah denounced this irreligious treachery, warning the fools who hoped to play tricks on Yahweh that the Babylonians would now return.

Jeremiah was not simply denouncing the treacherous deceit of the slave-owners, he was reminding them that they were breaking one of the most important statutes of the Book of the Law recovered in the reign of Josiah. The matter was, he knew, grave enough in its rejection of the whole idea of Israel as the community of free men chosen by Yahweh to invite disaster. The most likely source of punishment was the return of the enemy army. He therefore announced the gloomy future to the people of Jerusalem.

This was too much for the members of the ruling class. They went to Zedekiah:

'Put this man to death, he weakens our will to resist the Babylonians. He is a traitor.'

'Do with him as you wish.'

Jeremiah was taken to the barracks and thrown down a deep unused well and there he stood in the mud waiting for death. News of his imprisonment came to Ebed-melech, one of the chief councillors, who was a friend of Jeremiah, and he went straight to the king:

'My lord, this is a great crime. Jeremiah will die of hunger there in the foetid well. Have him released at once.'

'Do with him as you wish.'

In order to rescue Jeremiah, two long home-made ropes were strung out of clothes and blankets and Jeremiah tied these round himself and thus precariously was drawn up from the bottom of the well.

Zedekiah, fumbling between policies as ever, arranged a secret meeting with Jeremiah:

'I want to ask your advice.'

'And if I give it you'll hand me over to my enemies again.'

'No. You shall live.'

'Very well. All I can say to you is what I have always said. Surrender and at least save the lives of the people who have survived the siege.'

'If I surrender, then the quislings in the Babylonian camp will make a mockery of me.'

'No. That is an unreal fear. I tell you that if you persist in standing out against Babylon, there will be a mockery more bitter than that for you. Your womenfolk will be led away to Babylon and as they pass you they will sing:

> You trusted them,
> they urged you to resist—
> where are they now
> when you are covered in dirt?'

Zedekiah rose and would not continue the audience. He said only:

'Do not let anyone know that I have talked to you. Tell them that you asked only to be left at liberty or at least kept from your enemies. You are confined to the court of the guard.'

The Destruction of Jerusalem

The Babylonians defeated the Egyptians and returned to the siege again. After eighteen months the population was weak and tattered, famine was an enemy that could not be kept outside the walls. The Babylonians made a breach and occupied Jerusalem. Zedekiah ran for safety. Taking his bodyguard he went by night through the palace gardens and rode towards the Arabah. The Babylonian pursuers caught him in the plain of Jericho and brought him to Nebuchadnezzar who was encamped at Riblah.

There the king was bound in chains and made to witness the execution of his sons. This was his last sight in life for immediately after this his eyes were put out and he was sent to die in Babylon. Then followed the sacking of Jerusalem by the Babylonian soldiers, they staggered home laden with booty as the ruins of Jerusalem smoked behind them. The palace had been destroyed, the Temple had been burnt down, the burning pillars and the bronze were broken in pieces and carried away; Jerusalem had become a heap of rubble.

The governor of the new Babylonian province of Judah resided at Mizpah, the town where the men of Israel had first said to Samuel, 'Give us a king'.

BIBLIOGRAPHY

Alt, Albrecht, *Essays on Old Testament History and Religion*, Eng. trans. R. A. Wilson, 1966.

Beyerlin, Walter, *Origins and History of the Oldest Sinaitic Traditions*, Eng. trans. S. Rudman, 1965.

Bright, John, *History of Israel*, 1960.

Eaton, J. H., *Obadiah, Nahum, Habakkuk, Zephaniah*, 1961.

Eissfeldt, Otto, *Old Testament Introduction*, Eng. trans. P. R. Ackroyd, 1965.

Gray, John, *I & II Kings*, 1964. *Legacy of Canaan*; Supplement to *Vetus Testamentum, V*, 1965.

Hertzberg, H. W., *I & II Samuel*, Eng. trans. J. S. Bowden, 1964.

Knight, G. A. F., *Hosea*, 1960.

Kraus, Hans-Joachim, *Worship in Israel*, Eng. trans. G. Buswell, 1966.

Marsh, John, *Amos and Micah*, 1959.

McCarthy, D. J., 'Treaty and Covenant', *Analecta Biblica*, 21, 1963.

Montgomery and Gehman, *Kings, International Critical Commentary*, 1951.

Mewinckel, Sigmund, *The Psalms in Israel's Worship, I and II*, Eng. trans. D. R. Ap-Thomas, 1962.

Nielsen, Eduard, *Shechem*, 2nd revised edition, 1959.

Neth, Martin, *Exodus*, Eng. trans. J. S. Bowden, 1962. *History of Israel*, revised Eng. trans., 1960

Rowley, H. H., 'Elijah on Mount Carmel', *B.J.R.L.* 43, 1960-1, pp. 190-219. 'Hezekiah's Reform and Rebellion', *B.J.R.L.* 44, 1961-2, pp. 395-461.

Scott, R. B. Y., *Solomon and the Beginning of Wisdom*, Supplement to *Vetus Testamentum, III*, 1960.

Segal, J. B., *The Hebrew Passover*, London Oriental Series, 12, 1963.

Skinner, John, *Prophecy and Religion*, 1922.

Somervel, R., *The Parallel History of the Jewish Monarchy*, I and II, 1901.

Porteous, N. W., *Royal Wisdom*, Supplement to *Vetus Testamentum*, III, 1960.

de Vaux, R., *Ancient Israel*, Eng. trans. John McHugh, 1961. *Studies in Old Testament Sacrifice*, 1964.

Vawter, Bruce, *The Conscience of Israel*, 1961.

von Rad, Gerhard, *Genesis*, trans. J. H. Marks, 1961. *The Problem of the Hexateuch and other Essays*, Eng. trans. E. W. Trueman Dicken, 1966. *Studies in Deuteronomy*, Eng. trans. D. Stalker, 1953.

Weiser, Artur, *The Psalms*, Eng. trans. H. Hartwell, 1962.

INDEX

Aaron, 88f., 116f.
Abel, 98f.
Abel-Meholah, 131
Abi, wife of Ahaz, 163
Abiathar, 34, 43, 53, 56, 59f.
Abigail, 33f.
Abijah, son of Jeroboam I, 118
Abijah, son of Rehoboam, 119f.
Abimelech, 105f.
Abishag, 59, 61
Abishai, 38
Abner, 23, 38f., 111
Abraham, xii, 2, 8, 70f., 78, 91, 96, 103, 117, 130, 132
Absalom, 49, 51f., 57f., 62, 80, 115
Acco, 9, 65
Achan, 91
Achor, 160, 166
Adad-nirari III, 151
Adah, 99
Adam, 96, 98, 102
Adonijah, 59f., 62, 171
Adoram, 107, 113
Agag, 20, 21
Ahab, xiii, xiv, 122f., 128f., 133f., 136, 138, 140, 143, 144, 147, 165, 167
Ahaz, 162f., 165, 166, 168, 174, 176, 182, 184
Ahaziah, son of Ahab, 134f.
Ahaziah, son of Jehoram of Judah, 138f., 141, 143, 144
Ahijah, 68, 108, 118
Ahimaaz, 57
Ahimelech, 31, 32
Ahinoam, 34
Ahithophel, 52f.
Ai, 91, 193
Amalek and the Amalekites, 19, 20, 21, 34f., 37, 88f.
Amaziah of Bethel, 157
Amaziah of Judah, 151f., 153
Ammon and the Ammonites, 16, 46, 48f., 111, 178, 181, 203
Amnon, 49, 62
Amon, son of Manasseh, 185

Amorites, 91
Amos, 126, 154, 155, 156f., 166, 167, 187
Anathoth, 61
Aphek, 13, 125
Apiru, 84
Aqaba, 64, 87
Arabah, 67, 206
Arabia, 64, 151, 153
Aramaic, 182
Arameans, 136
Araunah, 58, 64
Ark of the Covenant, 3, 13, 40, 41f., 59, 65f., 108, 117
Ark of Noah, 100
Arnon, 135
Arpad, xii
Arvad, 179
Asa, 120f.
Asahel, 38
Ashdod, 7, 41, 42, 153, 176, 179, 181
Asher, 115
Ashkelon, 7, 37, 178, 181
Ashtaroth, 36
Ashurbanipal, 184f.
Ashur-nasir-pal II, 123
Assyria and the Assyrians, xii, xiv, xvii, 123, 133, 159f., 163f., 167, 174f., 178, 179, 182f., 188, 195, 197, 199
Athaliah, 133, 138, 144f., 171
Azariah of Judah, 193
Azekah, 20, 204

Baal-Melqart, 123, 127, 128f., 142, 143f., 155, 158, 160, 186
Baal-Zebub, 134, 142, 145f.
Baal-hazor, 50
Baasha, 121, 124
Babel, 101f.
Babylon and the Babylonians, 102, 175, 178f., 197, 200, 202f., 206f., 207
Balaam, 3
Barak, 9